DATE DUE FOR RETURN

Once a Jolly Bagman

ONCE A
JOLLY BAGMAN

memoirs

Alistair McAlpine

Weidenfeld & Nicolson
LONDON

With all my love
to my daughter Skye

First published in Great Britain in 1997 by
Weidenfeld & Nicolson

The Orion Publishing Group Ltd
Orion House
5 Upper St Martin's Lane
London WC2H 9EA

A catalogue reference is available from the British Library

ISBN 0297 81737 X

Typeset by Selwood Systems, Midsomer Norton
Printed in Great Britain by Butler & Tanner Ltd, Frome and London

The coat of arms chosen by the author. The central section is the arms of the McAlpine family. The supporters on either side represent the author's interests in gardening, collecting, Australia, birds and animals. The motto was taken from the last few words of *The Desire and Pursuit of the Whole* by Baron Corvo.

CONTENTS

ILLUSTRATIONS

INTRODUCTION

In 1942 I was born in the Dorchester Hotel. My bottle came with room service. The birth by caesarean section was not easy and I recall my father telling me of how the gynaecologist took him to one side and said, 'Things are bad, I may have to make a choice. Am I to save the child or the mother?' My father chose the mother. Happily, we both survived.

My life as a child was luxurious and it has not changed drastically since then. I suffered none of the setbacks that are supposed to build the character of young people. What I had I took for granted, not really knowing where it came from or why it was there. My life was a helter skelter of discovery; my imagination ran riot. Even when I left a childhood of playing with my rabbits, guinea pigs and budgerigars, all of which I kept in large quantities, I never realised that life had changed. As I moved in one bound from the community of a country life, home and school into an urban and harsh world of construction sites, I did not realise that there was a change, for the people who worked on the sites at the time were, for the most part, my extended family.

As I grew up I was taken by my father onto building sites and can easily remember being frightened, as a small boy, by the noise of the compressors that drove the pneumatic hammers. From then on, I hated heights. My father used to send me the weekly issue of the *Muck Shifter* at prep school. I tried to love the culture of giant bulldozers and earth movers, but I was just not terribly interested in it. Yet it was the world in which my father went to earn his living and it was where I was to go to earn mine.

In time, as I moved into the world of politics, what was certain became uncertain. I changed, like all explorers, as I discovered new enthusiasms and encountered new risks. As I expanded my own world, I moved from safe to dangerous territory. As I learned of these new worlds, I grew in intelligence and I hope in sensitivity and slowly my philosophy of life began to form. I realised that success was not everything, that failure too has its rewards, and that it is one's folly that is the best teacher, that happiness is not a goal with its own end and that contentment is often a state of mind that cares nothing for others. I learnt to ride the roller-coasters of joy and misery. I learnt that friendship and love truly matter, that they are not troubles to be lightly taken up and just as lightly put down again. For the first time, I began to think.

Once a Jolly Bagman

My Mother

My mother was a strong woman – strong in her opinions and in physical courage. She was fanatical in her loyalty to the people she liked. For those she disliked, however, she had almost total contempt. She was my friend and my protector when I was a child and there was a close bond between us. I amused her, made her laugh, which she enjoyed. We shared the same rather silly sense of humour and could both see the absurdity of situations that others believed to be serious.

An early memory of my mother is of her coming into my bedroom at night to kiss me before she and my father left for an evening at the theatre. She was tall and wore a full-length dress of green taffeta cut low above her breasts. She carried a mink stole and a *petit-point* evening bag. Her pale brunette hair was neither long nor short, rather it was curled in a series of loose waves breaking around her face. She wore emerald clip earrings, a string of pearls and an emerald, square cut and large at her chest. She smiled at me and as she leaned down the smell of her perfume filled the room, lingering long after she left as I lay in the half-sleep that the innocence of childhood gives.

My mother and father married when she was eighteen and he was twenty. Marriage gave my mother security because until then her life had been that of a nomad: her parents seemed unable to make up their minds whether they would live in Canada or Britain, Devon or London, Scotland or England, and they upped sticks and moved at the smallest excuse.

My parents were germane cousins: my grandmother's first husband, who died, was my father's maternal uncle; my mother and her sister were the offspring of my grandmother's second marriage. My father was married to both of them: first to my mother for fifty-seven years, then to her sister, who died shortly after his death in 1990. My father's family had always felt a responsibility for my mother's family, and the two families, while often geographically distant, always kept in contact.

In 1928, when my father told his father that he was attracted to my mother, who was then living in Vancouver, and said he would like to visit her, my grandfather, a stern Scot, felt that such an expedition might be considered a commitment and so invited my mother and her family to stay in England. Always keen for a reason to travel, they came posthaste.

Within weeks my parents were engaged and then married. Lyttle Hall, near Redhill in Surrey, was acquired for them and they set up home a mile or so from my paternal grandparents. My paternal grandmother kept an eye on how my mother ran her house. A young footman, Wilfred Harris, was despatched from my grandmother's home to serve as my mother's butler. He stayed with my parents almost all his life before retiring to Australia. My mother was furious, as she had always fully intended to die before her staff retired. A lady's maid was also sent from my grandmother's household. My mother, a raw, unsophisticated eighteen-year-old from Canada, was shocked to find that this woman was in the habit of putting the toothpaste on her toothbrush, ready for use in the morning and evening.

The war changed everything. Lyttle Hall was requisitioned in 1941. It stood on the escarpment overlooking the Sussex plains that led to the Downs and then the coast. This escarpment was the last line of defence before London, its civilian population therefore had to be evacuated. Thus my parents' property was taken over, at short notice, by the army.

At the time mother had two small children and was pregnant with a third. She was worried because she had already lost three children in the course of previous pregnancies. She had no home and my father, a civil engineering contractor working in the family firm, was away all day and most of the night, building airfields and munitions factories. Houses in the country were practically unobtainable, particularly big houses, which had mostly been taken by companies who had moved their offices from bomb-threatened London. My mother needed a large house because, along with my parents and their family, evicted from Lyttle Hall and its cottages were the wives and children of all her staff, whose husbands had gone to the war. These people and their children looked to my mother for accommodation.

Petrol was obtainable on a ration and that ration took you nowhere; trains were cold and erratic; Britain was fighting for her life. My mother tramped the countryside and, either by persistence or luck, finally found a house and a farm in the Chilterns behind Henley-on-Thames.

The house, called Benhams, was bought at an exorbitant cost by my grandfather William McAlpine and became my parents' home for the rest of their lives. It was, at that time, only a few years old and had been designed by an architect who must, I suppose, have been a follower of Lutyens. A red brick house, it stood in what was then a modest garden which my mother greatly enlarged. There was a pair of cottages and two transportable buildings were added to accommodate the tribe that moved with my parents. The views from the house were stunning, across beech woods of the Chilterns to Windsor and beyond to the Hog's Back in one direction, across a valley to the fields of the farm in another. Benhams was the most comfortable of houses. Of neo-Georgian architecture, its main rooms on the ground floor led one into another. These rooms were pine panelled, large and quite grand with old Turkish carpets and an assortment of nineteenth-century furniture and paintings. My mother was an enthusiast at sewing tapestry and the Victorian spoon-backed chairs were covered in her work, as were the footstools and assorted cushions. Benhams was not a beautiful house, far from it; its decoration then lacked both imagination and taste. Benhams was, however, a solid, reliable house, a house that reassured those who lived there, a home with an atmosphere of kindness. I was immensely fond of that house, perhaps more fond of Benhams than anywhere else that I have lived.

Along with her troop of camp followers, my mother moved and began managing the farm, which was called Dobson's. She loved that house and never intended to move again. Nor did she: her ashes are spread amongst the camellias in the wildest part of the garden that she devised and helped construct.

My mother's happiest time – or maybe the happiness was in the telling of it – were the war years. For the first time in her life she had a useful role to play, a role that was truly hers and not just that of consort to my father. As consort, she smiled at his customers, conducted his dinner parties, ran his household, listened to his problems and applauded his triumphs. This is not to say that she did not enjoy any or all of these activities, neither is it to underestimate the time, energy and patience that these activities demanded.

My mother set about running her farm, driving tractors and milking cows; evacuees moved in and land girls came at harvest time. She had many tales of those days: tales of the prize-winning Borzois that she bred, and a peach-stealing bulldog. A more unlikely animal to climb a peach tree than a bulldog it is hard to imagine. I remember her telling me of how she wrongly accused the evacuees who were billeted on our home of stealing the fruit, only to discover a few days later that it was our dog, which had acquired a taste for it.

My mother was particularly proud of her pedigree Ayrshire cattle. Fine beasts they were, light brown and white with a stately head of horns. The bulls were well known for their ferocity. My mother laboured over the cows' milk records, meticulously noting the production of each animal, trying always to breed beasts that produced not only more milk, but better quality milk.

I remember laughing so much that I tripped over my high chair and split my skull when my mother told the tale of how she went to fetch the cattle for milking and found them drunk. They had been feasting on a windfall of crab apples which fermented in their stomachs. Instead of a docile herd used to being driven with a light stick, she found that her cows were not only drunk, but aggressive. They pursued her and she escaped only by climbing a tree.

Our bulldog hated the cattle from the day a cow kicked him as the herd came in for milking. He sat and watched each day as they jostled each other on their way back to the fields. Then one morning he struck, jumping at the cow which had kicked him. Catching it by the lower lip, he hung on, swinging from side to side. There was a commotion, buckets of water were thrown, old grain sacks and besoms waved. The beast was finally freed and the vet called. Thereafter, dog and cattle were kept apart.

Butter-making was another job that my mother took on and I would watch her. When the weather was cold the hand-turned churn worked well enough and the butter was made quickly. When the weather was hot, however, my mother turned and turned that wretched handle and the butter never seemed to make. As a small child waiting for the first taste of the week's butter, minutes seemed like hours. Butter-making, however, was never really the same after the introduction of the electric churn. Neither my mother nor the cowman could get used to the idea of not covering the dairy floor in water, nor did they ever really understand how to use the new-fangled machine. The under-chauffeur Harry was called in, for anything mechanical was considered his department. As he fiddled with the churn, he suddenly started to jump about in a most frenetic fashion. He was not wearing rubber boots as he did not normally work in the dairy, and the electric current was going right through him. He was nearly killed as a consequence and the electric churn was consigned to a shed.

The war passed and the austerity of the postwar years turned to prosperity.

My mother particularly enjoyed Christmas; she was childlike in the pleasure that it gave her. Every part of the house had to be decorated. Together with Harris the butler she conceived the most intricate of decorations, which were different every year. I loved to decorate the Christmas tree with the glass balls that had survived so many Christmases. Attaching the fairy lights, however, was the prerogative of the chauffeur Mr Slopper, as were all matters mechanical and electrical.

On Christmas Day my mother usually woke up first at about four o'clock, despite the fact that she would not have gone to bed much before two. We all opened our presents together in my parents' bedroom, a ceremony which lasted about two hours. This was followed by a breakfast of scrambled egg, cold York ham, sausages, bacon and a variety of other fare, served in silver dishes in the dining room in front of the Christmas tree. Then the table was extended and relaid. My mother put the crackers on the table. These crackers became more magnificent each year. They always came from Harrods and my mother spent a fortune on them. Harrods was aware of this, for when it imposed a rule barring dogs from the store, my mother was exempt. This privilege turned out, in my view, to be a liability, for when we turned up at Harrods to do our shopping, complete with her dog, the doormen always tried to turn us away – communication between the management and the doormen, it seemed, was lacking. In any event, we had to wait while the Managing Director was asked whether we were really allowed to take our dog into the store. As we progressed with the rather elegant long-haired Dachshund called Russet, my mother's favourite dog, in almost every department except, of course, the one that sold Christmas crackers, we were stopped and questioned by floor walkers. My mother had a natural instinct to oppose bureaucracy and, in particular, authority that tried to implement what she regarded as 'ridiculous rules'. She was, by nature, also extremely argumentative and loved nothing better than to have a good debate. She could, of course, have perfectly well left her dog in the car with her chauffeur. However, she had for most of her life taken her dog into Harrods and did not see why she should stop doing that just because the management were making rules to harass their customers.

In the early days of my life, at the end of the war, Slopper the chauffeur, a veteran of the First World War with a waxed moustache, always dressed up as Father Christmas and distributed presents to all the household and farm children, while their parents ate mince pies and sipped brandy. There were presents for everyone.

As the children grew, however, Christmas changed. Slopper no longer wore the red Father Christmas outfit; the farm children were fully grown and had left the land and presents were delivered to their parents by my mother. There were usually a turkey and a bottle for the man of the household and a carefully chosen gift for his wife.

My mother took a particular interest in the turkeys. There were about two hundred of them, carefully nurtured until Christmas by one of her gardeners. Then they were killed and plucked, and mother tied labels around their naked necks. Most she gave away; a few she sold. She had a list of those to whom she intended to give one of the birds and selecting one of the right size was important because in those days turkeys sometimes ran to a hefty forty or fifty pounds in weight and, consequently, would not fit in the smaller ovens. One year a turkey came to life and walked around our kitchen stark naked. These turkeys were placed, a few at a time, along with the other presents in the car for delivery. My mother and I set out on a journey, first to our farm cottages to make these deliveries and then around the village to visit friends and dependants. It was an age when you truly knew those who lived in your village.

In 1958 came a huge change. My mother had a fall. A simple matter, she tripped on a rug in her loggia, fell and broke her arm. In time the bones in her arm healed, but a pain remained in her back. From then to her death in 1987, she suffered the most excruciating pain. A string of different doctors, surgeons and quacks attended on her. They stretched her and for six months she lay in bed with weights attached to her ankles. They injected her in different parts of the body and gave her morphine, which made her feel as if ants were crawling over her body. They manipulated and massaged her. Sometimes the cures seemed to work; more often than not they failed painfully.

She was (wrongly) diagnosed as having sciatica. We now know that she was suffering from osteoporosis. Slowly her body shrank. This fine tall woman, with the most elegant fingers, became small and bent. There were moments of relief when she travelled to the South of France. She liked the mild winters and loved to gamble, sitting until the early hours of the morning at the Chemin de Fer table. Dry Martinis were her real obsession. Her dry Martini had to be just right, which meant that it had no Martini in it, or at least so little that it made no difference, and had to be served ice cold. My mother claimed that she could tell when there was a different barman at a favourite restaurant by the taste of her Martini. At the Chemin de Fer table her Martinis were brought to her by Casino staff, and sometimes even her dinner was served as she gambled.

The boundaries of my mother's life slowly closed in on her. Travel by car became painful, as getting in and out of cars became more difficult. Slowly my mother began to eat less and to drink more. The variety and quantity of drugs and cures she was prescribed for the wrong reasons took a terrible toll on her. Her energy and aggression, however, were still there, and you could see her frustration at not being able to do all that she had once done.

Her hobby had been gardening. She had worked away at her garden, always extending its boundaries into the rhododendron woods that surrounded Benhams. In the early fifties my mother had been obsessed with her rock garden and together she and I used to visit Waterers, the market gardeners, on the floral mile – a mile or so alongside the main road from Maidenhead to Reading where, on either side, a number of market gardeners were situated. At some stage I had suggested to her that when she built the rock garden at Benhams it might be made of concrete tubs filled with sterilised earth and covered with rocks. This way, I believed, we would avoid weeds. It was all a load of nonsense, of course, for the weeds grew like mad despite my plan. In fact I have since then never come across a garden that needed so much weeding. I used to earn pennies and sometimes pounds digging them up.

Instead of gardening, my mother pottered in her orchid house. For exercise, we built an indoor swimming pool next to her bedroom on the first floor at Benhams and she swam, but getting in and out of the pool was painful. She hated the idea of a wheelchair and walked slowly with the help of a stick. More frequently holidays were cut short and she was brought back to England in pain.

I only ever had two rows with my mother. The first came shortly after her fall, when we were in Rome together. There was a party of us and as we lunched in a Roman restaurant my mother kept taking food from my plate. I complained rudely and she took deep offence. I apologised later that afternoon and she said words that seemed strange to me at the time: 'I have always defended you from your father's criticisms.' I had no idea that my father had ever criticised me. Perhaps the irresponsible humour that my mother loved so much in me irritated him.

The second occasion was when my parents were staying with my first wife, Sarah, and myself for Christmas at West Green, my then home. My first marriage had broken down and I was to leave my wife, but in the foolish way of those in this sort of situation, I had agreed to wait until after Christmas before I left. Sarah insisted that my parents had to be told. We all stood in the drawing room at West Green, a beautiful double-cube room lit by candles, the fire roared, and flames streamed up the chimney. I told my parents of my intention to leave Sarah. Divorce for them was unimaginable. My mother stepped towards me and beat me about the head with her walking stick. Despite being well into my thirties, for a few minutes I returned to childhood and shed floods of tears. My mother never criticised my actions again.

Slowly my mother tired of life and a series of nurses came to look after her. Some were better than others, but all of them were strangers to a woman whose life had been spent in the company of staff who came to her in their youth and left in their old age.

During her last illness, I visited her in the Wellington Clinic. She looked tired and small, not afraid, but terribly sad. We spoke for a few minutes and then she talked at length with my wife, Romilly, to whom she confided that her life had not been a great success. As I got up to leave I gave unintentionally some indication of there being a smell in the room. Perhaps I sniffed the air or, maybe, my mother just imagined that I had sniffed the air. 'Do I smell?' she asked. A woman of fastidious personal habits, I could see the idea affronted her. 'No,' I replied, 'certainly not.'

My mother died two days later. I arrived at the hospital an hour or so after her death. Her body had been taken to another room and her private nurse had decided to embellish her face with grotesque make-up. I try not to remember my mother as that shrunken, painted figure dead in a hospital bed. For me, my mother always was and always will be that vision dressed in green taffeta and emeralds, smelling of heavenly perfume, who came into my half-sleep and kissed me all those years ago.

2

My Father

My father was often described as 'charming', yet for me that would be too easy a word to characterise this determined but gregarious and friendly man. There was no doubt that he was extremely kind. Indeed, his kindnesses were legion. He was also an extremely considerate man. For example, once a week he would telephone a whole list of widows, whom he had come across through work or family. These calls always took place on a Sunday morning, when he would sit in the library, the smoke from his cigar describing curling patterns in the air as he chatted easily to these usually elderly and often lonely women.

The library was very much my father's room in the house. He had collected books as a young man and the room was filled with leather-bound Nonesuch Press editions of the classics and, in contrast, an ungainly collection of biographies and thrillers.

My father was one of those individuals who are always friendly and, therefore, constantly meeting new people. It seemed, initially, as though these meetings were totally accidental, but my father turned so many of them to good purpose that I sometimes wonder if he did, in fact, have a master plan and had organised them. Perhaps he did, or maybe he just made it his business to be where the people that he needed to meet were to be found.

My father usually lunched at the Dorchester Hotel and when doing so, always arrived early and stood in the hall, greeting friends and acquaintances as they came through the revolving glass doors. The hotel was the brainchild of his uncle, Malcolm McAlpine. It was built in the depths of the recession in the 1920s and my family provided the finance. When, however, the customer could not pay us for the building, we took over the hotel and my family owned and ran it for over forty years. My family promoted this project to provide work for their business. The hotel was built of reinforced concrete and supposed to be bomb-proof. Eisenhower lived there when he came to Britain as Supreme Allied Commander in the Second World War, as did many other dignitaries throughout that time.

The Dorchester was my father's stage, where he performed with brilliance. His genius was to put together people who needed to meet each other. In return, they were happy to give him contracts to build them buildings. It was in those days that my father began to introduce me to his customers. He taught me how to handle them, how to entertain, how to make conversation with people with whom I often had little in common, except that I wanted something that they could give, how to acquire business through building up a personal relationship with others. My father never seemed to teach, but I would sit and listen to him as he talked, mesmerised. His secret, if he had one, was his ability to be fascinated by every small detail that his guests told him of their lives. My father truly fell in love with his customers – for him they were the most important people in the world and, somehow without his telling them, they realised that this was so. He never gave others the feeling that they were intruding on his life, that they were either a bore or an inconvenience. When you met my father he made you feel that you were the one person for whom he had waited all day. He was, however, desperately short-sighted and sometimes did not know to whom he was talking.

Each year he would entertain seven hundred of his friends to lunch a week or two before Christmas. It was a huge gathering of the rich, famous, and of his old friends, many of whom were neither of those. Invitations were, I believe, much prized. This lunch, which started during the war with twenty-five guests, became such a ritual that it is said that a Cabinet meeting was once postponed because it coincided with Edwin McAlpine's Christmas lunch. Certainly several Prime Ministers delivered the keynote speeches.

My father loved politics and although he never became a politician, he did enjoy the company of politicians. I can remember as a boy listening to such great figures of the age as Oliver Lyttleton, later Lord Chandos, and Percy Mills, to whom Harold Macmillan often referred as 'wise old Percy' as they held our dinner table in rapt attention.

Oliver Chandos was a big man, big in stature, big in voice and big in views: 'Little is the most powerful word in the English language,' he opined. 'Little can be used in so many different ways – you can

evoke sympathy or express contempt with the use of the word little.'
Nobody knew the value of flattery better than Oliver Chandos. He
often would say, 'Words of flattery are the infantry of negotiation.'

Percy Mills did not have the size of Chandos, nor did he have
Chandos's facility with words. He was taken from industry to organise
the building of the houses that Macmillan had promised the electorate.
His success was Macmillan's triumph. What Mills did not have in
size he made up for in energy; what he missed in rhetorical ability
he made up for with silence, giving his views in a growl at the end
of a discussion. He was, I recall, a jolly man.

My father's particular responsibility within the family business was
for the company's position in the nuclear power industry. He rightly
identified this industry as likely to cause the biggest alteration in our
company's fortunes and was remorseless in his fight to gain advantage
in the multitude of changes that successive governments introduced.
Due to his efforts our business prospered mightily whilst building
nuclear power stations. Unfortunately, it was in the end a losing
battle. While Macmillan was in power my father's plans prospered,
but then the rot set in with Harold Wilson, who allowed the setting
up of the Industrial Reorganisation Corporation. They reorganised
everything they could lay their hands on, including the nuclear
power industry. Charles Villiers was its first Chairman, Alistair Morton
its Managing Director. My father found the latter a most uncongenial
man.

Frustrated by dealing with Alistair Morton, my father attended on
Tony Benn, the then Secretary of State for Trade and Industry, in his
office. He was, as is the custom, shown by one of the Secretary of
State's staff into a waiting room. In time a bright-looking young man
in shirt sleeves carrying a mug of steaming tea joined him. My father
took this person to be a junior civil servant. 'Tell me what is the new
Secretary of State like?' he asked. Tony Benn replied that he *was* the
Secretary of State.

When Ted Heath became Prime Minister in 1970 events moved
further against my father and his allies. Lord Aldington was the close
friend of Ted Heath and Chairman of GEC whose Managing Director
was Arnold Weinstock. Weinstock at that time was very close to
Ted Heath's circle and, together with Aldington, had considerable
influence on how the nuclear industry would be run. My father was
by now Chairman of one of the Surviving Groups. His hatred (for I

have to admit that was what it amounted to) of Arnold Weinstock soon became completely irrational. Weinstock was not an industrialist, my father said, just a pawn broker. There was an element of truth in this, for Weinstock had made GEC the power that it is by buying businesses, selling off their assets and keeping the resultant cash on deposit.

Weinstock could do nothing right as far as my father was concerned. Once, he was invited to the Weinstock home where he was entertained to a working lunch. This lunch took the form of a barbecue by the Weinstock swimming pool; Arnold cooked the steaks himself. Unfortunately, my father hated steak, for he had terrible trouble with his teeth. For weeks afterwards he remarked to all and sundry about the tough steak that Weinstock had given him for lunch, as if this was a mortal insult.

My father was always forthright in his views. 'To irritate is to stimulate' was his approach to life. Always provocative, he told Ted Heath across Lord Thompson's lunch table at *The Times* in 1973 that he should resign and hand over to his Minister of Education, Margaret Thatcher. My father had met Margaret Thatcher at lunch with Airey Neave, but did not know her well. The reason for the meeting was to discuss the nuclear power industry. In those days, the Secretary of State had responsibility for Science as well as Education. He had been instantly impressed by her intellect and grasp of what was a tortuous subject.

It was Edward Heath's bad luck that my father happened to be his fellow guest at Lord Thompson of Fleet's lunch. Two years later my father was lunching with the executive board of the National Theatre and Denys Lasdun, their architect, when Lord Goodman recalled my father's remarks. He was amazed, he said, when Margaret Thatcher became Leader of the Conservative Party. 'We all thought that you were making a bad joke when you suggested the idea to Ted at Roy Thompson's lunch.' My father was often controversial, but he rarely made bad jokes.

My father was recommended for a knighthood by Alec Douglas-Home, inherited his grandfather's baronetcy, and was proposed for the House of Lords by Margaret Thatcher, where he took his seat in 1980. He was, all his life, a staunch Conservative and I doubt anything would have changed that view. When I joined the House of Lords in 1984, my father and I were the first father and son to sit there each in their own right.

My father loved the theatre. He could tell you the date of any London production and who starred in it. He and my mother regularly used to attend first nights and sometimes I would accompany them. We all went to the first night of *The Mousetrap* and then shortly afterwards we saw two other Agatha Christie plays that were on in London: *The Spider's Web* and *Towards Zero*. I was firmly of the opinion that *The Mousetrap* was the least exciting of the three. *The Reluctant Heroes* was another play that I enjoyed and I have always been surprised that nobody has adapted it for television. *Prince's Rhapsody*, with Jack Buchanan, was the first musical that I saw and I was mesmerised.

My father also loved theatrical people; I doubt if there was anywhere that he was happier than the Garrick Club. He would return home in the evening and tell us of how he had met Felix Aylmer, John Gielgud or Kenneth More, the son of George Roby, then a stipendiary magistrate, or other theatrical people. In my early teens I would go with my father to watch the Crazy Gang. I loved their smutty humour. My father knew Budd Flanigan and Chesney Allen and we usually went behind the scenes to their dressing rooms.

Living at Henley-on-Thames, we were surrounded by members of the theatrical world. Robert Morley, Richard Todd and Ronald Culver were a few, and they all used to come to our house. One of our close neighbours was the Shakespearean actress Yvonne Mitchell and her husband Derek Mounsey, the Drama Critic of the *Daily Express*. My father was highly disapproving of them, not because Derek Mounsey was a supporter of the Labour Party – many of my father's cronies were ex-trade unionists or Labour ministers – but rather because, at a general election Mounsey had tied a large red rosette to the neck of his bulldog. My father thought this an insult to the bulldog.

I can recall them coming to our house for cocktails one summer evening – I was nine or ten – and to this day I can see Yvonne Mitchell sitting on the low wall of our terrace. She was immensely beautiful. She brought her cousin with her, the youthful Keith Joseph. My parents took the view that he was really rather pompous. Much later I came to know Keith extremely well and I can only write that a less pompous man I have never met, nor – with the exception of Margaret Thatcher – was anyone else in politics more generous with their time or freer with their kindnesses to me.

Apart from the theatre, my father's great passion was horse racing. I hated racing. I could not get excited by gambling either on a race track or in a casino. I did not even enjoy the horses despite the fact that I have always loved animals of all sorts and once even tried to breed Welsh cobs. Spending time at racecourses was for me totally boring. My father's family, however, had all been keen on horse racing; his uncle had won the Grand National in 1921, a year when every other horse fell over, three of the jockeys remounting to finish the race. He had paid 700 guineas for Saun Spadah, the horse that won the race for him, and the Grand National Cup stood for many years in the entrance of our London Office – until someone stole it. Malcolm McAlpine, or Great Uncle Malcolm as he was called to distinguish him from his son Malcolm and my father's brother, also called Malcolm, was an avid racegoer. He always backed horses for a place. In time the bookmakers on the racetracks called him 'The Fishmonger'. Great Uncle Malcolm kept a record of every bet that he made in his lifetime. The turnover was well over £1 million, a prodigious sum in those days, although the profit was only a few thousand. He, it must be remembered, was gambling at a time before bookmaking had reached its current level of sophistication and if you were smart and well equipped with telephones you could take advantage of differing odds between the track and the bookmaker's office. What is more, there was in those days no Betting Tax.

My father owned a large number of horses, but few of them were really much good. None of this seemed to matter to him. Of course, he would have liked to have won a classic race, but the pleasure he got was not in winning but in watching his horses run. My mother remarked one day in a fit of frustration when she thought that his racing activities were getting out of hand that he could have as many horses as he liked, as far as she was concerned, but please, no more trainers. My father's habit had been that when he thought a trainer was having a tough time he would put a couple of horses with him just to help the poor fellow. The result of this generosity was a continual string of telephone calls, at all times of the day and night, as these trainers rang in to report the lack of progress of my father's horses.

My father's cousins, Malcolm and Robin, also kept race horses, as did his brothers. Robin was the only member of the family to have any serious success. My cousin Robin, like his father, kept a record of all his bets and when he showed an £80,000 profit he gave up gambling. My father kept no records at all. Lists and prices were not part of his nature. In his view, you could either afford to gamble or you could not. He raced for pleasure and gambled for fun.

He had a strict rule, which was that he would never go into a casino in London. His gambling was done in the South of France. He reasoned that if he was seen in London casinos he was in danger of damaging his reputation and thus his credit. In the South of France, at the beginning of each holiday, he would take a large wad of cash and split it into piles. These piles were the same in number as the days of his holidays. Then he would halve these piles and put the money into different envelopes, each dated, each marked 'afternoon' or 'evening'. In this way he limited his losses to a figure that he could well afford. Maybe there were trips to France that resulted in a profit. I do not, however, recall any.

If my father's racing activities were never particularly successful, he nevertheless enjoyed himself mightily. I imagine that half the fun he had with his racing was meeting his friends in the bar. He preferred to race horses over the jumps, where prizes were smaller and the people involved of better quality, or so he believed, than those who chased fame and fortune on the flat.

The McAlpine family had a particular bet that they placed on the horses. This bet was to back all the odds-on favourites, regardless of where they raced. You could place this bet at the rate of £1 a point or £1,000 a point. For a long time this bet had never failed. One day my father was at the races and a scruffy-looking fellow approached him. My father was always good for a fiver if you had problems and he imagined that this was what the man wanted. Not a bit of it. He wanted to repay my father for past generosity. 'They've fixed your bet,' he told my father. 'They're making false favourites.' The man saved my father and his relatives a fortune.

Television was not much favoured by my father until he discovered that not only could you watch the racing at one racecourse, but by changing channels you could see what was happening on another racecourse at the far end of the country. Within the year my father's bookmakers at Henley-on-Thames had installed a direct telephone line to my father and his television. Shortly afterwards (undoubtedly aided by the large sums of money my father had spent with him), Sam Cowan, a bookmaker in the then small town of Henley, opened a London office. My father was rather pleased by his telephone, for his calls to the bookmaker were free and he could also listen to what was happening on a third racecourse via the Bookies Blower and the telephone link. The idea that our family should sit over their meals and 'make' conversation with each other came to an abrupt halt just before two o'clock on Saturday afternoon, at which time my father moved to the sitting room where he remained, cigar in hand, until five-thirty, switching channels, a telephone tucked under his chin, with the *Sporting Life* laid across his knees and his head and shoulders shrouded in cigar smoke illuminated by the flickering black-and-white light of the screen. It is not hard to imagine how much his pleasure was increased when the broadcasts began to be in colour and he could spot by the jockey's colours how a particular horse, neglected in the race reader's commentary, was doing.

My father enjoyed racing, gambling and cigars in about equal proportions. Harris the butler had the same instincts. My father would give him a cigar and ask if he had any tips, after which my father could be heard on his bookmaker's telephone placing £50 each way for himself and a fiver each way for Harris. If the horse won, Harris kept his winnings; if the horse lost, my father paid the bill.

As for cigars, Christmas was always a time of tension for my father. His friends sent him cigars as presents – each year as Christmas Day drew near he would count these cigars as they accumulated. From one friend a hundred, from another a hundred and fifty. If an expected box failed to arrive he would grumble for days. If this year produced more than last, his delight knew no bounds. One year my father discovered that more cigars had been sent by the bookmaker to Harris than to him and there was friction in the air for several days. My father was always quick to forgive and as quick to forget, unless he took a grudge against someone, in which case that grudge could last a lifetime.

All my father's life he worked for our family company. I know that at one stage it was his ambition to leave and set up on his own. It was not lack of courage that stopped him, rather my mother, who did not want even to contemplate the upheaval such a change would make to their lives. In the dark of the nights during the early 1960s I could hear them arguing about this as their bedroom in London was next to mine. My father gave up much in his life for my mother. However, in the event, he probably made the right decision not to go out on his own, for my mother was just starting the illness that from then on dominated their lives.

When my mother died in 1987 my father was never the same again. They had been married fifty-seven years and the last thirty of them she had been in terrible pain. In retrospect, I realise that my mother's illness probably greatly curtailed the possibilities of my father's life. She, during those years, cannot have been easy to live with. I have, however, no doubt that he loved her very deeply and she returned that love. In the few years my father lived after my mother's death, he remarried. His new wife was my mother's sister. My own relationship with him changed dramatically from that point on. From being a father and son who were extremely close, we became estranged.

When I look back on my relationship with my father, I have to admit that I took too much for granted. While I am sure that I knew my mother extremely well – indeed, every nook and cranny of her character was familiar – I realise now that, close as I was to him, I barely knew my father. This is a fact that I regret, for he was I am sure far greater than just a man who made life fun for those around him.

3

My Childhood

I cannot blame either of my parents for the shortcomings in my life; the days of my childhood were blessed. My family was extremely wealthy, close knit and loving. We – uncles, aunts, grandparents, cousins, brothers and sisters – all lived within a few miles of each other. My maternal grandparents lived in a flat in Fountain House, a substantial building on Park Lane. When in London, my parents lived there, two floors above them.

My elder brother Bill built a house on my father's land and lived there with his wife, Jill. When I married, I bought a house that adjoined my father's farm. My maternal aunt and uncle lived on other farms of my father's, first at Turville and then at Medmenham, both villages not far from Henley-on-Thames. Never a day would pass without my father telephoning his parents. Never a day would pass that I did not ring my parents.

My younger brother David and I are four years apart in age. As children we spent much time together and are very close. My elder brother is six years older than I and although I love him deeply, we did not enjoy the companionship that existed between my younger brother and myself. Our childhoods were separated by virtue of the fact that he was always just leaving as I was arriving. My sister Patricia is six years older than my elder brother. She was married by the time that I was six, so as a child I hardly knew her.

There were no tragedies in my childhood. The people around my parents were immensely kind and, I suppose, spoiled me. My parents never hit me; only once did a nanny spank me. Happily she was a temporary nanny, as I was deeply offended by her action. It was not the pain that upset me but the affront to my dignity.

I did not suffer hardship in any form. I had illnesses. I once nearly died of pneumonia and can recall the doctor and my mother talking while they believed I slept. 'He is not out of the woods yet,' the doctor said. While this illness was uncomfortable, it did not frighten me. As a child I felt totally secure.

Since I was born in 1942 I can remember little of the war, and such memories as I have I am unsure are true. I remember V.E. Day, when bunting was strung between our gateposts, and one morning towards the end of the war, when the Germans were sending V2s across the Channel. My nanny had taken me to see the pigs. We heard the V2 approach and nanny thought it a good idea to shelter in the pigsty. The pigs believed it a good idea to cavort in their yard. At the moment when the V2's engine stopped, there was a collision between pigs and nanny. Seconds later we heard a crash as the V2 exploded a mile or so away. The iron roof on the pig shed rattled and then nanny and I repaired home to clean ourselves. The pigs, well, they were I believe bitterly disappointed, for they imagined that we had brought them lunch.

I can also recall a searchlight position beside the road from our farm to the town of Henley-on-Thames and the anti-aircraft guns in Hyde Park and American soldiers, whom I was told to address thus: 'Have you got any gum chum?' They gave us children sweets, a rare commodity in Britain at the end of the war.

Moments of happiness from later childhood, however, still come to mind with perfect clarity. Our morning started at breakfast, a family ritual that commenced when the gong was sounded by the butler and we all hurried down to the dining room. My mother sat at one end of the table. Usually my father had already gone to his work and my elder brother sat at the other end. When he was away at school I sat in his place. My sister was always late. Breakfast was a considerable meal with silver entrée dishes lined up on the sideboard. There was always a large choice, ranging from kedgeree to kidneys.

Often I played in the woods with the children of my family's employees. We would play amongst the rhododendrons, the branches of which had grown so closely together that you could walk on top of them. We would walk in the woods, picking the bluebells that flowered in profusion, and primroses that grew in the glades. The summers seemed long and hot, the winters short and filled with log fires and Christmas. I remember lying in my bed sleepless on a hot summer's evening and hearing the birdsong broken by the conversation floating up from the adults as they sat and talked in the garden below.

We had in those days a Clydesdale cart horse, a grey mare called Shenee. She pulled the cart that carried the wheat sheaves. We children sat on top of that stacked cart, making fortresses with the straw as the farm hands pitched the stooks up to us. The whole household turned out for the harvest. The tractor pulled the harvester that cut and bound the wheat into sheaves and as it slowly circled the field, making the block of standing wheat smaller with each circuit, the farm hands and neighbours closed in carrying guns. We, the children, stayed with our picnic on top of the wagon. The rabbits hiding in the diminishing patch of wheat broke cover and there was a battue as the hunters fired their guns. The dogs would bark and the onlookers cheered.

The farm workers had little money because their pay was low, but they had food and housing. Their pleasures were the pub and the days when there was a shoot or a hunt in the district. There was a community in the village of Fawley Green in those days. When one of my father's workers was ill, my father organised for proper medical attention; when a farm worker's wife had a baby, my mother arranged for baby clothes to be given to her.

My family's household was made up of a lady's maid, Mrs Harris, and her husband, our butler. My mother was very fond of Mrs Harris. Over the years an incredibly deep bond grew between the four: the butler, the lady's maid, my mother and my father and they helped and consoled each other at times of distress and trouble. I am unsure how satisfactory life was for any of them after they parted.

The cook, Mrs Peters, was married to the gardener. She looked and behaved as a country cook should. Asked 'What's for lunch?' she would reply, 'Windmill Pudding. If it goes round you'll get some.' Peters, the gardener, was assisted by two under-gardeners.

The chauffeur, Slopper as he was known to the family, Mr Slopper to the staff, had worked for my great uncle and then for my father. He died in my father's employ and his son still worked for my parents when they died. Trained by Rolls-Royce, Slopper had been in the army driving the first armoured cars in Persia and the Middle East. His squadron of Rolls-Royce armoured cars had been sent to save the Tsar from the Russian Revolution. Slopper did not have a lot of time for the Tsar, or for that matter any other Russian. During the First World War he had lost an eardrum and entertained us children by blowing cigarette smoke out of his ear. He taught me to drive, which must have been a trial for the poor man, then in his seventies, for I failed my driving test eleven times. I did, however, learn to double de-clutch when changing gears which will, I am sure, be a tremendous help to me if I ever have to drive a Rolls-Royce from the early years of this century. The other aspect of driving that Slopper took very seriously was the hill start. He would place a matchstick between the wheel and the road, then you started the car and drove forwards. If you carried out this manoeuvre to perfection, the matchstick remained intact. These refinements to the art of driving were, I am afraid, wasted on me for my problem was telling where the road began and the pavement ended on the car's blind side.

Television, in my early childhood, was banned in our house, since my mother regarded it as an impediment to conversation. I was on very friendly terms with the butler Harris's son, Georgie, who used to invite me round to their cottage to watch the television. *The Black Ace* was my preferred viewing. A story of early aviation, of biplanes with open cockpits, the villain would be making his escape when the Black Ace appeared behind him in the rear cockpit, and a terrible struggle followed. Once a week we had film shows, with Harris the butler working a sixteen-millimetre projector. The film hire distributers were a company called 'Ron Harris' – I always believed that my family's butler was a big shot in the film industry.

In time my father discovered that television showed racing and the film projector, with the weekly episode of *Tarzan* followed by a George Formby film went, much, I am sure, to the disappointment of the children from the farm and those of the household staff who gathered with their parents in the darkness behind the projector to watch these shows. Instead, a large television set was installed.

The wireless, however, had always been acceptable to my mother. I remember well listening to Bertram Mills' Circus on the wireless. On one occasion, a performer fell off the Wall of Death. The commentator described how this man drove his motorcycle round and round the inside of a tube. Faster and faster he went, both his motorcycle and his body parallel to the floor. The excitement in the commentator's voice was intense ... Then, oh my God ... There was truly a deathly silence followed by a faltering explanation about how elephants are trained. I learned later that the man died.

The wireless in those days did a lot for the English language, for real events were described. Today, with television, we just look. In the evening, when my parents' guests arrived for dinner, I would peer through the banisters of the landing, watching, listening to what they had to say and when they had all arrived and were out of sight it was bed for me with a plate of biscuits and a glass of Ovaltine as I listened to *Dick Barton, Special Agent*.

I attended an infants' school in Baker Street in London for a time – up a long steep staircase. I was collected each morning at the entrance of Fountain House in Park Street by my father's groom, Macauley, who brought a pony and trap to take me to school. The pony was called Gypsy – a savage brute that would, given half a chance, rather eat flesh than hay. I rode this pony in Hyde Park with my father when I was not at school. My father's horse was called Starlight, a fine bay gelding, a hunter, but blind in one eye. Macauley was tall, elegantly dressed and sported an orange handlebar moustache. He would sit atop a large grey mare waiting for us by the fountain in Hyde Park. My father and I crossed the road and mounted our horses. On one occasion, Starlight bolted with my father, frightened, I imagine, by a lorry that had crept up on his blind side. Hell for leather, they went straight down Rotten Row. Macauley very wisely, in my view, hung onto my pony, Gypsy, who had it in mind to join this wild chase. Onto the scene came the Household Cavalry, smart as new paint in their shining breastplates and horsehair plumes dangling from their helmets. My father and Starlight hit them head on, straight between their ranks. The cavalry scattered, horses heaved, troopers were thrown to the ground – there was mayhem.

The trap that took me to my school in Baker Street returned at twelve o'clock to take me back to Park Lane. One time, on our way past the American Embassy, a wheel came off and Nanny Fletcher and I were thrown into a heap. Macauley set about repairs and we walked home. Shortly after this, I moved to a school in Henley-on-Thames called Rupert House. Nearby was Rupert's Elm, the remains of a tree where Prince Rupert had hung a dozen or so Parliamentarian soldiers during the Civil War. I was fascinated by this tree for I was, at the time, most concerned with ghosts.

At six I was sent to a prep school, Sandroyd near Tollard Royal in Wiltshire. I was the youngest boy in that school and as a result the masters and most of the boys were very kind to me. At just six years old, I was something of a curiosity. I cried myself to sleep for weeks at the beginning of each term. It was not that I hated school, just that I loved my home. The boys wore purple caps, grey flannel shorts and jackets. Each holiday, we made a pilgrimage to Rowes of Bond Street, a school outfitters. I hated being fitted for clothes. New shoes were pure torture for me then and, indeed, still are. In later life I did a deal with my father. We bought six dozen pairs of Gucci shoes that fitted us – we had not only the same size feet, but also the same shape – black loafers for which Gucci charged more as we wanted them without any brass ornaments. My father wore the shoes first, I when they were beginning to age.

Holidays were filled with people, and on Sundays, church followed by a cocktail party. At church we had our own pew, the one behind the local squire. At least it was our pew until a retired civil servant with a knighthood came to Fawley Green, when we moved back a row and he sat behind the squire. Rather, he sat behind where the Squire, Margaret Mackenzie, would have sat if she had ever come to church. Margaret Mackenzie had the gift of the living, but seldom attended services to test the quality of the parsons whom she appointed. It was a formal church: if anyone arrived after the service had begun, the opening door would squeak and the whole congregation would turn and watch as the latecomers found their seats.

My parents kept what amounted to open house. There was always a place at our table, always enough food to go round if someone arrived unexpectedly, or decided to stay on for a meal. No friend of mine or my brothers and sister was ever turned away. My mother played tennis in the mornings with my father and their friends; in the evening they played Bridge or Canasta. In the summer, if the weather was good, we ate our lunch beside the swimming pool that was several hundred yards from the house. Platters of food were carried there by Harris and all the help he could muster. I was trained to serve at table along with my brothers at an early age. Harris was a good teacher and taught me how wine and food should be presented. He also taught me how to open a bottle of port by cutting off the end of the bottle's neck with a kitchen knife. We seldom sat down to lunch with fewer than twenty people. At the weekend, when the weather was good enough for swimming, people would arrive all day long and swim, have a drink or meal, and leave again.

When my parents travelled to London I was left in the country. I stayed with my Aunt Nancy and her husband on a farm that my parents owned high in the Chilterns, amongst their beech woods and only a mile or two from our home. I cannot, in fairness, say I hated those days, for my aunt and uncle were kind to me, it was just that their home was not my home. My cousin, Anne, their daughter, was two years older than I. In the fashion of older children she believed it was her duty to tell me what to do. She may have been right, but I hated that and consequently I hated her. She was also a lot cleverer than I, and a better horse rider. She was fearless and I, a total coward, could not see the reward in taking what I regarded as an unconscionable risk in jumping over logs on a horse. To me there was no point to it at all. My mother was of the view that riding was good for children: it gave them exercise, and while they were out riding they could not be at home causing trouble. At one period we had a riding mistress called Pam, as a substitute for a nanny.

My younger brother David and I rode every morning around the fields of the family farm, jumping over bales of straw in the summer, wooden poles in the winter. We were taught to ride properly, taught to look after a horse and how to behave at a gymkhana. I never won a prize as my heart was not in it.

At prep school we rode two afternoons a week on ponies that were savage; ponies that bit and bolted; ponies dead on their legs that you needed to kick to get them into even the slowest form of locomotion; ponies that lunched off the hedgerow as we moved along; ponies with a penchant for heading straight for trees with low branches. School had every type of pony so well known and described by Thelwell. These ponies had only one thing in common: when they were turned towards home, they forgot about eating hedgerows, or trying to bite their riders, or even trees with low branches. These ponies that walked in their sleep became, as if by magic, bundles of energy with only one purpose; as if commanded by some invisible Master of Horse, they all set out for home at a dead run. How I hated those horses and at the age of five was quite prepared to couple the home of my cousin Anne, with my hatred of those ponies.

I did, however, love westerns. This my mother and I had in common. We would set off to the cinema at Henley or Marlow to watch a western at the drop of a local paper with a western advertised in it. Once we went to both cinemas on the same day, first to Marlow to see *High Noon* with Gary Cooper as the fearless marshal prepared to give up love for justice and duty, then on to Henley to watch Cooper again, this time as a scout working his way across Florida pursued by Indians in *Distant Drums*. *Shane* was a much-heralded film at the time, although my mother and I thought it a very poor thing; the star, Alan Ladd, a complete wimp. We liked our westerns hard and tough. My mother had only one complaint about these westerns: she could not stand the fact that cowboys kept their hats on when they went into buildings. She took some trouble to explain to me that such behaviour was the height of bad manners. My mother was very strong on manners. Once when she came across me eating a currant bun at the crossing of Henley's two main streets she really took me to task. 'Never eat in public,' she instructed.

My experience of horses was not at all bad. Once a week we rode slowly across country to the village of Hambleden. With careful planning it could be reached without going any distance on a road. We made our way through the beech woods of the Chilterns. For me, we were in the high country of Montana or woods of Nevada; the hills and valleys of Buckinghamshire became the foothills of the Rockies. We turned along a leafy track through the beech woods away from the ridge of the Chilterns, down a valley with the farm where my uncle and aunt lived and began to catch glimpses of the village of Hambleden. There was no hurry; it was an easy ride, with just the woods and the slow swish of undergrowth as our ponies tugged at a branch, or pushed another aside with their flanks. In the spring there were primroses and bluebells, masses of them, great pools of colour. No one came this way apart from the occasional forester. I rode with the riding mistress, Pam, and my brother, but I rode alone with my thoughts.

Hambleden was a small village, with the big house and its attendant dower house, a church and a smithy. We came to see the blacksmith, the smell of burning hoof as the red-hot shoe is fitted, the roar of the bellows as they forced wind amongst the coals, turning them bright red in the furnace as the shoe is heated again and knocked into a tighter curve. The blacksmith held my pony's hock between his legs and trimmed the hoof, fitting the red-hot shoe again. He drove home the nails with certain strokes of his hammer and with long-handled pincers nipped the points of the nails that protruded from the upper side of the hoof. He dropped the pony's leg, stood straight and rubbed its back, patting its rump as I led it away. Pam gossiped with the smith; David and I played, the ponies hitched to a nearby railing. Then it was home again, back up into the Chilterns, through the great beech woods, woods that were not always friendly, woods that frightened my cousin Anne and I when we strayed into them. For these were woods with shadows that hid behind massive trees, woods with patches of darkness and deep undergrowth, woods where unquiet spirits played. We ran as fast as we could to my aunt's house, tearful and terrified.

Whilst I was attending Rupert House I lived with my aunt during the week, moving home at weekends. As if this was not bad enough, my parents used to send me to Scotland each summer. The pretext for this visit was that I enjoyed Scotland. While I have an immense admiration, indeed a love, for the idea of Scotland and most things Scottish, I did not, in those days, enjoy the reality of the place. I stayed with my godfather David Paterson on a farm just outside the town of Ayr not far from the Castle of Dunure, a ruin filled, I was convinced, with ghosts. There were ghosts on the hill and in the farmhouse. They lurked in the ruins of castles all along that coast; they frightened me and they fascinated me.

As a treat I was taken to Butlin's Holiday Camp outside Ayr. In retrospect I am rather glad that I was given this experience, for despite the fact that the holiday camp was a cold and in my view thoroughly unattractive place, I find that these days my sojourn there has become immensely useful to drop into a conversation about the world's grander holiday resorts.

I travelled to Ayr by Dakota from Northolt to Prestwick. My playmate on my godfather's farm was a small, red-haired girl who, convinced that I was English, was determined to humiliate me. 'Show me your muscles,' she demanded, and I did, bending my arm hoping that a small lump would appear. Thwack! The wretched child had hit me where the muscle ought to have been. 'Can you walk across the burn on this wooden plank?' I asked, and as she tried to cross the burn I tipped her in. 'My father will leather you right around the farm,' she shouted as she set off home, a somewhat bedraggled but in her anger heroic figure. 'You've spoilt my new kilt.' I went in fear and trembling for some weeks lest her father catch me without the protection of my godfather.

In the barn I watched the farmhands killing rats with sticks as they fled from under a pile of sacks. One ran up the trouser leg of the little red-haired girl's father, and we laughed and he laughed. I travelled on the tractor as they made the stooks at harvest time. I attended the cattle auctions held beside the railway station in Ayr. Once, after an auction, I was taken to lunch in the Station Hotel. We ate minced meat, or at least they ate minced meat. Mine rolled and rolled around my mouth, becoming an inedible and tasteless bundle. We sat and sat. Some of the adults left. In time, my godfather and I sat alone, a barely touched bowl of mince between us. He, with a hard look, insisted that I eat the revolting stuff. I, with a dogged determination, said that I could not. The mince followed me home and at each meal it reappeared until Mary, my godparents' housekeeper, suggested that I give the inedible stuff to the dog when no one was looking.

I loved Mary and we visited castles together. There was Culzean, the house of Eisenhower, with its great circles of swords and guns on the wall of its grand staircase. A masterpiece by Robert Adams, it was for me at the time just a castle, but amongst the best that I knew, far better than Stirling, or even Edinburgh. The ramparts at Culzean were poor things by comparison with those great castles, but the guns and swords had caught my imagination.

Dunure Castle was ruined, but romantic, placed atop a small fishing port. Mary and I sat in the sunshine and ate ice creams, and I asked her of ghosts. When it rained we made expeditions to Robert Burns's house and the Brig' o' Doon, where there was a hotel where we ate and looked at the bridge through the dining-room window. I could see Tom O'Shanter crossing that bridge, drunk beyond belief, the devil holding his horse's tail. Mary and I travelled to Edinburgh and I bought tartan presents for my parents.

Mary made me potato cakes and Scotch pancakes; she played my games with a wild enthusiasm as we ran around the small, windswept garden in front of that white-painted, long, low house. Once, we went to the cinema to see a film about a boy who ran away, joined a circus and then caught typhoid. For several nights afterwards, I was convinced that I had contracted the disease. Mary comforted me and Mary reassured me. I enjoyed my days in Scotland, days of walks on the hill and picnics. My godparents' house was comfortable. They had no children, so they were, I suppose, a bit put out by having a small boy about the place, but they took my presence in good part. It was only afterwards that I realised how much they must have had to put up with as they played the parts I allocated to them in the fantasies of my childhood.

I returned many years later to that house for the funeral of my godfather. His wife wept as he lay in an open coffin surrounded by the men with whom he had drunk, bought cattle from or to whom he had sold farms. Stern men, they stood silent as the dominie recited the tale of my godfather's life. I loved my godparents and in particular I loved their housekeeper, Mary, but I was not happy there any more than I was happy at my school, as I preferred living at home. I could never really understand the reasoning that said because my parents had to leave home for business or pleasure, I had to leave as well. Why did I have to stay with these other people when I could well have stayed at home?

The first family holiday that I can clearly recall was a visit to Bournemouth. We stayed at the Branksome Towers Hotel, in the Tower Suite. Each day my nanny and I took a path through the Branksome Chimes to the beach. The beach in those days was defended by a high barricade of scaffolding interlaced with barbed wire. Signs warned of the dangers from landmines. One day the path was closed. There had, we were told, been 'a terrible murder'. The murder in question was indeed a terrible one, committed by Heath, a sadist and mass murderer.

We – the whole family and hangers on – set out for Bournemouth in our large, wooden-bodied Rolls-Royce shooting brake. Hitched behind this stately vehicle was a trailer normally used for transporting pigs. The trailer was filled with baggage; the shooting brake filled with people. The journey from Henley-on-Thames to Bournemouth is only about sixty miles, yet we were equipped as if we were setting out on a transpolar expedition.

Just after passing Basingstoke we pulled off the road onto a layby, which was edged by a golf course. There was not much traffic on the road so the place was peaceful. Slopper climbed from the shooting brake and stood smartly to attention as he opened the vehicle's door for my mother. She rearranged the children and climbed out. One after another we followed her as Slopper opened the other door for my father. Then the unpacking began and a picnic rug was spread on the grass, containers of food and drink laid out. The family had their lunch.

The Tower Suite at the Branksome Towers was luxurious by the standards of English hotels, but it did have its drawbacks. There was virtually no food in the hotel, and the electricity in the rooms was metered. This presented no problem to us, for we had brought our food with us and an electric stove to cook it all on. Slopper rigged up the stove and we set about cooking breakfasts of sausages and eggs – just one of the benefits of living on a farm. My sister sat up until the early hours of the morning before we left, determined to use the last of the money put into the meter.

We often went to Bournemouth for our summer holidays, some-times staying at the Branksome Towers, sometimes at the Palace Hotel. I particularly remember one occasion, when my sister had just become engaged. She wore a two-piece bathing suit. What a scandal. We were all deeply shocked: such behaviour was nearly unknown in Britain, let alone Bournemouth. On another memorable occasion we received a case of bananas. They were objects of wonder; I had never seen a banana before.

When I think about it, my sister's fiancé was also an object of wonder to a small child. An officer in the Life Guards, Robin Borwick was young and dashing, wore armour and rode a black horse. Neither he nor my sister had very much of a sense of humour, at least not as far as the practical jokes of a small boy are concerned. Paradise for me at that time was Hamley's toy shop in Regent Street. Visiting Hamley's, I headed straight for the conjuring department, where they kept the practical jokes. I had noticed that Robin Borwick always cut the white of his fried egg from the yolk, leaving it on the side of his plate. One morning at breakfast he was handed a plate of fried eggs and bacon. He cut the bacon with no trouble. Then he started to cut the egg and it shot across the dining room table. Quickly, he retrieved the egg and tried again, but the same thing happened. By this time the poor man was covered in embarrassment and tried for a third time. The table was covered in bacon and rubber fried egg.

My sister's wedding was spectacular. All my family were there, as were the household staff, the farm staff and the staff from my family's business. Then there were friends, hundreds of them. Robin Borwick wore his uniform and a guard of honour from his regiment stood, swords drawn making an arch, as the bride and groom left the church. The reception at the Dorchester was a triumph and all the farm staff, the household staff and staff from the family firm tucked into the food, particularly the champagne. Strong men who could down twenty pints in an evening and as many whiskies with them, became tipsy after a few glasses. The guard of honour became paralytic, falling all over the place, each armoured soldier landing on the hotel's marble floor with a resounding crash. Even my young brother David got tight and poured orange juice down a guardsman's boot while the poor fellow was in deep conversation.

Once, rather uncharacteristically, my parents decided on a bicycling holiday in Scotland. We stayed at the Trossacks Hotel at the foot of

Ben An, each day setting out on an expedition. I was perched on the handlebars of Nanny Fletcher's bicycle. It rained most days and when the rain cleared the midges homed in and attempted to eat us alive. Some days we fished from a boat on the loch. I never caught any fish, nor do I remember anyone else catching any. After a long trip across the loch we arrived at the village of Stronachlachar. My father, a great optimist, who I am sure felt this return to Scotland disappointing and no comparison with his youthful days in that country, asked an old lady – she seemed old to me, she was in fact probably about thirty – 'Where can we get a cup of coffee?' 'The woman replied, 'You'll get nae coffee in Stronachlachar.' Those sentiments pretty much summed up our Scottish holiday.

I was seven years old before I travelled outside England and my first journey abroad was one of considerable excitement. We went to the South of France. This was to me an enchanted land. In the days before air travel was the normal means of transport we went by train, and for as long as I live I shall never forget my first journey from Victoria station, where the Blue Train was drawn alongside the platform, bursting with people. In those days travelling was a grand affair for the rich. The station master, complete in tailcoat and top hat, shook us all by the hand and wished us well. The officials of Thomas Cook, in smart uniforms, directed porters who appeared to heave great cabin trunks as though they were as light as shopping bags. Chauffeurs and maids attended us and many of the other travellers, fidgeting with the details of the baggage. The sleeping car attendants greeted us with an enthusiasm encouraged by the expectation of a tip.

To a small child it was all a world of wonder, complete with the mystery of steam that seemed to spout both from the engine and between the carriages. The coaches were dark blue, resplendent with gold lettering, and drawn by a mammoth engine. As we sped through the Kent countryside, luncheon was served. We were always a large party – my brother and sister, a nanny, my aunt and uncle, and several hangers-on, along with my parents.

Lunch over, the Blue Train drew into Dover, and thence aboard the cross-Channel train ferry. We had a cabin reserved and sat there, watching the sea – in those days it was more of an exciting novelty than an inconvenience to travel between Britain and the continent. A knock on the cabin door announced the Captain's steward, who issued an invitation to take tea with the Captain on the bridge.

At Calais the Blue Train left the ferry and set out apace for Paris, arriving at the Gare du Nord at about six o'clock. We children always stayed on the train as it chugged its way around the city, while our parents and their friends set out in evening dress for cocktails at the Plaza Athenee and then to dine at the Tour d'Argent, rejoining the train around midnight at the Gare du Sud.

Our compartments became our bedroom. Bench seats became bunks, tables became wash basins and lavatories, or rather the receptacle for a large china pot. I slept fitfully that night, and with the light of morning edging the blind, I could not lie still any longer. The blind, once released, shot upwards on its roller, its movement ending in a noisy clack, and there were the bright blue sea, the orange rocks and giant cacti. At least they seemed giant to me, for the only cacti that I had ever seen were miserable, sickly things two inches high in a minuscule clay pot that I had bought at a garden fete. The Blue Train swayed along the twisting track that borders the Mediterranean into tunnels where the smoke filled my compartment, out of the tunnels with the smoke flying free like a war pennant atop the train. It was, I think, the brightness of the light, the sharpness of the sunlight that made the landscape seem so very different. I could, as far as I was concerned, have arrived on the moon.

Other trips were made to Switzerland in the years after the end of the war. First we went to Gstaad, on skiing holidays. I hated the snow, and I still do. I think I can predict snow, for as soon as the horrible stuff is in the air I feel sick. My father loved Switzerland and the Swiss. I did not, and do not, love either.

My father had many friends in Switzerland, made through his Deputy Chairmanship of the Dorchester Hotel, which had always been managed by a Swiss. In fact, when my family first owned the hotel, knowing nothing of how to run such a place, they enquired as to who were the most famous hoteliers in Switzerland. The Bonn family was recommended to them. Switzerland was, at that time, the home of the hotel industry, and the Bonn family the doyens of that industry. However, the Bonn whom my family hired to run their new hotel was – unknown to them – the only member of his family not to be engaged in the hotel industry. He was a cavalry officer in the Swiss army. Only years later, after he had made a great success of the Dorchester, did my family discover this.

The London Bonn's first name was Anton and he became famous not only for running a splendid luxury hotel with military discipline and the precision of a Swiss watch, but also for arranging credit for his British customers at a variety of Europe's most famous watering holes. Those of his British customers who travelled could enjoy their time spent on the Continent and settle their bills in London at the Dorchester. While this seemed a sensible and convenient system that demonstrated an enthusiasm for European cooperation that we are all urged to display today, it was, in the second half of the 1940s, highly illegal. Currency control gripped those who wished to travel in its icy grasp, a currency control that lasted until Margaret Thatcher abolished it in 1979. The Dorchester Hotel became famous for these activities and soon the heavy hand of the law descended and the directors were prosecuted. My great uncle, the Dorchester's Chairman, who was completely unaware of what had been going on, had to pay a heavy fine. Bonn, however, never really understood what he had done that so upset everyone.

My family were always welcomed by hotel keepers in Switzerland. After all, they had been sending them all those customers, and the Bonn family in particular were pleased to see us. Their family ran the Station Hotel at Basle, where half the station is in France and the other half in Switzerland and, on my first trip, as we cleared French customs we were greeted by Anton Bonn's brother and led to the hotel's dining room. They knew the deprivations that British families had suffered and determined in some part to make up for them. The table was covered in freshly baked rolls, black cherry jam and pastries. Omelettes and bacon appeared as if by magic; platters of cold ham were presented and entrée dishes of sausages surrounded by heaps of mushrooms. We all tucked in, and then came the chocolates. Nanny Fletcher ate everything she could lay her hands on and for an encore vomited the food from the middle of the bridge across the tracks, all over the visiting train. No one minded: we were British; we had just won the war. In those years we went to Davos for Christmas. I wanted Christmas at home.

Winter was not the only time that we made the pilgrimage to Switzerland. In the summer we stayed at the Berganstock on Lake Lucerne. The weather was usually awful, thunder rolling up the lake towards Vitznau. The beach at the Berganstock was a short stretch of pebbles infested with mosquitoes, reached by a funicular for which you had to pay. I have never really forgiven the Swiss nation for the meanness that they demonstrated to me as a child. Their meanness was in no way personal, in fact, as individuals the many Swiss who were my family's friends showed us remarkable generosity. The meanness of the Swiss is congenital. The charging for reaching a hotel's beach when you were staying as a guest in that hotel I regard much in the same light as if they had imposed a charge on using the hotel's lifts. It was, however, in Gstaad that I encountered the truly congenital meanness of the Swiss. The chambermaids in the hotel used to remove the handles of the bath taps after they cleaned the baths in the morning, replacing them late at night as they turned down the beds after you had gone downstairs to dine. Only one bath a day was allowed in the Switzerland of the late 1940s.

Holidays as a child, while usually spent in the utmost comfort, were never the happiest moments of my life. I much preferred to stay at home, where I had around me my own possessions and the people whom I knew and loved. Strangely, when I grew up, I felt and still do feel an irresistible urge to travel.

4

Schooldays

My education at Stowe was, in the formal sense, a disaster. I left, I think, with three O Levels; it may have been only two. In the event, this failure has served me well as I am able to criticise John Major's total lack of intellect with impunity. John Major is given to attacking those who criticise him, and who have achieved honours at Oxford or Cambridge, with the accusation that they patronise him. I suffer no such disadvantage as I was on building sites and drinking in pubs whilst Major was still at school trying to pass any sort of exam. I have always believed there is no need for a formal education so long as you have the wit to realise that you must acquire an education as you go through life.

Whilst at Stowe I was bored by Latin, fascinated by geometry and judged a disaster at English. I regret that I never discovered until much later how I could use those subjects later in my life. My geometry is now out of date, but visual alertness has stayed with me, and as for English, no master I met at Stowe would have given me other than very long odds on earning a living by writing.

Stowe's gardens were my passion. I did not realise it at the time, but as I idled, I wandered amongst masterpieces of architecture. In the days when I attended the school both the grounds and the buildings were in decline. Columns had been removed from William Kent's Temple of Concord to build a new chapel. The architect, William Clough Ellis, thought nothing of this piece of vandalism anymore, I suppose, than he thought about the missing staircase from his new building for the school's Chatham House, where an iron stairway was later bolted onto the outside of the building's rear elevation, in sharp contrast to its neo-Georgian façade, after he realised one had been completely forgotten in his original plans.

It was, I think, the air of dereliction that permeated the gardens that fascinated me: the lakes overgrown with reeds and choked with weed; the damaged grottoes, sea shells plucked from their walls; the Monument to the British Worthies, the busts of our nation's heroes and heroines each with their nose broken; streams that no longer ran; gardens, like the Japanese gardens, no longer recognisable as such; the Gothic castle, then used as an armoury to store the ancient Lee Enfield .303 rifles that we carried as we marched in the Corps, urged on by a tuneless brass band.

I was a particularly useless boy soldier: I could not march in time: 'Who do you think you are, Fred Astaire?' the sergeant from the Ox and Bucks Light Infantry would shout at me as I shuffled my feet, trying to regain the step. I never really forgave Harold Macmillan for reorganising the army, so causing Stowe's Corps to be transferred from the civilised supervision of the Coldstream Guards to the ungodly Ox and Bucks Light Infantry, who marched at 180 paces to the minute and spoke a language as unintelligible to me as Serbo-Croat. 'You look like an 'og,' their sergeant major would shout at me as the elegant Algy Cluff, who commanded Stowe's Corps, would preen himself in his spotless uniform, its trousers with creases like knife edges. My turnout, however hard I might try, always looked as if I had slept in it and slept badly.

Each year we had what was called a Field Day. First, we would parade in front of some great dignitary, and then that dignitary would move amongst us as we carried out military duties, such as cleaning our rifles or taking a Bren gun apart. I usually tried to be the second half of a Bren gun team. There was always great competition at the beginning of the day to carry the Bren gun, a heavy but glamorous weapon, but few boys other than I ever wanted to carry the wooden rattle that simulated the sound of the gun firing. As the day went on and the Bren gun became heavier for my companion to carry, he always wanted to swap tasks. My reward for the lack of a glamorous job was in having to carry only the light wooden rattle, from which I refused to be parted under any circumstances.

On this particular Field Day we were inspected by the late Lord Mountbatten. In order to give the best of impressions, a small group of the scruffiest boys was told to cook lunch. I lit the fire and got out my billy can and on this metal dish that serves as both cooking utensil and drinking vessel, I cooked several pieces of liver. They were just about ready when Lord Mountbatten arrived. Normally, I suppose, he would not have shown any great interest in a bunch of cooks. This time, however, he walked straight up to me, took the fork out of my hand and without a word ate all the liver, which I had been greatly looking forward to eating myself. That afternoon we paraded to bid him farewell as he took off in his helicopter. Sadly his departure was an anticlimax, for someone had stolen a vital part of his helicopter's engine and he had to return to London by car.

I hated the Corps: climbing trees and sliding down ropes from cliff faces was not my idea of fun, nor was wading through lakes up to my neck in muddy water, for I am short and in those days was shorter. These games were not just fun to entertain schoolboys, for as we practised war we knew that in time we would all do our National Service and likely see active service. Each day we read in our newspapers of the rising tensions in the Middle East that eventually led to the Suez Crisis.

My house master at Stowe was a parson called Windsor-Richards who, unsuccessful as a civil engineer, had taken to the Church of England and the trade of the schoolmaster. We had much in common, for he liked a pheasant or two for his dinner and I liked shooting them.

Windsor-Richards was engaged in restoring the gardens at Stowe. I would do anything not to play rugger or cricket, so I joined his team of recalcitrant sportsmen and we set about building a dam to reflood the Oxford Water, a lake that spans the main drive to Stowe House. Over this lake is a ravishingly beautiful bridge by Vanbrugh. It was only later, when I learned about construction, that I realised how little Windsor-Richards knew about engineering, for the reinforcement in his concrete dam consisted of any old iron, rusted or not, on which we could lay our hands. However, the lake filled with water and Windsor-Richards' dam stood sound as a rock.

My father liked Windsor-Richards. A man who enjoyed a dry Martini and understood something about construction was just his cup of tea. Windsor-Richards had great plans for the garden at Stowe. Lakes were to be dredged and their banks repaired. The temple roofs that were now heaps of mouldering lathe and plaster; the walls that were in danger of collapse; the overgrown gardens, and the delicate job of repairing those noses of Britain's worthies were of no interest to Windsor-Richards. He, like so many of his former calling, liked to move large quantities of earth, or muck as they called it. My father arranged for Windsor-Richards to have the necessary equipment. A small crane complete with a dragline was delivered to Stowe, and with it a bulldozer and a van. With this equipment came Frank Porter and his son-in-law, Dennis. Frank drove the dragline and Dennis made himself useful. Many years later Dennis became my driver and worked for me until 1976. At Stowe, however, Frank, a short and plump Cockney, and Dennis, a Clint Eastwood look-alike, were my tutors. They taught me to drive a dragline, an operation which in the hands of an expert seems quite simple, but which is far more complicated than might be imagined. The bucket, a heavy steel affair with teeth at its mouth, is pulled close to the crane's cab with a wire cable. A second cable from the crane's jib is tightened at the same time, then the first cable is released, allowing the bucket to swing away from the cab. At the furthest point of the arc described by the bucket, you release the second cable and the bucket drops like a stone into the earth. You then repeat the first part of the operation and when the bucket full of earth is at the cab you repeat the second part of the operation, having first turned the crane through ninety degrees. The earth should at this point be deposited in a neat heap or in a lorry.

I always enjoyed driving draglines. It was, I suppose, a dream of most small boys to be allowed control of a powerful piece of machinery. To drive one of these cranes, or for that matter a bulldozer, needs all the coordination of hand, eye and mind that is learned playing cricket or rugby. I spent most of my spare time working with these machines. Dennis also taught me the rudiments of driving a van and I used to race around Stowe's extensive grounds on a network of private roads. All went well until I nearly ran down the new Headmaster, Creighton Miller, recruited from Fettes to put some moral fibre into the idle and scruffy boys that infested the lackadaisical Stowe. Amongst his first acts was to send my construction team packing, so Dennis and Frank Porter put their bulldozer and their crane on a low loader along with all their spare equipment, which was considerable, and set off down Stowe's elm-lined avenues to London.

As well as the landscape park, perhaps the greatest after the park at the Palais de Versaille, there was also the main house at Stowe, built by Vanbrugh. As I sat and stared at the ceiling instead of learning to decline a Latin verb, I looked at a masterpiece by Robert Adams. But I did not love Stowe or its buildings; they just happened to be part of my life. When, a few years ago, I became a governor of the school I met many of the masters who had taught me. With the benefit of experience I was better able to judge their ability and I am bound to say I was not impressed. Nor did I hate Stowe; I just preferred being at home. As I look back on those years it seems to me that there was a loneliness in my life, yet I had, I remember, many companions.

The summer holidays were an adventure the year I left Stowe. I was free. I did not have to worry about exams; they were no longer an issue, for I had a job. I was to become a civil engineering contractor in the way that my great grandfather had been a civil engineering contractor, that my grandfather had followed that calling, as my father was a civil engineering contractor, as my elder brother was a civil engineering contractor, indeed, as a multitude of uncles and cousins, removed and not removed, had been and were civil engineering contractors. I barely knew what a civil engineering contractor was, but I was to become one.

At Stowe I had wondered whether I might become an architect. Such a profession fell within the orbit of family acceptability, whilst to suggest that I became a writer or a painter, or even an art dealer was out of the question. Not that I wanted to be any of these things, for it was firmly fixed in my mind that I should be a civil engineering contractor. However, I did voice a wish to become an architect. Those who taught me were amazed that my father, whom they regarded as an intelligent man, for his success was manifest by the cars that he rode in and the size of the cigars that he smoked, could not realise that he had a son who, to put it succinctly, was 'thick'. 'Your son,' these teachers told my father, 'is not clever enough to become an architect. He will not pass the necessary exams.' They were right in that I would not have passed those exams. They were, however, wrong about which exams I would need to pass. I do not blame them, for they sent me off into the world an innocent with no preconceived educational ideas and the world that they sent me into was a vast college where I set about identifying teachers, preying on their generosity both with their time and their wisdom.

I have always been lucky, but one piece of my luck that I did not discover until twenty or so years after I left Stowe is that I am dyslexic. My dyslexia has left me doubly blessed, for what I lacked in my ability to read and spell, I made up for with an active imagination. As for reading, I did not read before I was eleven, but like a child kept back from a feast, I tucked in with a wild enthusiasm when I had the chance. I read and read. My hatred of sport allowed me the time and I read whenever I should have been playing games. I read when I should have been doing my Latin prep.

Changes in life are apparently brought about by circumstances, but fate is a far subtler creature. It is the people whom you meet who really change your life. In my case it was Sherman Stonor, latterly Lord Camoys, who sowed the seeds of change in my brain. To me, in that summer of 1958 when I left Stowe, Sherman Stonor seemed old: I was a youth and he an immensely sophisticated adult. He liked me and he did not think that I was stupid. In fact, he gave me the impression that the reverse was true. He was not interested in civil engineering nor, I suspect, was he really interested in work of any kind. I spent a lot of my time at his magic home, Stonor Park.

I use the word magic not in any sense of literary extravagance. I use it for it is exactly the right word to describe the Stonor Park of my youth. Beside the small chapel attached to the left-hand wing of the house is to be found a ring of sarsen and pudding stones put there in prehistory, the earliest sign of habitation on a site that for over nine hundred years has been, and still is, occupied by members of the Stonor family. Nearby are the old stables and a group of cedar trees, amongst which Sherman Stonor is buried, his grave covered with a slab of slate as broad and heavy as the man himself. The left wing of Stonor Park holds the library, which stretches the length of it, barrel-vaulted and lined with bookcases. Amongst it reading tables, chairs and globes the Stonor children and I played our childish games. And as we played there was always the feeling that others who were not visible played with us.

The garden at the back of the house was reached through a gallery that ran the length of the house on the first floor. The gallery was hung with portraits and against its walls were cabinets that held ancient flint axe heads and pottery shards found in the grounds. At the far end of the gallery was a conservatory filled with comfortable chairs and rare, scented geraniums. The garden runs away from the rear of the house up the hill to a gate that leads towards the deserted Dower House and was then half kitchen garden, half lawn, the two separated by a bank of laurels. Nothing about Stonor was properly kept; there was the air of decay wherever you went in that house and its grounds.

I loved Stonor; I loved Sherman and his wife Jeanne, a woman whose face was of the palest white and her hair jet black. She wore spectacles with bright blue frames and blue tinted lenses. Jeanne, given the opportunity, could become a monster, striking terror into the minds of those who crossed her. However, she was always kind to me. Happily I have always had a sense for danger and an inclination to stay away while danger is abroad. Jeanne Stonor was an aggressive conversationalist given to the extreme statement. She tended to go round the table attacking each male guest in turn. You could never defeat her for I am sure that she never listened to a word anyone else uttered. One night, dining with my parents, she became involved in an argument about religion. Suddenly she announced that we would ask the Pope his opinion. We all rose from the table and moved to the next room, where we watched and listened in pure amazement as Jeanne Stonor telephone the Pope. After a few minutes she was put through to His Holiness.

Of Jeanne's five children, the three I knew best were Harriet, Georgina and Bobby. Bobby was the exact contemporary of my younger brother, while Georgina and Harriet spanned my age, one a year older, one a year younger. I was madly in love with Harriet, a love that was unrequited. In those days she was perfect: small and slim with long auburn hair, rosy cheeks and dark eyebrows. There were more flashy girls about: Susie Methuen, whom Harriet's brother Thomas pursued with boundless energy, was tall, elegant and devastatingly attractive; Joey Clover, another friend of mine, was athletic with a delight in fun. Harriet was reserved and there was something fragile and terribly vulnerable about her. As she grew older, she fell for the charms of a spotty but elegant young fellow from Eton, a close companion of the late Prince William. I could not stand the sight of this young man, who was in the habit of combing his golden locks in public. During childhood how extreme everything seems. People are wonderful or hateful, love is so deep, hate so lasting, and then like the early morning mist as the hot sun of life rises through the years, all of this goes away and it is as if these emotions, these images of the past, were nothing, just ghosts that wander in a busy memory.

We were all wonderfully childish in our lack of responsibility. On a couple of occasions we nearly got into trouble, once when a stray banger set light to a hedge that abutted the house. Luckily we were able to put out the fire before it set light to the building. Another time, I put a banger underneath the chaise-longue of Sir Malcolm Sargent, who was sunbathing in only his bathing trunks. It exploded and so did the famous conductor. 'Little boy, do you not realise that I earn my living with my ears?' I did not realise that. Small boys are notorious for their stupidity and I was no exception. Apart from that, it was the great conductor's bottom that was in danger not his ears.

In the winter when we could not play in the woods or the gardens as the light failed early, we played the game of Murder, turning all the lights off and squeezing into a cupboard or under a table while the murderer searched for us. I must admit that Stonor Park was a far better venue for this game than Benhams, for I always felt there that, although we children played alone, far more people played the game with me than just the other children.

The Stonors were a quarrelsome and eccentric family. Seldom would a meal in their home end with the same people with whom you had started at the table. Julia, the oldest, was emotional and I am afraid suffered from being the eldest. Blame more often than not found its way to her. Thomas, the eldest boy, was set to star from an early age. Now Deputy Chairman of BZW and Deputy Chairman of Sotheby's, he is destined to become the Queen's Chamberlain. Selected by the Foreign Office when he left Eton, he was despatched to Nepal, then a primitive country in the midst of a complicated political crisis, to be the tutor to Nepal's Crown Prince, Birendra, now the King of Nepal. When he used to stay at Stonor he came many times to swim in my family's pool where he was, he claimed, a sea god, which was somewhat surprising, for Nepal is nowhere near the sea. I remember some energetic young girl pushed the sea god's head under the water and pronounced to the amusement of all of us that the Crown Prince was mortal. The Crown Prince cried, and the youths in the pool displayed an indifference to royal tears.

In as much as her sister Harriet was fragile and gentle, Georgina was the opposite. She had a workmanlike approach to life, was good humoured but a thoughtful and serious woman of extremely strong character – the sort of woman that you would not tangle with unless you had a good reason. There was a lot of her mother in her, while Harriet took after her father.

This was the cast that lived in the enchanted Elizabethan mansion built in a valley amongst the Chiltern hills. These were the people who played parts in my childhood. They lived in a house amongst the fallow deer that ate the sweet grass of their park land that has lain uncultivated for a thousand years. This family, one skip ahead of poverty at the time I knew them best, were the tutors who taught me as I changed from a child to a man. Stonor Park, their home, was the school where I learned those lessons.

Sherman Stonor was a man who was endlessly fascinated by life and all that filled the world, whether it be a rare orchid or piece of Gothic revival furniture. Often I travelled with him in his Jaguar XJ150 to see a particular carved church doorway many miles away or some other great curiosity. He was one of life's natural educators, his mind was filled with a million pieces of useless but fascinating information mixed with childish stories that only the telling made funny. Sherman was, above all, a kind man.

Sherman's great delight in those days was the same as mine – fireworks. We were forever planning firework parties and, thrown at almost any excuse, they were truly magnificent displays. There was nothing that this family did that I was not fascinated by and so I watched and listened and I learned. When you are staying in a house party, Sherman Stonor told me, and you wish to visit a girl in another part of the house, always crawl on all fours. That way you avoid creaking floorboards. 'Does that work?' I asked. 'Yes, but it has a drawback,' he replied. 'When I did that I crashed head first into another man doing the same thing and coming in the other direction. We looked at each other in the dark and both turned around and crawled back to our rooms.'

Sherman Stonor's qualities and drawbacks exactly mirrored those of my own father; they were alike in many ways. Both of them were interested in people; they both, I suppose, collected people. Around the lunch table at Stonor Park were always seated the interesting, the famous and the downright obscure. And often, it was those from obscurity who had that snippet of information that is really worth having.

I sat at that table on many a Sunday, mesmerised by the likes of Betjeman and Piper, Osbert Lancaster and Graham Greene. There were Ambassadors, visiting statesmen and cabinet ministers, amongst them Lord John Hope, the son-in-law of Somerset Maugham. I remember only too well the day that the architect Guy Morgan shot Lord John Hope, then the Minister of Works. Morgan, a fellow guest, hit the minister squarely across his backside, happily at some distance so the force had gone out of the lead shot. Nevertheless, the minister did a little dance of pain. By good fortune this social blunder happened during the last drive before lunch, so Sherman was able to save Guy Morgan, an irascible Welshman, from the embarrassment of being sent home. Tactfully, Sherman arranged for the afternoon's shooting to be abandoned and extra port at lunch to be drunk instead.

Eartha Kitt came to lunch one Sunday at a time when she was at the height of both her fame and physical prowess. For some reason she elected to demonstrate gymnastics on the kitchen table, to the delight of Sherman and myself and the distress of Catrina, the Spanish maid and cook, left in the dining room. Miss Kitts' husband, a one-armed manufacturer of sanitary ware from Texas, stamped his foot in anger. 'Where has she gone?' he shouted as he pounded the dining-room floor. He was lucky not to vanish himself, for the timbers were past their best.

Mia Farrow came to lunch. She was then the sixteen-year-old star of *Peyton Place*, the first American soap opera to be shown on British television. Her visit was of immense interest to a trio of wine merchants who attended at Stonor with great regularity. The brothers Jervaise, priests of some eminence and equally eminent historians, sat and held hands, breaking away only to take up a knife up and scrape the remains of the lunch from the fronts of their cassocks, then popping into their mouths the food that they had recovered.

Then there was the family priest, Father Smith. He hated me with a passion, perhaps because I was guilty of dumb insolence or perhaps because he disapproved of Protestants mixing with his flock. In any event, it all came to a head when Harriet remarked how far she had walked to church in Cannes while she was on holiday with my family. Father Smith scowled at me and then said accusingly, 'You let this child walk alone in that town?' 'Not a bit of it,' I replied. 'I walked with her and waited outside the church.'

How certain one is in youth. Then I saw a great gulf between our religions. Today that gulf is long behind me; in maturity I find the forgiving nature of the Catholic Church a considerable comfort. Filled with anger at my insolence, the priest turned to me and spat, 'When you address me, you can call me Father, or Father Smith or even Joe.' I cannot in truth recall what his Christian name was, but I am reasonably sure that it was not Joe. He went on, 'What I cannot stand is to be referred to in the abstract by you.' With this, he turned and strode out of the room. I am cursed with a desire to giggle when I am nervous. To giggle was not appropriate at that moment.

The most fascinating part of the Stonor house for a young boy such as myself was the attic. I spent some time in the attics, browsing amongst the great curiosities that were stored there, the most spectacular of which was a stuffed wild boar shot in the Chilterns at the beginning of the nineteenth century. Once I came across a cache of weapons, wheel locks and sporting guns, amongst which was a strange pistol broken into several parts. It was at that time my pleasure to restore old weapons; I also collected them and this pistol fascinated me. I took it at first to be an Arab pistol, but as I cleaned away centuries of dirt I found that it was of European manufacture, its lock marked with the initials R.A. and dated 1614. I showed it to a number of friends and they confirmed my view that it was a Scottish Snaplock pistol. So off to the Tower of London I went with this trophy. I was right, for soon the experts at the Tower agreed that this was not only a Scottish Snaplock pistol, but the earliest one known. The Tower made an offer of £300, a large price in those days. Sherman turned this down and some years later the pistol fetched many thousands of pounds at Sotheby's.

In those days I used to enjoy shooting at animals, a habit that I have long since abandoned. I have no desire to stop others killing animals and I recognise that others may well enjoy testing their skill against defenceless birds and beasts. In defence of field sports, I recognise that these activities hold together what is left of our country traditions. The hunt and the shoot bring country people together in a way that cannot be replaced by political meetings or bingo. However, the days when young men needed to be skilled with a firearm are long gone. Modern military skills are best acquired playing video games. The days when it was sooner or later important for young men to know the skills of woodland and stealth are long past. Today's world is about missiles and technology, nimble fingers and brains that work as fast as lightning. The countryside has gone. It would be far better to concrete the whole place over than leave it in the hands of pretend countrymen who extend cottages to mansions with money from the insurance or stock markets. Men like Sherman Stonor, true countrymen, are mostly long gone. Today you need only to attend a shoot to see the difference. They are peopled by so-called sportsmen dressed in Barbours and green wellingtons, who take more ammunition out for a day's shooting than they kill birds in a season. Sherman Stonor was so different: he wore an old tweed jacket, took no more than a pocketful of cartridges. Birds would fly over his stand and Sherman would glance at them, not even lifting his gun. Then, as happens in the Chilterns, a pheasant would break cover and with the wind in tail, rocket towards the stratosphere. Sherman would look up, his gun and body became one fluid motion as his back bent, his feet moved, and his gun hit his shoulder. One shot and the pheasant would fall far out on the plough behind his stand.

In the 1970s all changed at Stonor. The family quarrels knew a bitterness that had never been there before. Sherman Stonor inherited a fortune from his American mother, a woman who disapproved of him and once remarked, when Sherman caught mumps, that at last the good Lord had intervened and hopefully there would be no more children. Sherman changed as his circumstances changed. He drank and spent money with abandon. More importantly, he felt the need to perform. It would be so easy to write that Sherman Stonor's life was wasted, but to write such words would be a travesty of the truth. Sherman Stonor was as necessary to civilised existence as any great aria or poem. The fact that Sherman Stonor, one of a strange breed of Englishman born beyond his time, existed, only shows how we have lost something of great importance from the fabric of our nation in the struggle to be part of a modern world. Once, sitting at the dining-room table of Stonor Park, I heard the conversation turn to the conservation of rare animals. The argument about these endangered species rumbled on: how best to ensure their continued existence; whether it was indeed even necessary to do such a thing. Then a voice spoke up. I do not recall whose voice it was, but the words have stayed with me always, for the truth of them cut right to the heart of the matter. 'Protect endangered species, indeed. The Government should protect the Stonor family, for they are an endangered species far rarer than white gorillas.'

5

Working in the Family Business

My family's company offices were the ground and first floors of Fountain House, its entrance at 80 Park Lane. On the first floor was a suite of offices occupied by the partners, hung with the portraits of their predecessors. My cousin, Robin, had the first office, then there was Miss Palgrave's office, as she was the secretary to the partners. My Great Uncle Malcolm sat at a desk in the boardroom and his sons Kenneth and Malcolm H, as he was known, had identical desks at the other end of the room. My father used the next office. All these rooms were decorated in the same fashion: walnut veneer panelling in the main office and boardrooms, with walnut furniture upholstered in green leather, and dark green carpet. The corridors were cream, as were the general offices. My first memories of these offices as a small boy came from the ritual of attending on Miss Palgrave to collect the pens and pencils, the writing paper and notepaper that I would need at school. The family and the business were in those days one and the same thing. The family worked in the business and the business worked for the family, there was nothing else. Everything that involved them seemed to happen at 80 Park Lane. A year or two after I went to work on the building sites, I was invited to attend my first Directors' meetings and for the next two years I sat in on all the meetings of the partners. I did not contribute, nor was I expected to do other than sit and listen. I was there to learn how my family's business was run.

Those were the years when I learned about human nature, how very different the men inside the boardroom were from those on the building sites. I learned just how much each group of men depended on the other. My working life was male dominated at that point, for women did not come near construction sites and the female members of my family did not contribute to my family's business. Indeed, women in those days were anathema as far as business and the male members of my family were concerned. My family went to great lengths to exclude daughters and daughters-in-law from any possible involvement in their business affairs. No daughter could inherit any part of their business nor, for that matter, could any widow inherit her late husband's shares. In its strange way, this system worked.

The sun shone the day in 1958 when I arrived at the Shell site on the South Bank of London's River Thames. I was not new to this site as I had spent time there in my school holidays. On one occasion I had been terrified out of my wits as I went through the airlock to the tunnel face where the miners worked way below the Thames under compressed air. It wasn't the compressed air that frightened me, rather the medical examination I had to undergo before I was allowed into it – I was terrified of doctors and am still frightened by the very thought of having an injection.

I sat with a dozen or so miners who wore just vests, trousers and heavy boots. They worked hard these men, their job was dangerous and they were well paid for doing it. We sat shoulder to shoulder in the air lock and it took about thirty minutes to change the air pressure to that at the tunnel's face, and then another thirty minutes on the way out. We walked along the tunnel. Segments had been made watertight, but water still seeped in at the face and a pump kept it at about an inch deep. Electric lights were strung from the ceiling, a railway track ran down the centre, the atmosphere was heavy with the smells of oil and sweat. The sound of the pneumatic spades, used to cut the clay, rang backwards and forwards in the tunnel. I was fifteen and terrified.

On that morning in 1958 I climbed from my father's chauffeur-driven car and was directed to the site office. In a utilitarian meeting room sat John Sheenan, Manager of the Sir Robert McAlpine and Sons Ltd London Area. A tall, sturdy, red-faced man, he was something of a legend in my family. Inclined to drink, he once told one of my older cousins his fortune in no uncertain manner. The occasion was the firm's annual staff party, which took place on my father's farm, Westfields, whose fields ran alongside the Thames at Medmenham. Several hundred of the staff had arrived by steamer from London. There were marquees filled with food and drink in plenty. The afternoon was the time for children's sports. I can recall being forced to run in a three-legged race at an age when I was having trouble standing on two. As the day wore on the sports came to an end and the men settled down to the crack (the term used by Irishmen for reminiscing, not an illegal white substance stuffed up the nose) and serious drinking. It was at this point that my older cousin fell foul of John Sheenan and I must say I did not envy him the experience, for John Sheenan was indeed a formidable man when sober, but when the drink was on him and he was angry, he was a terrible sight to behold. My father was very fond of John Sheenan who rang him to apologise the next morning. However, it was clear that Sheenan must go, so when my great uncle rang my father to demand John Sheenan be dismissed, my father was able to say that he had already done so. Sheenan spent a holiday in Ireland and, the heat taken out of the situation, my father then re-employed him on his return to London. Taken back on in a junior capacity to save the faces of all concerned, Sheenan's natural talent soon had him back in charge of my father's department.

John Sheenan offered me a cup of tea and a biscuit, introduced me to the head timekeeper, a man by the name of Callaghan, and sent me on my way.

On my first day on a building site, the manager told me one of life's great truths. 'You are lucky,' he said, 'for you are young. No one expects you to know anything.' He was right. At sixteen I knew nothing and that was fairly obvious to all whom I came across. 'Turn what seems to you a disadvantage to advantage. Never fear to ask questions.' I took his advice for I could see wisdom in his face. Sam Hull was his name, an iron man whose handshake could bring you to your knees. He was, in his twisted way, as straight as a die. He did not see things as other men saw them. His philosophy, half biblical, half common-sense, was leavened with a natural cunning, tempered by the cold winds and sleety days on constructions sites. I was a callow youth whose schoolmasters had, if they had taught me anything, succeeded in removing from me any idea that I might have a mind capable of constructive thought, or that I had a memory worth the name. They had convinced me that I was both idle and stupid. It was for me the greatest gift that they could have given me, for when I arrived on the building sites, the men who worked there expected a youth convinced of his own brilliance. I learned from these men because I knew nothing, I needed to learn. I learned from them because I wanted to learn. I have always had an endless curiosity.

I worked in an office with a dozen or so other young timekeepers. Our duties involved getting to the site by seven-thirty a.m. to book the men on, and checking each man twice a day, morning and afternoon. This checking was done physically, so you took your time book with a list of 250 or so men and walked where you could, scrambled or climbed where you had to, around the building site until you had a tick against each name. Then at 6 o'clock you booked them off again. If a man was a minute late for work you docked a quarter of an hour's pay from his packet; if he was half an hour late you sent him home. The trouble usually arose on the afternoon check when men who had lunched too well at the nearby pubs were somewhat irritated if you sent them home as being not fit to work. I learned the most important aspect of my trade in those days as a timekeeper, learning the name of almost everyone on the site; furthermore I began to form opinions as to which were hard and efficient workers and which were layabouts. I got to know the foremen, their strengths and weaknesses. I learned about the families of these men, their problems and their triumphs. Many of them had worked for my grandfather, known as Mr Willie. I hardly knew him, but from my childhood memory he was a hard, stern man not given to playing with children, unlike my maternal grandfather, a school teacher and sometime employee of Tetley's Tea, his wife's family business. My paternal grandfather was a tough man, who in his early years could knock down any man that he employed, and often did. Construction in his day was a wild industry. His sternness, I believe, came from the knowledge of just how hard life can be. He was serious because being serious had served him well.

His father, the founder of my family's business, was born in 1847 and became a wage earner at the age of twelve, working in a coal mine on the Duke of Hamilton's estate. By the age of fifteen he was at work at the coal face near Coltness. By 1867 Robert McAlpine had married Agnes Hepburn, daughter of an elder of the church. The Hepburn family were stone masons and quite grand. Their next-door neighbours were the Livingstones, whose son David was the renowned missionary. Robert McAlpine, a bricklayer, was looked down upon by the Hepburns. Supposedly to impress his future father-in-law, he learned to read and write and got himself a job with a local builder, where he earned eighteen shillings a week with an extra twelve shillings for overtime. House builders in those days were known as Corks, for they bobbed up and down as and when work was available.

Robert, seeking secure employment, signed on at the Motherwell ironworks, where he earned more than double working on Sundays as a fitter repairing the brick linings of the furnaces, an extremely unpleasant job carried out in horrendous conditions. It seems that he was careful with his money and that this made an impression on the local bank manager, who offered to lend him the money to set up a business as a building contractor. He refused the offer and said that he would prefer to postpone his start in business until he had the funds himself. By 1869 he had achieved this and his first contract was the repairing of a chimney, for which he charged £2 9s. After a number of small jobs he won by tender the chance to build a signal box. It took him ten days and he cleared £50 profit. He financed this contract by borrowing £11 from the local butcher and pawning his watch.

Soon Robert was heavily engaged in house building. He worked with a team of labourers who mixed and fed him with his mortar. He regularly laid over 2,000 bricks a day himself, starting at four in the morning, and worked late into the night preparing his work schedule for the next day. One of his labourers was his firm friend, Keir Hardie, who later became the first Labour Member of Parliament and a founding father of the British Trade Union Movement. By the age of twenty-seven Robert McAlpine was employing a labour force of over a thousand men. His passion, however, was astronomy and he acquired a considerable telescope with which to watch the stars. His business prospered and soon he was earning £8,000 a year. He bought himself a fine house and consumed books as he set about acquiring an education.

The clan spirit that Robert McAlpine's Highland ancestors had brought with them when, after the 1745 rebellion, they were forced to migrate to the Lowlands in search of work, was still strong. Many of those who worked for him were his relations. It is true to say that the same clan spirit exists in the McAlpine family today. There has always been a tradition in the business of employing the relatives of their employees and I hope that this will always be the case. Four generations on from the original Robert McAlpine, the business is still owned by the McAlpine family and a strange sense of unity still holds us together. It will take more than several generations of southern living to kill these Highland instincts.

Robert McAlpine was amongst the first contractors in the world to use concrete. In fact he became so obsessed with the material that he acquired the nickname 'Concrete Bob'. He obviously had a cordial relationship with his employees, for they arranged a high tea for him in Hamilton town hall. These men shared his enthusiasm for concrete and after they had presented Robert's wife with 'a massive necklet in gold', they sang a parody of the 'Charge of the Light Brigade' which went thus: 'Forward the building trade, Forward! Our hero said, for building with concrete is a step onward. Was he a man destroyed? Not though the critics said that he had blundered. His not to make reply, his not to heed the cry, he did but do and try, houses of concrete and by the hundred.' McAlpine's bank manager, who attended this occasion, was reported as being highly impressed. Next my great-grandfather bought a carriage and pair then became a local councillor.

In 1878 the Glasgow Bank failed and McAlpine, along with most of the other businesses in Glasgow, was ruined, but he immediately set about recreating his business. His great breakthrough was winning the contract to build the Singer sewing machine factory in Glasgow. Meanwhile, he was remorseless in his efforts to educate himself. He took up with a well-known local botanist and together they made a study of grasses. Mineralogy also caught his attention and he set about learning about metals with a passion. A contemporary wrote of him: 'I discovered that he had a great craving to dive into the mysteries of nature', and that they (McAlpine and his friends) dis- cussed 'many of the subjects which only a few people generally talk about, such as the mystic, the Occult, the psychic, or spiritualistic.' Much later Sir Arthur Conan Doyle, who had the same interests, became one of Robert McAlpine's close friends. Dr Milroy, a com- panion of my great-grandfather who had studied the ancient Greeks, recited for him the songs of Homer and claimed that he 'fell in love with some of the Gods and Goddesses'. 'Often,' he wrote, 'Robert McAlpine would address me thus: "Come along, tell me more about blue-eyed Athena."' There is no doubt that he was a Highland romantic. A friend reported that Robert once said to him, 'I forget concrete and building when I hear a great musician – music takes me close to the grandest things in life.'

He described himself as 'a seeker after knowledge for sheer pleasure of the thing. I realise there is as much mystery in one atom of matter as in all the astronomy of the skies.' He added that he was 'also a firm believer in the power of the spirit behind matter'.

Robert McAlpine from middle-age became a vegetarian, because of his antipathy to killing animals and birds. I never met him and I can only judge how he looked from his portraits. What I know of this remarkable man has come to me by word of mouth and from that evidence. The following quotation from Reginald Pound's unpublished book seems to me more likely than not a fair description of the man: 'By then middle-aged, he had the dynastic look and bearing often seen in the Highlands, where the holder of a clan name enjoyed the prerogatives of membership of a family, regardless of his or her place in the wider social scene. Robert McAlpine carried himself like a Chieftain, without reference, so far as is known, to the romantic possibility of his descent from King Kenneth McAlpine, who united the Kingdom of the Picts and the Scots c. 870. His office staff, and some of the older outside men, habitually and fittingly referred to him as "The Chief". As part of his Highland inheritance, he was supposed to be fey. He claimed to have seen apparitions of his dead mother and that these apparitions had sustained him through the harder parts of his life.'

Robert McAlpine had, at the turn of the century, progressive views on the lot of the working man. He believed that the workers were entitled to a fair wage and somewhere of good quality to live. He was amongst the first employers to have resident nurses and doctors on his large civil engineering contracts. He also believed that if a man was not well fed, he was unlikely to work hard.

The illiterate twelve-year-old Robert McAlpine had come a long way from the Lanarkshire coal mines to become the founder of a successful dynasty. When his youngest daughter married Lloyd George's, the then Prime Minister's, eldest son, he had reached a place of influence in British national life that the Elder of the Kirk Mr Hepburn, who had looked down on the young bricklayer, could not possibly have envisaged. Robert McAlpine, however, not only could imagine this outcome to his life, but he did imagine it and what is more he had the energy, dedication and sense of purpose to make the product of his imagination a reality.

When I arrived at the building sites many years after my great-grandfather's death, stories of his doings still circulated. They called him in his later years 'the Umbrella Man', for he always dressed in a dark suit, wore a bowler hat and carried an umbrella, which he used without compunction to belabour anyone whom he considered was not working properly. One morning, arriving at the construction site where his company was building a power station, the old man spotted a gang of labourers digging a trench. They were not, in his opinion, working with enough enthusiasm, so he set about them with his umbrella and when they complained, dismissed them. Going to the office, he informed the works manager of what he had done. There was a strange air about the office and a number of whispered discussions took place, during which a delegate was elected to tell the old man that he had just dismissed a gang of workmen employed by the Gas Board.

In those days men worked encouraged by the carrot and the stick. The foremen, and for that matter members of my family, carried tickets that they gave out to men who seemed to be working especially hard, which entitled them to a bonus. Those who slacked received their cards on a Friday. Among those who worked for my great-grandfather was Patrick MacGill, one of the last tramp navvies, a man who later became a poet and writer. In his book *The Children of the Dead End* (published in 1915) he describes many of the experiences that he had working on the site of the Kinlochleven aluminium factory while it was under construction by my great-grandfather's company. The construction industry of those days was a brutally hard place to work. MacGill describes it thus: 'A sleepy hollow lay below, and within it a muddle of shacks, roofed with tarred canvas. The time was five o'clock in the morning; the night shift men were still at work and the pounding of hammers and grating noises of drills could be heard distinctly. The day shift men, already out of bed, were busily engaged preparing breakfast, and we could see them hopping half naked around the cabins, carrying pans and smoking tins in their hands, and roaring at one another as if all were in a bad temper ... The muck was caked on the bare arms, and a man, by constricting his muscles firmly, could break the dirt off his skin in hard dry scales, the hair stood out strongly from their cheeks and jowls, some were walking about the huts naked, the false modesty of civilisation was unknown.' MacGill goes on: 'Our picks and shovels froze until the hands that gripped them were scarred as if by red-hot spits. We shook uncertain over our toil, our sodden clothes scratching and itching the skin with each movement of the swinging hammers. Near at hand the lead Derrick jibs whirled on the pivots like spectres of some ghoulish carnival, and the muck barrows crunched backwards and forwards, all the dirt and rust hidden in woolly mantles of snow.'

By 1958, when I first went to work on a building site, much had changed. The Shell site opposite Waterloo station had just passed through one of the fiercest and longest strikes that the contracting industry had ever known. After a series of disturbances intended to disrupt the construction of Europe's largest office building and the Shell Oil Company, both symbols of capitalism, my family had taken the decision to close the site. Three and a half thousand men were dismissed and the site was closed for six months or so, after which it reopened and my family chose the men whom they wished to re-employ. This caused a ruction dubbed by the press 'The Battle of Waterloo'. Three thousand or more pickets came from all over Britain to stop workers getting onto the site. There was considerable violence, but in time the pickets went and work was resumed. My family had won a battle that has left our business virtually strike-free ever since.

The great strike was led by the Behan family. Dominic Behan actually worked on the Shell site and a better looking sort of workman you would be hard put to find. His brother Brian and the playwright, Brendan, roused the strikers with their oratory. I watched them at their work one sunny September afternoon as they addressed an audience of building workers on some vacant land opposite the site, next to the Festival Hall. The workers sat and ate their sandwiches in the sunshine as they listened to Brendan Behan haranguing them. 'What do you imagine that old McAlpine does when he gets home at night? Sit and pick his toenails? No, he works out more ways to make a profit, ways to put more blood on bricks.' This utterance, however, did not have the full bite of which Brendan Behan was capable. For instance, after the opening night of his play *The Hostage* at the Royal Court theatre, a member of the audience approached him with the words, 'I loved your play Mr Behan, but I didn't get the message.' Behan replied, 'What do you think I am, a bloody postman?'

The tail end of summer that year, 1958, was wonderful. I had found a new world, I revelled in the giant cranes, the thump of pile drivers, the rattling of kanga hammers as they cut away concrete, the roaring of bulldozers as they moved earth 100 feet below the streets of London. I climbed to where the steel erectors worked high above the concrete gang and watched as they moved concrete with vibrators–concrete that had come up the twenty-odd storeys through a pipe, pushed by a concrete pump, concrete mixed in the giant batcher plant. That building site had a life of its own, an energy, a hustle, a hurry to be finished.

I did, however, have a fear of heights and suffered from terrible nightmares as a result. I would scream in my sleep and scream and scream. Alone in my parents' flat, I would wake with the bedclothes tied in a knot around me as I lay on the bedroom floor. If my parents were there, my father would wake me. Once in my sleep, I lifted my bed and put it against the door. My father pushed and could not get in; by this time awake, I could not move the bed as it was far too heavy. Often I would find myself on the balcony of my parents' flat six floors above the street. Once, I remember, I was locked out in rain, waking drenched to the skin. What surprised me most about my terrible screaming was that none of the neighbours, who must have heard these screams, ever called the police or even rang our doorbell.

Slowly Christmas drew closer, the weather changed and in the New Year the cold winds blew down the Thames. Sleet would fall on the men who worked on the high steel, nails would freeze to the fingers of the joiners fixing the shutters that held the concrete in place until it set. There was very little protection from the weather on building sites. I tired of the food in the site's canteen, and began to eat my lunch in the Wimpy bar on Waterloo station. Long into a Thursday night I would sit, trying to balance my time book.

It was the responsibility of the timekeepers to make up the pay packets by hand, counting the cash, working out the hours and calculating the bonuses, and then filling the pay packets. The problem was to get the right money into the right packets. If you found that you had even a few shillings left you had to start all over again. If you were short of money, then it must come from your own pocket, so needless to say you counted it all again. Ten-shilling notes, half-crowns, two-shilling pieces, shillings and sixpences, pennies, half-pennies and farthings – each of them had to be in the right packet and the totals must balance.

At first I took the tube from the South Bank to Hyde Park Corner, then I walked to Fountain House, where I lived with my parents. I knew nobody in London and usually ate my dinner and went tired to bed. When winter came the tube filled with passengers and I started to walk home across Hungerford Bridge, Charing Cross Road, Soho and then through Mayfair to Park Lane. At first I walked straight home, but soon I lingered in Soho. I ate my dinner in a steak house and watched the prostitutes and the pimps. I quickly learned that if the ladies of the night were remotely attractive then they would take your money and leave you waiting on the pavement. I learned that clip joints were just that: whatever they offered they never delivered. I drank modestly in the pubs, more for company than pleasure. I wandered amongst the street theatre of London in my builder's boots and donkey jacket, the grime of the building site over my face and hands, my hair discoloured by concrete dust. I was another worker from a building site.

By the next winter, the Shell Centre was much changed. The ganger men and the labourers were mostly gone, the pile drivers had moved to the next contract, the monotowers – tall steel frames with a heavy crane on top of them, where I used to climb the 110 feet up vertical iron ladders to see the driver in his cab – had long disappeared. I used to stand beside their drivers and watch as he swung the crane on its steel towers and luffed the jib to lift a load of timber or scaffolding from a lorry high onto the building to where the shutter hands and scaffolders worked. All this had been replaced by joiners fixing the fancy panelling of the executive offices, electricians, plasterers and painters – materials were moved by lifts fixed to the outside of the building.

The Shell Centre is a vast place with its own power plant, shooting range, squash courts, swimming pool, concert hall, all below ground with acres of car parking – two thirds of that giant building is underground. In those days there was a night shift running on the site and I was transferred to work at night rather than day. Once I got used to working at night it suited me very well, for the few girls whom I knew were working but not terribly serious during the day, and were free to take long lunches. At night it was another matter, for they were mostly in the habit of going to parties to which I had not been invited. Generally I got home at seven-thirty in the morning, slept until twelve o'clock, got up, bathed and then took one of these, in my eyes at least, beautiful young girls out to lunch. I always felt, and I still do, that a good lunch is a far more satisfactory affair than a heavy dinner. My lunch guests went back to work and I came home for a snooze before setting out for work at five-thirty p.m.

The South Bank was a busy place at night, with people coming and going across Hungerford Bridge from Waterloo station, or arriving for concerts at the Festival Hall. Felix Topolski, the painter, gave parties in his studio under the arches of Hungerford Bridge, just a stone's throw from our site offices. We, the office staff, used to sit and watch the celebrities arrive as we took our tea break. One party that

Princess Margaret attended was a riotous affair, ending in the police being called. As a young man, I thought Princess Margaret wonderfully beautiful. Much later in my life I used to meet her occasionally at dinner parties.

Many years later, now a member of the House of Lords, I had just attended the opening of Parliament. By chance that evening I was next to Princess Margaret at dinner. I asked her had she enjoyed the ceremony – a silly question, and she said so. No, she had not. The only fun she had had that day was when the royal family took it in turns to try on the crowns. 'My father's crown fits me so much better than my sister, The Queen,' Princess Margaret informed me.

I asked if I could smoke my cigar, which I suppose was an equally silly question, for the Princess had smoked cigarettes all the way through dinner. 'Yes,' she said. As I started to light it, she snatched it from my mouth. 'You have no idea how to light a cigar,' the Princess informed me, a remark which I took rather badly as at the time I was smoking half a dozen cigars a day, cigars, I may say, of rather good quality. 'My father taught me to light cigars,' she informed me, which is a strange coincidence, for my father taught me how to light cigars and whilst he was not a king in the regal sense, he certainly was a king amongst cigar smokers – his collection of cigars, running into hundreds of thousands, was all perfectly stored at various cigar merchants in London. As a matter of interest to those less well versed in cigar smoking than either the Princess's late father or my late father, the way to light a cigar is to apply the flame of the match to the flat end, only removing the covering of the round end by pressing either side of it with your finger, causing its cap to pop off, after the cigar is alight. In this way the end of the cigar that you put to your lips remains perfectly dry. If you slobber over a cigar, then the result will be an attack of serious wind.

By midnight most of the fun left the South Bank. The violinist who played in the archway that led from the railway station to the concert hall, his choice of venue giving his music a resonance that was incredible, packed away his violin, changed his coinage into a bundle of bank notes at our office and set off for home. We builders of the night were left to our work, except, of course, for courting couples who often sought privacy in that lonely area. In order that they should enjoy privacy, one of the foremen had erected a hut attached to the site's hoarding. This hut was small and had a bench seat across its back wall. Couples came and sat on that bench and, imagining that they were unobserved, conducted their courtship. This considerate foreman had drilled a hole in the wall of the hut so that he and his mates could see and hear all that went on between these lovers.

There was, I think, more fun to be had working on the night shift than working the normal daylight hours. In the early hours of the morning we would slip across to Covent Garden for a mug of coffee laced with whisky. I loved the emptiness of those London nights, the way that they began with revellers going home to bed and the way that night begins its ending with the water carts in the streets and porters carrying boxes of flowers in the market. It was a joy to see these great bundles of flowers on the stalls of the old Covent Garden. It may not have been the most efficient way to distribute flowers and plants, but it had great style. That Christmas I bought boxes and boxes of different coloured carnations for my mother. The house was filled with them; every surface had a vase of carnations.

For the first time in my life I came across the lonely people of London: not the tramps who slept rough in the summer and found shelter in the doss houses during the winter but the bag ladies who used to walk all night going nowhere in particular, never arriving at a destination, just walking and walking until with the dawn they vanished into the bustle of working London. Another character of the night was Diamond Lil, a woman of vast proportions who would show her breasts and let the workmen feel them for half a crown. She was reputed to have worked the Brighton train as a young woman. When I came across her she worked the subculture of the arches of the Hungerford railway bridge and Waterloo station. Diamond Lil was a cheery soul who always appeared to delight in her occupation.

With the dawn and the first of the commuters from Waterloo station came the Happy Wanderers Band. They arrived by limousine and entertained the commuters, who walked like zombies across Waterloo Bridge, with their music. The Happy Wanderers' limousine collected them as the commuter rush came to an end. The proprietor of the flower stall at the entrance to the station was one of the first out and about. 'Now's the time to die, flowers are cheap,' he would call. The commuter zombies passed him and I doubt they heard his words. They might stop occasionally to buy a handful of daffodils or the like, a present purchased in the morning, perhaps for a member of the typing pool. On the way home they might stop again, a bunch of roses purchased in the evening, perhaps for the wife in recompense for thoughts incurred during the day of that youthful incumbent of the typing pool.

One morning our cement silo exploded. Cement flew everywhere. The City zombies walked like grey snowmen as a result. It was part of my job to handle complaints. That day we must have set off a boom never to be repeated amongst tailors, because we replaced so many suits. Once an irate businessman complained that a building worker had tipped a bucket of water on his head as he walked past our site on his way to Waterloo Bridge and work. I knew its contents, for I had used such a bucket many times. These buckets were placed on every floor of the building to save the workmen a walk to the lavatory. This was the way with building workers: they all thought the businessman's predicament a great joke. Those who worked on building sites imagined that they were a blessed race, free to live their lives much as they wished; they were not in the strait-jacket of convention that imprisoned businessmen. Building workers were free, proud men who viewed the zombies, whose regular lives were work and wife, with contempt.

Often I would stand with one of the foremen and watch the concrete gang as they worked under the great arc lights that illuminated the whole site. We would gossip about life and I learned the tales of the construction industry, of power stations long built, of the fights and the practical jokes, the tragedies, the deaths and the black humour that pervaded the construction sites in those days, of the cruelty that came from that humour and the mateship that men felt. Construction was a hard but wildly romantic world. Most of the men who worked for my family in those days had always worked for them. Often their fathers and sometimes grandfathers had worked for McAlpines. I met many foremen and workmen who had known my grandfather well, even some who had met my great-grandfather. These men were big men in every sense of the word, tough, hard, but emotional men, with names like Paddy Torpey, Andy Walsh and Hughie Dougherty; men with hands like shovels; all men from Donegal, Colchmuich and Kerry. I was told my grandfather believed that Irish men were the best workers, Scots the best supervisors and England the best place to work in. These men came in families and they worked as a family with us. Their sons and cousins were always sure of a job. If men were needed to work over a weekend on an emergency job, the likes of Paddy Torpey could recruit a hundred or so on a Friday night in the pubs of Camden Town. I was fascinated by these men and the tales that they told. I enjoyed their company and it was with their passing that I lost my enthusiasm for construction. John Sheenan, who was in charge of my education in those early days, told me a great truth about these men. 'Never,' he said, 'appeal to logic. Always appeal to their emotions.' The strange aspect of these people and their culture is that the folklore which they told and retold – for a favourite tale was never too much told – depended on an oral tradition and it was the way these tales were told that gave them their humour. Now they are lost, gone with the men who told them.

6

Out and About in London
and Other European Cities

As I look back on my early days in the construction industry, I realise just how patient my family were with my approach to life. I, on the other hand, was desperately impatient: nothing could be done with enough speed as far as I was concerned. Every problem had an answer and I could never understand why others failed to see solutions that were, to me, so obvious. My father once told me that his secretary, Miss Palgrave, had said that I did not suffer fools gladly. She was right only in part, for in my arrogance I did not suffer fools at all and I felt that I was, at that time, the sole judge of foolishness.

I was restless as a youth, always wanting to do different things and things differently from others. I was, as I gained experience, given responsibility for several building sites in London. In those days our cranes were everywhere and we dominated the market. My family were the first people to apply the principles of civil engineering to building contracts. Our contracts were always run by an agent who was a trained engineer, whereas the agents working for other builders were usually trained as carpenters and bricklayers. I travelled between these sites all day, attending meetings and endlessly walking around the works to encourage the various managements on these contracts to greater efforts. I cursed my father, who had the terrible habit of always arriving on one of the contracts under my control just after the men had started their tea break and he would grumble that the crane was still and the job silent.

It was my habit at this time to invite a girlfriend to the theatre most evenings – in those days a young man would have many girlfriends and in the main these girls were friends in the true sense of the word.

Young people in the late 1950s and early 1960s did not enjoy the promiscuity that became commonplace a few years later. To attend the theatre, it was normal to wear a dinner jacket if you sat in the better seats. Afterwards we would go to dine at the Dorchester, where there was a cabaret. For many years my father, who was the Deputy Chairman and then the Chairman of the hotel, took an interest in arranging these cabarets. Usually they were composed of a singer or a comedian, followed by a conjuror or juggler and dancing girls. My girlfriend and I would eat our dinner, dance, watch the cabaret and then I would return her to her home.

One of the regular guests at the Dorchester was Jack Cotton, who could truly be described as a property tycoon. He lived in the hotel along with his fine collection of Impressionist paintings. He was always kind to me, often stopping to say 'hello' and gossip. In retrospect, I have come to believe that it may have been my female companions who attracted his attention. Jack Cotton did, however, give me one invaluable piece of advice. 'Young man,' he said, 'never try to over-tip a head waiter in order to get his goodwill and the best table. It is a waste of time and very expensive. Give a large tip instead to the cloakroom attendant, for when you entertain a guest and hope to impress him so that you can do business, the first person you meet will be the cloakroom attendant. This attendant will always remember your name because few people ever give a large tip to a cloakroom attendant. You will be greeted by this man and fussed over, so by the time you reach the domain of the head waiter your guest will be so impressed that how you are treated from then on is immaterial.' Cotton sat almost every night in the Dorchester Terrace Room with his mistress, an elderly grey-haired lady, and they appeared barely to speak.

I seldom went out to parties at that stage, for I did not know many people who gave parties. I enjoyed the company of individuals and small groups. Another of my favourite night spots was the Blue Angel, a smallish very dark night club where you could cuddle as you danced. The cabaret at the Blue Angel was introduced by Nöel Harrison. I used to eat Chicken à la King there, a wonderful dish rarely seen on a menu these days. If the weather was clement after I had returned my companion to her home, I would visit the night shift on one of the sites for which I was responsible. On one particular night, when the summer had wandered into what should have been winter and the night was warm, I stood on the scaffolding three storeys above where the night shift were working, that is twenty-seven storeys above the ground if I looked outwards. After a while I noticed a man climb up the ladder beside me. As he turned and addressed me with considerable aggression, I could not help but notice that his breath stank of raw alcohol. This man informed me that it was his intention to throw me off the scaffold. Indeed, he said, he probably would throw both of us off the scaffold. 'Why?' I asked. He had been sacked, he said; there was no future for him; his life was one of despair. I knew this man: he was a hardworking labourer who had spent the early part of the evening in the pub. No doubt the foreman had sacked him as much for his own good as ours, and equally without doubt he would be re-employed the next night. It seemed, under the circumstances, a great waste for him to jump off a scaffold from twenty-seven storeys high. I was also somewhat reluctant to accompany him. 'Sack you,' I said. 'Impossible. You are one of the finest men that I employ. How could anyone be so stupid as to sack you? I don't believe it.' We climbed one after the other down the ladders to the ground. My mistake was to go first, for the wretched fellow put his feet on my fingers at almost every step. When we were firmly at ground level we searched for the foreman. 'Did you sack this man?' I asked. 'Yes,' he replied. 'Then put him out the gate.' The man resisted and the foreman hit him between the eyes. The next night, however, the labourer was back at work and greeted me like a long-lost friend.

How the construction industry has changed. Labourers dress well and drink less, the night shifts are gone and so have the remnants of that strange culture. One day, as I was just leaving the site of Smithfield Market, which the company were then rebuilding, I was accosted by a certain Jack Hussey. Accosted is probably not the word to describe having someone grab you by the lapels of your suit. Hussey was a part-time wrestler and full-time ganger man, and was generally in charge of organising the muck lorries. You needed to be tough to do that job, for muck lorry drivers were a violent lot, not much given to waiting around. Hussey, it seems, had been sacked and I may say not before time, for likeable as he was, he caused endless trouble with his propensity for fighting. What he wanted to know was why he had been sacked, and then he said he intended to kill me. I doubt if he was serious, but I did not put a lot of faith in his ability to avoid killing me by accident. I quickly invented a fiction. 'Sack you, Jack? I had to. It was the only way I could save you. The

Revenue has been asking questions. I had to tell them that you have gone back to Ireland.' Hussey shook my hand until it hurt, embraced me until my ribs almost cracked and, with tears in his eyes, thanked me. Jack Hussey was still thanking me as he set off for the train and the next boat back to his homeland.

More and more these days, I spent time with Irishmen, drinking in pubs, listening to the crack. I used to visit the site in Lombard Street where we were rebuilding the Clydesdale Bank. Behind the bank was a pub, a pub which, as was the habit in the City of London, closed at about 7 o'clock. Now 7 o'clock is about the time serious drinking gets started in pubs near building sites, so the upstairs room was kept open and we drank and talked. Beer was followed by chasers of whisky; pints and pints of beer were accompanied by a string of chasers. I enjoyed pubs in those days and I visited a great many of them, from the Denmark Arms in Brompton Road to the Prospect of Whitby just off the Mile End Road. The East End of London was then still a dangerous place. The doors to houses in Cable Street were reinforced with sheets of iron and had steel plates with peepholes in them.

I was working in the East End demolishing buildings, of which Martineaux's sugar refinery was one. Most of the steel that came from these buildings we sold to a scrap merchant, a Pole with pink and chewed ears called Tony Horsika. He was about five foot tall and when drunk could, and indeed often would, stand on his head while he smoked a cigarette and blew smoke rings from his mouth. Horsika always insisted in paying for the metal he bought in cash, which came in a suitcase and was usually presented by a very drunk Horsika to my father when he made a site visit. The appearance of all this cash caused endless confusion in our accounts department as, on one occasion, did my idea that we should pay the drivers of the muck lorries in cash.

We had just won the contract to excavate the Barbican site and at the same time we were contracted to pull down what remained of the buildings left after the terrible fire caused by bombing in the war. The site was about twenty-four acres, filled with basements and cellars, a number of which had people still living in them. The haulage firms formed a ring. They would not shift our muck for under eight shillings a cubic yard. We were to be paid eight shillings to dig and haul that muck. In those days a contractor made his profit by varying the prices for the amounts of hard and soft material to be moved. On the Barbican site our surveyor Stan Hailes felt that the client's surveyors had underestimated the amount of hard material, for which we would be paid something of the order of twenty-seven shillings to dig. We priced the hard material high, and the soft material low, so our tender figure came out by far the lowest. When the job was remeasured and it was found that there was, in fact, far more hard material than expected, we made a considerable profit. However, regardless of this outcome, eight shillings was too high a figure to pay for haulage. We were being blackmailed by the large haulage firms, so I drew a sum of money from the office and paid six shillings cash to whoever would take the muck away, hoping to attract the independent owner-drivers of lorries. All and sundry turned up and, of course, they mostly had the wrong licences – in those days to haul gravel or muck you needed a B licence. These licences were hard to obtain, which gave a virtual monopoly to the large companies.

In one day, admittedly the best day, we moved over 2,000 cubic yards of muck, a prodigious quantity when you consider that this was a London building site. All, however, did not run smoothly. Many of the haulers were immigrants and recently arrived in London. They were, it was rumoured, financed by Shirley Bassey. These men were enthusiastic, but not well tutored in the ways of the capital. It did not seem to matter a lot to them where they tipped this earth. Rumour had it that the strange mound at Hyde Park Corner came from the Barbican, as it appeared overnight, much to the surprise of the contractor who was working on the road intersection there. A trench, newly dug by Murphys along Oxford Street during the day, was filled up by lorries from our site during the night.

Amongst those with lorries working on the site were lorry drivers employed by Bill Edrich. Famous England cricketer he may have been, but that cut little ice with either me or my foreman, Paddy Torpey. We were in the business of moving muck and moving it fast. If a lorry broke down and blocked the queue, we moved it out of the way with a bulldozer. Edrich felt that he were not being treated with the respect he deserved. Some of the freelance drivers had found a spot in which to tip muck that clearly no one else knew existed. An area of pristine ground – no fence and no potholes – it was a perfect place to leave unwanted material. It was also a perfect place to play football and the local police were in the habit of doing just that. All hell broke out. The illicit drivers abandoned their lorries and headed for the metaphorical hills, complaints flew fast and furious. 'I will change the man in charge,' I told the client. Paddy Torpey went and Dick Torpey arrived and still there were complaints. 'I will change the man in charge again,' I told the client. Dick Torpey went and Tom Torpey arrived. 'This is ridiculous,' said the client. 'All you are giving me is the same bread with a different jam.' Again I changed the man in charge and we still went on shifting muck until it had all gone.

My family owned at this time a painting and decorating business that prospered with the building boom and I was given charge of it. The man who ran the business day to day was a tall, well-built Scotsman by the name of Alec Wardrope. We got along together remarkably well having, amongst other things, a shared interest in boats – not in sailing them, rather in buying them. We went to boat shows and we studied boat magazines; we made trips to the Essex marshes to look at old hulks; we visited West Country fishing ports to view redundant fishing boats. Take it from me: if you ever get the feeling that you wish to buy a boat, go outside and walk around until that feeling goes away. A boat is a luxury that ranks alongside divorce as amongst the biggest expenses in which a man can indulge.

In time I bought a boat, a disused MTB, which I suppose was only marginally less stupid than the 200-foot mine sweeper that I had set my heart on. I imagined myself racing across the waves and Alec Wardrope joined in this fantasy. Two years later we sold the MTB untouched. When you touch a second-hand boat you only make it worse. It is like a woollen jumper in which you have cut a strand of wool. You give it a pull and away it comes in your hand. Pull again and again and you have nothing left. Each repair that you make to an old boat only reveals another area that needs repairing. Far better build a new boat than repair an old one. The company that we ran together was called Balcloutha after the house my great-grandfather once owned – the word Balcloutha is Gaelic for Mouth of the Clyde. Apart from straightforward painting and decorating, this company manufactured fibrous plaster mouldings and also worked in fibreglass.

There was at that time in Britain a programme to rebuild the slaughter houses and meat markets. The largest of these was the first stage of rebuilding Smithfield. Balcloutha had acquired the rights to a patent slaughter house floor from Germany, the best example of which was in Hamburg, so Alec Wardrope and I set out on a trip.

We combined visiting the Hamburg slaughter houses, to look at their floors, with a visit to Stockholm to see a patent sprayed plaster, and then to Milan where a mosaic finish called Grissitti, which we had an interest in, was to be found – it had been used to face the Pirelli building.

First we visited Stockholm, where the weather was brisk and fresh. We assiduously toured building sites during the day and turned down the offer of seats at the opera to tour night clubs at night. It was folly to miss a performance at the Drottningholm Palace Theatre. I have since been there several times, but I was young and ignorant. Stockholm passed without trouble. Even Hamburg passed without trouble, despite finding ourselves in a club where Germans did unimaginable things to a donkey. At one of the clubs we visited, we were seated behind the bar, I imagine because the place was over full of customers. Between both of us were placed two not very attractive hostesses. In the night clubs of Hamburg, which all seemed to open at about breakfast time, it was the habit to sell you a glass of beer and chaser of schnapps both at the same time. I drank the beer, but lined up the full glasses of schnapps in order to keep count of the number of beers that I had consumed. The hostess, spotting my intention, poured my schnapps, all ten of them, into the beer of a man with his back to the bar. This man from England looked as if he was on holiday with a rugger team. Soon the poor fellow turned and, picking up his beer, downed it in one long draught. A few minutes later his beer fortified with schnapps downed him. As he slid from his bar stool he mumbled that beer had never done this to him before.

Then it was on to Milan, where we spent our time examining the Pirelli building. I had, at that time, never heard of the building's architect, Gió Ponti. I was truly impressed with his work; indeed, it has made a lasting impression on me. I thought then, and I still believe, that the Pirelli building is amongst the most elegant buildings in the world. It was a shame about the Grissitti finish, however, which started to fall off some years later. It was due, I am sure, to no fault of Gió Ponte's, for the same thing happened to me when I stuck this stuff on buildings in Britain.

That night we dined in the arcade near Milan's Cathedral. Prostitutes lined the streets like guardsmen. We finished our dinner, hailed a taxi and gave the driver the name of a club that we had been recommended to visit. The taxi driver drove around the city for the best part of half an hour before dropping us within yards of where he had picked us up. 'Why are we here?' we asked. 'We're right back where we started.' The driver pointed at a doorway and sure enough there was an illuminated sign with the club's name. Feeling a bit stupid we did not argue, but simply went inside. Before long we were joined by two girls and two bottles of champagne. We discovered that these women spoke English and two more bottles of champagne arrived. Most of the previous bottles had run amongst the ice in the champagne bucket when the girls turned the bottles upside down long before we had finished them.

Soon we entered into the spirit of the thing. Champagne kept coming and the other customers and their selected women started leaving. We were the only two men left in the club when one of the girls told us she desperately needed help. 'Help', we said in chorus, we're just the chaps to help you. She needed help for she was being held prisoner by the proprietor of the club. This was a rather different sort of help from that which we had in mind. The girl started to cry and her colleague joined in. She, too, it seemed, was a captive. The club appeared to become filled with men, who now surrounded our table. 'Stand up,' I said to Alec. Now he was not exactly a giant, but he had spent his life on construction sites, much of it as a bricklayer. When this formidable Scot rose to his full height the encroaching Italians hesitated. We left the girls and a bundle of notes behind as we backed to the door, out onto the street and – whether by chance or because he had no other customers – into the same taxi that had brought us there. The next day we set off for London, poorer, exhausted and perhaps even wiser men.

After our exploits on continental Europe my life began to change. As I grew older my father began to introduce me to the concept that you could not make money out of construction unless you first persuaded someone to give you a contract to construct a building. Of course, you could tender for work and quite often we did tender successfully. St Thomas's hospital was one such contract. The Ministry of Health first employed the hospital's own staff architect. A pleasant man, he was soon judged inadequate for the job and York, Rosenberg & Mardel were appointed. My father agreed that we would stop work on the hospital and let our cranes stand for one year while Rosenberg got on with the planning. I regret never having met Mr York, who was the moving force in the partnership. He had died of throat cancer just before I came into contact with his firm. Eugene

Rosenberg I knew well and often I would go to their offices in Greystoke Place, an elegant building caught between a disused graveyard and a pedestrian cut, off Fleet Street. Hanging on the walls of this building were York's collection of paintings, mostly by British painters of the 1940s and 1950s. There were several early paintings by William Scott that were particularly fine.

I always had some difficulty in understanding Eugene Rosenberg as he tended to change the normal order of words when speaking. I believe he liked me, for we got on well together, seldom being unable to resolve the endless disputes that arose over the building of St Thomas's. There was, however, an irresponsible quality about Rosenberg that irritated the hell out of his partners, two of whom, Brian Henderson and David Alford, became, and still are, my friends.

David Alford and Brian Henderson loved food and drink. The Etoile in Charlotte Street was a favourite haunt of ours. One day as we lunched, a heavily built man in loosely fitting black jacket, black tie and striped blue shirt with a stiff white collar ambled over to our table. He had a poor quality cigar burning in one hand and a glass full of brandy in the other. Brian Henderson introduced him as Cedric Price, a fellow architect. Cedric Price sat down and our long friendship began.

Cedric Price is the most remarkable of thinkers. His architecture is many years in advance of the generation who now are heralded as Britain's best architects. For instance, his Fun Palace designed for Joan Littlewood, but sadly never built, was the building that influenced Richard Rogers' Beaubourg Centre in Paris and his Lloyd's Building in London. No one had, until Price, suggested the idea of putting the guts of a building on the outside. The difference between Price and Rogers is, however, fundamental for Price put the services on the outside of his Fun Palace so that the building could be taken apart and moved, or merely destroyed, for he does not believe in longevity of buildings. Rogers, on the other hand, put the services on the outside of his buildings because they looked nice that way, although he might with justice argue that doing so saved internal space.

Cedric Price has an honesty of purpose that frightens people who might pass work his way. He is, like so much great talent in Britain, a commercial failure, not because he is commercially unsound, rather because he will stick to a point that he believes in. His conscience is his own, it has not the flexibility in it to make the life of those he works for easier at the expense of principle. He is one of the very few truly principled people I have ever met. In a country that delights in the second rate, promotes the flashy and fashionable and, without fail, continues to put in high office men with a record of continual failure, there is little place for Price. Time, however, will be Price's friend, for as the years pass his importance will grow in the minds of those who think about architecture. I am sure Cedric Price will receive the most glowing of obituaries; his work will be praised, his archives plundered and long after he is dead his buildings may even be built. His ideas will be perverted and words put into his long-dead mouth. Meanwhile I am proud to be his friend and grateful that he took the time to be my tutor in so many aspects of life. Each morning, for many years, Cedric Price and I would take breakfast together. Starting at seven or seven-thirty we would argue, he a left-wing Socialist, I a right-wing Conservative. Some people go each morning to a gymnasium in order to limber up. I used to argue with Cedric Price to get my mind in shape. After these sessions, replete with eggs, bacon, sausages and fried bread, my mind alert, I would head for the Central Office of the Conservative Party, where I worked for fifteen years.

David Alford, Brian Henderson and I used often to lunch at Le Poulbot in Cheapside. Our lunches were long, the food and wine of the best quality, but our time was not wasted on gluttony. We discussed art, painting and sculpture, architecture and design. We gossiped about our mutual friends and I learned because I listened to what these two men had to say. One lunchtime at the Pulbot, so enthralled were we in our wine, food and conversation, I believe in the reverse order, that the time passed without notice. A couple came and sat down at the next table. Brian Henderson remarked to them, 'You're late for lunch.' They replied, 'We're about to eat dinner.'

We talked of travel, but seldom of politics. I believe both Henderson and Alford voted Labour in the 1960s but by 1979 they were Conservative voters. The experience of Socialism had changed their views. This is why, I believe, Britain every once in a while needs a Labour government to teach us what Socialism is really like, for it is often beyond the memory of many voters to remember when Britain last had a Socialist government. And if, by chance, that new Labour government turns out to be Conservative in thought and deed, so much the better. Then the Conservatives will have truly triumphed, for the whole point of politics is to convert your opponent to your way of thinking. I have no interest in keeping a particular bunch of men and women of a political persuasion in office just for their own benefit.

I learned, at lunch with Alford and Henderson, that you do not sell someone an idea by continuously batting on about it, nor do you make converts to your idea if you guard it tightly, insisting that no one else may use it.

Lunchtime became for me the most important part of the day. It was then that my father entertained developers and architects, quantity surveyors and engineers. I ate with him often, usually in the Terrace Room of the Dorchester, modelled on the Terrace Restaurant in the Tivoli Gardens in Copenhagen. The head waiter was an Italian called Tony Torrone, his assistant a Cypriot called George. When George took your order he would start with the words, 'The steak and kidney pie on the trolley is wonderful,' and then add, 'The chef has told me that I have got to get rid of it.' My father had so many lunch appointments that after a while he employed a sometime property developer, Jack Lundy, to help him get through the list of those he had to meet. Lundy worked on commission and was known as my father's second stomach. My father was immensely able at getting work and at that time over two thirds of our turnover came from negotiated contracts.

As I grew up and entertained on my own I was more often than not joined at lunch by Peter Scott, a young man in our business and a protégé of my father's. He had been appointed by my father to run the family's London building department at the age of twenty-nine, having worked for my family, except for a break when he went to the war, from the age of sixteen. He started work for the princely sum of ten shillings and retired at the age of sixty-four. Peter Scott and I became very close; in fact I believe that we were telepathic. We worked as a team, he the practised builder, I the entrepreneur. To say that Peter Scott was a son to my father would be no exaggeration; certainly he was a second father to me. I found it easier in those early days, perhaps more so than later on, to form very strong friendships, and such a friendship was mine with Peter Scott.

Another of our favourite places to eat was the Coq d'Or. I was often taken there as a small boy. The proprietor Mr Sartori was, at the time the hotel opened in 1930, the head waiter in the Dorchester Restaurant. His manager, Charles, had worked at the Mayfair Hotel, where he was in the banqueting department, and had supervised my parents' wedding reception in 1929. The wine waiter, a dignified gentleman called Gallo, was the brother-in-law of the second waiter in the Dorchester Grill. The restaurant, long and narrow, every table a wall table, was soberly decorated. It has now become the fashionable Stratton Street restaurant Langans.

In those days the bar of the Coq d'Or had a large rotisserie at the back of it on which chickens turned in rows. Max Joseph, when he bought the Coq d'Or, removed the rotisserie and its chickens. Along with the rotisserie went Sartori and Gallo, followed after a few years by Charles. Great restaurants are not made by décor or even by brilliant chefs; it is the people who work in a restaurant, combined with the people who eat in that restaurant, who make it truly great. Remove either and an era is passed. The place may well serve brilliant food and have equally brilliant service, but something has gone along with those people, that something which made the place memorable.

One property developer who seemed to have an unusual success in the late 1960s and early 1970s was Eric Miller. That success, however, turned to abject failure by the end of the 1970s. I was always fond of Eric Miller, or Sir Eric Miller as he became in the notorious 'Lavender Paper' Honours List produced in 1976 by Harold Wilson, but supposedly compiled and written on lavender notepaper by Marcia Falkender. I liked both Harold Wilson and Marcia Falkender. They were extremely kind to me in the mid-1970s. In any event, it was a resignation Honours List, which is supposed to include the names of those who have helped a prime minister. He or she can put the names of their cooks, or Chef de Cabinets on that list, just as the fancy takes them. Indeed, Harold Wilson was entitled to put the name of anyone he wanted to on that list, whatever its colour. At a meeting in Central Office when this apparent scandal broke, there was great excitement among the staff there. They set off after Harold Wilson's blood like a pack of hungry mongrels. 'Wait a minute. Just wait a minute before you start attacking Harold Wilson and his Honours Lists,' advised Lord Thorneycroft. 'I received my peerage on a Wilson Honours List.' There was a shocked silence in the room. Marcia Falkender was Harold Wilson's secretary and it seemed to me the most normal thing in the world that she should have jotted down a few names as an *aide-memoire*. Who cares? Perhaps they were her suggestions.

In the matter of Eric Miller, however, there were problems. His name was on the final list and he had been allowed to come far too close to the workings of government. He knew too much about the workings of the Labour Party and contemporary Socialism in general. In an injudicious moment, Harold Wilson had made Miller the Treasurer of Socialist International, the organisation that coordinated the activities of Socialist parties around the world. More importantly, however, Miller got into financial trouble.

The problems with the friends of prime ministers only start when those friends need help. Eric Miller needed help. There was a revolt in his company board room and a group of directors, headed by Lord Mais, were keen to get rid of them. Raymond Mais had done this kind of thing before; he was a natural cuckoo. Bring Raymond Mais into your company and he would, as sure as cuckoos' eggs become little cuckoos and little cuckoos become large cuckoos, push you out. My father had warned Miller of this, who explained how wrong my father was about the man. The board met with the shareholders and Lord Mais addressed them all. Then Sir Eric Miller stood up and gave his address, starting with the immortal lines, 'It is true that I have made a few mistakes, three of them are sitting behind me.' Lord Mais won, Sir Eric Miller lost. A few days later, he was found shot through the head in the garden of his home; that day was the holiest holiday in the Jewish calendar. Neighbours were convinced that they heard two shots fired. I have always had my doubts about the manner of his death.

The generous, overly obliging Eric Miller when he was in financial trouble became a threat, for he was a man who expected help from those whom he had helped. His wife, Myra, was a classic Jewish beauty. Life with Eric Miller could not have been easy. Myra, however, showed nothing but the greatest dignity, often under extremely adverse circumstances.

Eric Miller was a surly, moody, difficult man, but immensely kind when he felt like being so. One night in 1973 my telephone rang at about ten-thirty at night. I was already in bed. 'Eric here. Would you like to go and listen to Ella Fitzgerald?' There was nothing that I would rather do. We arrived at Ronnie Scott's and the place was packed. The head waiter greeted Miller like a brother. There was, however, no empty table, nor any likelihood that there might be one. 'But for you, Mr Miller,' as he was then, 'there will be a table.' And there was one very quickly. I watched as the head waiter strolled up to a couple sitting at a table near the stage. He leaned forward and whispered to the man, who turned and spoke to his female companion.

He then rose and walked out of the room to a telephone kiosk, where he waited, holding a telephone to his ear. Seconds after he had left the restaurant, the head waiter went over to the woman and spoke to her. She rose and headed for the telephone kiosks. Waiters, moving with well-trained ease, stripped the table as we were ushered towards it. The man and the woman tried to return, but their passage was blocked. We listened to Ella Fitzgerald, who was fantastic. At the end of the performance, Miller took me to her dressing room, where she threw herself around him like an old fur coat. The poor woman's eyes were so inflamed from smoke that she could barely see. This, she told me, resulted from many years of singing in smoky atmospheres. It took, she said, a couple of hours each night to get her eyesight back.

On another occasion, again the telephone rang as I was just falling asleep, this time near midnight. 'We're going to Paris tomorrow. I will pick you up at seven o'clock.' True to his word, and somewhat to my surprise, Eric Miller arrived at the door of the house that I had built myself in Hans Place, Knightsbridge. We drove in his Rolls-Royce. He sat in the back with Reginald Maudling who lived opposite me; I sat in the front with the chauffeur. After about twenty minutes we arrived at Battersea heliport, where we waited for a helicopter to take us to Heathrow. At that time helicopters landed a long way from the main terminal and the three of us climbed from the helicopter to a car that drove at a snail's pace around the airport's perimeter road to the terminal. We cleared Customs and Immigration then, back aboard the car, we set off again to a private jet that waited for us. 'We will have a slot in half an hour,' the pilot told us and, true to his word, at ten o'clock we took off. It had not, I suppose, occurred to Eric Miller that if we had used the services of British Airways we could, by this time, have been in Paris.

The flight took about forty-five minutes and we were served breakfast by a beautiful, long-legged girl, whose legs would have been perfect in a night club but became an inconvenience in a small jet. Then we went by car to the Plaza Athénée where we arrived at about twelve-thirty. 'We are to lunch with the Chairman of Perrier Water,' Miller informed us. As we drew up at the Plaza Athénée and climbed from the limousine Miller had hired for the trip, a beautiful woman put her head out of a first-floor window and shouted, 'Hello Daddy.' The three of us looked up. Eric Miller waved and Reginald Maudling and I looked at each other. Who was this beautiful creature who had appeared so suddenly? It was, in fact, Eric Miller's daughter. What she was doing there, at that moment, I have not the least idea but Miller put it down to chance. Inside the Plaza Athénée, caviar and vodka were ordered, Eric's daughter joined us and we all tucked into a large tin of Beluga caviar and several glasses of vodka. This party lasted some time and it must have been well past two o'clock before we arrived at the headquarters of the organisation that bottles Perrier water. The Chairman greeted us as if we had arrived exactly at the right moment and after a glass or two of Dom Perignon we were taken up a spiral staircase at the end of his office. This was no ordinary spiral staircase, nor was his any ordinary office. First of all, it was nearly fifty feet long and perhaps half of that as wide, decorated in a sumptuous fashion. The spiral staircase was not one where you duck your head as you climb, rather it rose slowly with shallow steps set in a grand curve. Upstairs was the Chairman's private dining room. The table was set with antique cutlery and fine glass. There were so many of these glasses that they looked like regiments assembling for a parade; the parade that they had been prepared for was, in fact, a parade of the finest wines. Liveried butlers hovered; their white-gloved hands appeared as if from nowhere to change a plate or fill a glass; the meal went on and on.

As we ate the conversation ranged across a whole spectrum of subjects. At no time did I get even the remotest hint of why we were there. Reggie Maudling clearly did not know why we were there either; indeed I doubt if this rather grand French industrialist, who was our host, knew why we were there. His functionaries who lunched with us gave no hint as to our purpose and I began to wonder if Eric Miller really had any idea why we had come all this way to lunch. No word was said during the whole meal that could possibly have been of any significance. I knew why I was in Paris with Eric Miller; he had building contracts to let and I was determined to win them. If, in fact, he had suggested lunch at Morrie Blooms in the Mile End Road, I would have gone with him. Now, I like a lunch of salt beef at Blooms, but I have to admit that the munificence of this captain of French industry was something else. The lunch was not wasted on me, for it was my first experience of how the grand figures of French industry lunch while at work. I had eaten in many board dining rooms in England but found nothing that remotely compares with this experience.

Strange as my day had been, all this was only a small example of

Eric Miller's excesses and eccentricities. Our plane took off from Orly without delay. More caviar was served and with it more vodka. The leggy French girl, our hostess, repeated her impersonation of the Hunchback of Notre-Dame in the small cabin. Eric Miller sent for the pilot and was soon deep in a whispered conversation. The pilot returned to the cockpit and the aeroplane banked steeply. I began to feel a little strange and, looking out the window, I could only see cloud where once there had been bright blue sea. Reggie Maudling, who sat opposite me, turned a pale shade of green and I feared that we were about to witness a replay of his lunch. Eric Miller sat and giggled as he informed us that we were flying upside down. We continued to execute barrel rolls the entire width of the Channel. I asked Miller why we were doing this. His reply was that he wanted to show me what a good aeroplane we were flying in.

As far as I was concerned the only trouble with Eric Miller was that he did not like paying for the buildings that I built for him. The chief bone of contention between us was Fulham Football Club's new stand. I went to the opening match there. I hate football, so I took a cigar to pass the time but so great was the crush I could not get it from my pocket to my mouth, let alone light it. Eric Miller went to immense trouble to avoid paying for this stand. He promised, and he promised. Dates for payment passed and new dates were agreed. Still Miller did not pay. This debt was now an embarrassment to me, for I had told my family that I trusted him. As in the way so often with those who owe you money, Miller became impossible to speak with over the telephone. The only solution was to ring Myra and tell her of my problem. 'Eric has lost his voice,' Myra informed me. 'It's not his voice I need. Just as long as his right hand still works that will be fine by me,' I replied. 'I don't want to speak to him, just to get him to sign a cheque.' Miller rang me back within minutes. A meeting was arranged and I attended at three o'clock in his office. I was greeted by Mick the butler, who gave me a Monte Cristo magnum cigar and a glass filled to the brim with Chivas Regal. Miller did not arrive. Determined to see him, I sat there with three more giant cigars, six more whiskies, Mick would not take no for an answer.

At seven-thirty that evening Miller arrived. Mick the butler embraced Miller; Miller embraced Mick the butler. 'I must just go and see my secretary,' Miller said. 'By all means,' said I. Time was no longer important to me, but getting that cheque was everything. Back came Miller and as he sat down, Mick the butler put a large brandy at his right hand. The secretary put a pen and the cheque beside him on a table. The secretary bade Miller and myself good night. Mick the butler handed Miller a cigar. At this point, Miller leaned forward and signed the cheque. I leaned forward to take it from him. He held his hand to stop me. Raising his glass, Miller toasted the payment of his debt.

I returned his toast and then as I watched, Miller juggled with his cigar, the lighter and the brandy and dropped all three. The brandy went all over the cheque, and his signature swam towards me. The cheque, now useless, was torn up and another promised for the next day. I left, drunk and dispirited, into the night. I never saw Eric Miller again. A few weeks later he was dead. I liked the man, for with all his disagreeable qualities, he had great charm. Crook or not, it didn't matter, the world was the richer for Eric Miller's life, and many people remember him with gratitude. Some people believe that much of what Eric Miller did was dishonest. The Labour Party were the beneficiaries of much of Miller's largesse and if they did not know where it came from, or the terms under which they received both help and money, then they should have known. How strange it is that the Labour Party, who benefited from Miller's activities more than any other person or organisation, chose to forget that the man had ever existed. Such is the nature of politics.

My days on construction sites were happy and carefree, for I worked in a family business and my father, along with his brothers and cousins, carried the responsibility for that business. I often used to go out with my friends in the evenings, sometimes we would drink and gossip all night, taking breakfast after visiting the markets in the early morning before going to work. My father was an immensely tolerant man and on occasions I must have tested that tolerance. He slept badly, often waking to make tea for my mother and himself. Sometimes he would walk down the corridor of the flat to collect a bottle of soda water from the cocktail cabinet. One particular night, as he walked towards the cabinet, a piece of furniture the size of a wardrobe, veneered in burr walnut and lined in chrome and mirror, I was lying on the floor trying to seduce Linda, the daughter of the Agent General from Alberta. Linda was an extremely good-looking girl with red hair and an athletic body; she was also a most entertaining companion. Luckily, as it turned out, I was not making much progress, as she found the idea that I might want to sleep with her hilariously funny. In any event, my father, who, as I have written, was terribly short-sighted, walked straight past us, collected his bottle of soda water, turned around and left. I do not know to this day whether or not he saw us lying there with our clothes in considerable disarray. He never mentioned this incident. He did, however, suggest that if I were to work long hours I might try going earlier to bed. 'You can't burn the candle at both ends,' he said.

I had many girlfriends in those youthful years. They were mainly the daughters of friends of my parents or girls who lived around Henley-on-Thames where I spent the weekends or what was left of the weekends. The construction industry worked on Saturdays until about four o'clock and one Sunday in four – more if the weather was good, for success in construction is more dependent on the weather than almost anything else. On summer weekends we swam in my parents' pool; my friends and I would often go to a nearby pub for some supper and then come back and swim again.

Shortly past my twenty-second birthday, I married Sarah Baron. The service was at Holy Trinity, Brompton Road and the reception at the Dorchester Hotel – eight hundred people came to the wedding and the reception afterwards. At six that evening we left the Dorchester to stay in the Forte Hotel at Heathrow. The next day we set off for Beaulieu on the Côte d'Azure. After fourteen years, the last two of which we were separated, the marriage ended in considerable bitterness.

Sarah Baron was never a particular girlfriend of mine, rather she was the companion of my younger brother, her contemporary. Her parents were friends of my family, her grandfather a friend of my grandfather. For years Sarah Baron was just about the place, coming on holiday with my brother and my parents or coming to stay at our house in the country with her parents. It was in Paris that she changed. Her mother had sent her to Paris to be what people wrongly call 'finished', when what they mean is in fact 'started'. I visited Paris one spring and took Sarah out to dinner. This child was now a pretty woman, smartly dressed and well informed. Soon afterwards Sarah came back to London. I can recall her walking in the snow that winter, her clothing the height of French fashion, where English girls at that time, especially the ones who lived in the country, were dowdy by comparison. Sarah Baron wore long black leather boots with stiletto heels. The country girls wore brown gum boots and

duffle coats. Sarah Baron was the smartest thing that I had ever
seen. She was sixteen; I was twenty-one. We married almost a year
later, just after her seventeenth birthday. On our return from the
South of France we lived in a cottage on my father's farm, by the
Thames at Medmenham. I had bought an old vicarage opposite the
church at Fawley Green, but work needed to be done and we could
not move there for a year.

Why did I marry when I was so young? I asked that question of
myself often enough in the years that followed. The answer, I am
sure, is that I was tired. I had spent six years on construction sites,
six years of living amongst rough, hard men. Drinking in pubs,
wandering the streets, I had seen and heard aspects of life that my
contemporaries who were still mostly at university had never even
dreamed about. I had become involved with artists and architects;
my friends were years older than I was; I felt grown up. In truth, I
was still a child, with all the selfish, destructive instincts of childhood.
I was not constrained by the need of a job; I had a job. The lack of
a house did not make me stop and think, nor did I wonder if the
time was right for marriage. I was brought up with the idea of
marriage and children, so I bought a house and settled down to
married life with much the same natural instinct that takes a young
duck to water.

I lived in the country, leaving every morning at about five-thirty
to pick up my elder brother and then driving round to pick up my
father at about six o'clock. All three of us lived on the edges of my
father's land at Fawley Green. We then drove to London, which in
days before the M4 was completed was about an hour and a half
away before the rush, several hours if you travelled during the rush.
We breakfasted at seven o'clock in my father's flat, leaving to be on
the building sites by eight. I had finished my work by seven most
nights and drove home, whilst my father and brother usually went
by train. I would arrive home between eight-thirty and nine. Weekends were spent in the country with friends. Just at the time in my
life when I was beginning to become involved in art, just as I was
beginning to understand and enjoy artists with their Bohemian
lifestyles, I found that I had trapped myself in what seemed as time
went by to be an endless and cloying domesticity.

By my marriage to Sarah Baron I had two daughters. I did the
best that I could in a material sense for both these girls and their
mother. Now I have three grandchildren, a boy and two girls. I have

never met my grandchildren, nor have I seen my daughters for some years. How different my life is from those early days of marriage. How uncertain is human behaviour and the outcome of events.

7

Art, Artists and Collecting

I, along with one out of every three adults in the western world, am a collector. Collecting has always been in my blood; I think perhaps it runs in my family. My father collected racehorses; my mother Staffordshire pottery incense burners in the form of small houses; my elder brother steam railway trains and everything to do with them; my younger brother collects wine and military uniforms. I as a child collected stones, fondly believing them to be Roman arrow heads. I also owned fragments of Roman pottery, dug up on the London building sites and brought home as presents by my father. I inherited from my maternal grandfather a Canadian sheath knife and a poisonous snake in a bottle. My elder brother gave me a Japanese sword and my mother various old guns.

As a child I haunted the shop of Mr Giles in Henley-on-Thames' main street. It was a treasure chest and a few shillings could buy a masterpiece, or so I believed. That, I am afraid, is the belief of every collector. It is hope that keeps the collectors collecting. Dealers should know this and take care never to destroy that hope, for it is from collectors that the dealer earns his living.

Despite this childhood passion for collecting and arranging objects in an orderly fashion, it was not until I was twenty that I took any interest in painting and painters. This passion that I have for 'art' and the art world arose in the most unlikely way. The plastering and painting company, Balcloutha, that I helped to run, needed a London showroom to sell its fibrous plaster mouldings. That showroom needed antiques to liven it up and I needed to deal in antiques, for no better reason than I was completely fascinated by the whole world of antique dealing. Alec Wardrope and I opened such a shop in Sloane Street. My family tolerated what must have seemed the most extraordinary eccentricity for a youth who was supposed to be learning about the construction industry. My father was supportive of the venture, my cousins generous in their muted protests. The shop needed to employ someone to restore the antique furniture before it was offered to the public as it was often acquired in rather poor condition. Such a person was found. His name was John Heath. Tall with rough and dark good looks, he looked like a gypsy. A moody man, he was by training a painter, who earned his living restoring furniture. He drove a van with no doors, which he soon exchanged for a second-hand refrigerated lorry that he converted to living accommodation. For a hobby, he played the guitar and frequented Finches, a pub in the Fulham Road, the haunt of artists. Heath was actually rather a good painter, but his work has never been commercially successful. He did, however, know about paintings and the people who painted them.

I went with John Heath one summer morning to a gallery behind Marble Arch where, for the first time, I came across abstract painting. I found the idea of abstraction irresistible. I loved the freedom, the colour, the complexity of its forms and, indeed, the total lack of recognisable form in it. There were no famous artists represented by this gallery nor, I suspect, were any of the works I saw there ever to become highly considered. I did, however, with the help of John Heath, discover a new world. After working for me for a couple of years, John Heath packed his van and set out for Cornwall. I doubt he realised quite what he had started that summer's day.

Dealers in those days were different from dealers today. Apart from anything else, it was the pure volume of their stock that made them different. Mendleson, a picture dealer in Soho's Poland Street, had a whole house full of paintings, mostly canvases cut from their frames and piled in heaps. Mr Mendleson looked like the Jew that he was, but a Jew from another age – small skull cap, long hair, long beard and long coat, his back slightly hunched. He could show you his stock, piles and piles of it, and after you were black from head to toe with grime from sorting through these piles, he would look at the paintings that you had picked out. The best he would not sell, the rest he would put a smart price on. His shop, or home, in Fulham Road was the same. In the end, it burned down and all the paintings that he had been saving went up in flames. I never really liked Mendleson.

On the other hand, Leslie Scott, a German Jew with a shop in Motcomb Street and rather more stock than you would conveniently keep on premises four times its size, was a close friend. His stock comprised paintings and sculpture, glass, china, furniture, bronzes and silver, and he taught me much about dealing. He introduced me to German glass and Art Noveau silver, and I collected both for a while.

One morning he telephoned me. Could I come to his shop straight away? He had, it seemed, been offered £14,000 to quit his premises. This was a prodigious sum in the early 1960s. The snag, however, was that he must be gone within a week. 'What am I do with all this stock?' he kept repeating. He was in a terrible state. He wanted the money but not the trouble of moving the stock and I cannot say that I blamed him: to move it would, indeed, have been a nightmare. 'How much do you want for all the pictures?' I asked. 'A thousand pounds,' he replied. 'Eight hundred,' I countered. We settled and I had bought just over eight hundred paintings. I took them in a truck to my shop in Sloane Square, gave a fiver each to two young boys and instructed them to spread the word that pictures were for sale at three pounds each. We sold out in ten days.

Other dealers who kept prodigious amounts of stock included the Applebys in Bury Street, St James's, who had a gallery where they sold watercolours. Originally café owners near King's Cross, they discovered greater profits were to be won in art dealing. They used to put on mixed shows of watercolours several times a year. 'How do you choose the watercolours to show?' I asked. The reply: 'We just take the first hundred off the piles of stock.'

The Andrade family at Borgia Villas in Plympton had a row of houses stuffed with stock. From them I bought some of the later, heavier Staffordshire pottery figures. On one trip I purchased nine hundred figures for £900. The room that housed these figures was full from floor to ceiling. I just took the first nine hundred that came to hand.

E. Joseph's bookshop was a little like these other establishments but the proprietors, Sam and Joe Joseph, just put their surplus stock in store as it was never for sale. They sent it to Oxford during the war to avoid the blitz; they themselves moved into the Dorchester Hotel for the same reason. Their stock stayed in Oxford until well into the 1950s. By the time they came to sell their Oxford stock, as they called it, its value had skyrocketed.

These two old men would spend their day standing in the street reading books taken from the shelves outside their shop front. These shelves were loaded with books. 'Do you lose many books from shop lifting?' I asked. 'Quite a lot,' they replied, 'but it doesn't matter. The profit from the books that we sell from these shelves far exceeds those losses.' Each day, the pair stood there reading, looking like tramps; each night, they would dine in the Dorchester Grill, wearing their dinner jackets, looking like the vastly wealthy men that they were. Both Sam and his brother were very kind to me, taking time to tell me about books, and cautioning me about my follies.

In Paris, at de Nobele's bookshop in the rue Bonaparte, I bought a copy of Redouté's *Lilies* in a fine red armorial Morocco binding, and *Les Plus Belles Fleurs*, one of the rarest flower books. At the same time I acquired a third very fine illustrated flower book and a copy of a book illustrated by Van Spandonk. The last was not a botanical work, rather a book illustrating bouquets of various flowers that could be used as needlework designs. I showed all four of these fine books to Sam Joseph, who reprimanded me for paying too much for them. Two years later I sold them at Christie's, along with a large collection of botanical and natural history books. The titles from de Nobele fetched well over three times the price I had paid for them. De Nobele, who was in the Christie's salesroom at the time, and from whom I had bought many books over the years, turned away in disgust as the books were sold. He never spoke to me again.

In the Edgware Road was the shop of Percy German, a rotund and aggressive man, a dealer in guns. The rain could be pelting down and likely customers came into his shop, soaked during the short run across the pavement from the taxi. 'Can we look around, please?' they would ask. 'Only the goods in the window are for sale,' Percy German would reply. The shop was filled with goods – brass pots and pans, armour and weapons of all descriptions – but the customer was blocked from them all by the sales counter, located a few yards from the shop door.

I was about seven years old when I first visited this paradise for the gun collector. Percy German's wife used to sit in the vast area behind the counter with her dog. She was a kindly woman and often asked me if I would like to join her for a cup of tea. I spent hours listening to Percy German talk about his life as a dealer. Originally he had been a butcher, until one day he was offered a collection of arms and armour, twenty thousand pieces of it at one shilling per piece. He gave up the trade of butcher and took up dealing in antiques. I well remember a drawer at the back of his shop, where he kept a great quantity of wheel locks taken from broken guns, most of them immensely rare. Downstairs in his basement, Percy German kept a collection of an altogether different nature.

Pip Roberts was a waiter from the Savoy Hotel who became a dealer in antiques. At first he bought jewellery from the Savoy's customers, or customers' friends. During the war, when most people were selling whatever they had, Pip Roberts was buying. Whether it be books or clocks, it did not matter to him. I once bought a Cabochon emerald of nearly eight hundred carats from him and sold it again the same day. In the early 1960s you could buy in St Martin's Lane and sell in Bond Street, and make money in the time it takes to travel that short distance and do a deal. Dealers seldom left their shops, often they would not speak to each other, and old rivalries went back a long way.

Pip Roberts was an Italian with a penchant for fine Rolls-Royces and Bentleys. He spent a lot of his time in the salesrooms. His eye was brilliant and he could spot a fine gun no matter how heavily that weapon had been disguised by age or ill-use. His problem was that when he bid, other dealers, who knew little of the gun trade, followed his bidding, often going one bid more than he was prepared to go. One such dealer did this the whole time and, much irritated, Pip Roberts determined to teach him a lesson. He bought a badly broken, eighteenth-century Spanish gun, cleaned it, had it heavily engraved and lavishly covered in gold. Putting this refurbished gun back under the hammer, he bid on it. The other dealer matched him bid for bid, the price for the gun rose and rose. Roberts scowled and finally shook his fist at the other dealer. But the more he demonstrated anger, the more the other dealer bid. Then, with a sweet smile, Roberts shook his head as the auctioneer offered him one more chance to make a final bid. The other dealer began to look worried as this flashy fake was knocked down to him. Roberts turned to another dealer, standing beside him, and remarked, 'I cannot understand just why that fellow didn't buy that lot when it came up in Christie's a couple of months ago. He could have had it for a fraction of what he has just paid.'

The most charming of all those dealers in the early 1960s was Robin Braid Taylor. I always said, at the time, that if Robin Braid Taylor had ever had any money, the antique trade would have prospered mightily, for he was a man gripped with a compulsive urge to buy. Of mysterious background, he always claimed that his father had been the Governor of the Bank of India. He dressed impeccably, and although I know nothing of his education, it appeared to have been an expensive one. Tall and good looking, he seemed the perfect con man, with charm enough for a dozen such as he. He seldom arrived anywhere on time, but when he did arrive he seemed completely unaware that he was late. He raced about the countryside buying and selling guns and I used often to travel with him, to meet dealers and collectors. During those trips, not a moment would pass without him telling of some unlikely event that had taken place. The barriers between truth and fantasy were blurred for Robert Braid Taylor, but he was all the better a person for it. At one time he came too close to a group of submachine guns stolen from the American army and took a long holiday in Spain. He did, however, know a lot about his trade, which in those days was unusual.

The old curiosity shop in Beaconsfield was another of my haunts. Oliver Tribe, its proprietor, had been an actor manager but life had been hard on the boards, so he closed his touring company and set about selling its props as antiques. He was a short fat man with a bright red face, who spluttered a lot and could get quite angry without any real reason. His stock was eclectic, to say the least. I used to visit him first as a child and then as a young man. He always had the sort of goods that just might be worth a lot more than he was asking for them, but usually they turned out to be worth a lot less. He gave the impression that he did not really know their value. These goods were always remarkable for their quality and I have all my life been a sucker for quality goods.

In about 1961 Oliver Tribe telephoned me in London. 'Come at once. I have a pair of Colt revolvers.' I usually visited him on my way home for the weekend on a Saturday afternoon. 'You must come at once,' he insisted, and so I went. He informed me, as I arrived, that I was too late. The guns were sold and on their way to London. A knocker (people who earned a living knocking on house doors to ask if the occupants had any antiques or second-hand books for sale) had sold him the pistols for £100; Oliver Tribe had sold them for £200, minutes before I arrived, to an American serviceman stationed nearby. The knocker had bought the pistols in Cardiff. They had been in a fine mahogany case and had been given to an old lady by her son shortly before he died. The case was locked and there was no key and the old lady believed it contained nothing more than a set of knives and forks. When the knocker forced the lock, the old lady was horrified when she found guns and had accepted 50s. for them.

I returned to London, went straight to Pip Roberts and told him the story. He told me that he had just bought the guns in question, a pair of Colt Roots side hammer pistols in mint condition. They had ivory grips. On one of them the grips were carved with the portrait of Prince Louis of Bertheim, and on the other his coat of arms. The pistols had been inscribed and presented by Colonel Colt to the Prince in order to secure an arms contract during the Franco-Prussian war. The hinges of their mahogany box were silver and inside were packets of the original ammunition and the tools needed to load the guns. I bought the pistols for £2,000 and sold them, a year or two later, to Robin Braid Taylor for £5,000. He passed them on, no doubt at a considerable profit, to Keith Neal, the doyen of British gun collectors. Many years later I came across them again in the collection of Warren Anderson, the Australian property developer and Colt pistol collector. Anderson sold them in America for £250,000.

I met many dealers while I had the shop in Sloane Street, and bought a great variety of objects, including a vast quantity of old farm implements and carpentry tools from Wigington, an antique gun dealer in Stratford on Avon. I persuaded a friend of John Heath's, called Ivor Thomas, who was a sometime folk singer, to turn them into sculpture. In the end I sold them to Andreas Crane Kalman, who had quite a success with them, selling them as the work of the English primitive 'sculptor Thomas'. Now the price of country hand implements has risen so high I am sure that the owners of these sculptures are longing to take them apart so that they can put the original implements into Bonham's rooms.

In the early 1960s a friend, Paul Breakspeare, now Chairman of Breakspeare's Henley Brewery, worked for my family while he learned to be an architect. He married a beautiful model, started a family and left my family's business in search of more gainful employment, which he found in selling cement. Paul Breakspeare knew a different class of art dealer from those frequented by John Heath, and showed me the way to Cork Street. I was a bachelor at the time and Paul Breakspeare was a wonderful drinking companion, if a bit prone to accident. A man with a considerable sense of humour, he had nevertheless a naive streak to his character. When he worked on the construction sites he was the victim of both practical jokes and accidents. An example of the latter was when he visited his doctor suffering from severe constipation. The doctor prodded and poked and in time announced that Paul had swallowed too much cement dust, which, when mixed with natural fluids, had turned to concrete inside him. On another occasion, when working on a construction site in Baker Street, a labourer pointed out a tunnel under the street. He told Paul that there was something very interesting at the end of it and sent him down to take a look. In a flash several bricklayers set to work and built a wall across the entrance. After wandering around for a few minutes and finding nothing remotely interesting, Paul set off back towards the entrance. The entrance, however, was gone. He retraced his steps many times and still no entrance was to be found. An hour or two later the bricklayers demolished the newly built wall and a dazed Paul Breakspeare reappeared to the general merriment of all concerned.

Drinking one evening together, Paul mentioned a great friend of his, the sculptor David Wynne. Would I be interested in meeting him? Of course, I was in those days so taken with the idea of art that I would have gone anywhere to meet anyone. David Wynne lived in Wimbledon in a modest studio, with his beautiful wife Gilly, an artist's model who posed often for Russell Flint.

David Wynne was a wild and glamorous figure. A pupil of Richard Erlich and Jacob Epstein, he had an impeccable grounding in figurative sculpture, and a natural eye for form and balance. That day we started a long friendship. David was, quite frankly, on his uppers. He had no money; he was to have an exhibition at Tooth's Gallery the next year. His studio was full of work; his bank account empty. I talked with David for an hour or so – he is one of the best raconteurs of improbable stories that I have ever come across – and I was enchanted by him. That evening I bought four pieces of his work: a bronze of two sisters standing naked looking at each other, a bust of Yehudi Menuhin, a reclining nude girl and a white marble carving of a woman whom David called a Boulder Woman.

Paul Breakspeare and I helped David load the car with sculptures and we set off for London. There was something about David and his work that Leslie Waddington once described in this way: 'David Wynne is like a young girl who discovering sex realises that she is good at it. As a result, she is much better at sex than she might otherwise be.' When I look at David's work I can see exactly what Leslie Waddington means. I half agree with him and although David's work seems to go against every rule that is taught to students who would become sculptors, it has a beauty about it that defies definition.

While I have no time for most other sculptors working in the same genre, I regard David's work very highly, for inside each piece there is a spirit trying to break out. His works are not just dead lumps of bronze or marble.

In the years that followed I promoted David's work, introducing him to many of the customers for whom I was building. One or two of them commissioned sculptures for their buildings, the most extraordinary a gentleman called Armstrong. Mr Armstrong happened, by chance, to wander into my family's office at 80 Park Lane. My father, by a similar chance, walked in behind him. 'Can I help you?' he asked this small but bustling man. 'I am looking for a builder,' he replied. 'In which case you have come to the right place,' said my father, who took him up to his office and within an hour we were hired to build his University of the Radio Church of Good at St Albans.

I was sent a message to go and see this American gentleman at his British headquarters. About twenty of us sat down to lunch and a plate of roast beef, cabbage, potatoes and carrots, covered in a thick gravy, was put before each of us. Our host made no move to begin the meal and we sat in silence as the gravy grew a skin. One man picked up his knife and fork as if to start eating. 'Just one moment,' said Herbert G. Armstrong. Again we waited then, quite suddenly, Herbert G. Armstrong broke into a convoluted grace. The meal began. He talked of his university – Ambassador College, he called it. I asked him how he made the money that he was so generously giving away. Was it made out of oil or gold or even wheat? 'No,' Herbert Armstrong replied. 'Out of God. I am in the God business.' And so he was, being the proprietor, founder and leading light in the Radio Church of Good. Herbert G. Armstrong became one of David Wynne's greatest patrons, buying a number of vast sculptures.

In about 1961, while Tooths had an immensely successful show of his sculpture, I put on an exhibition of David Wynne's drawings at the Dick Temple gallery. Dick Temple and I had been at Stowe together. He is now London's leading dealer in icons but in the 1960s he was about London's only dealer in icons. On Friday mornings Sotheby's as a rule had a General Sale. Sotheby's was then a very different organisation: not at all grand, a small, intimate, slightly inefficient but friendly company. This Friday they were selling furniture, carpets, musical instruments and icons. In this sale was a sleeper. No one knew of it but Dick Temple. Both he and I went to

Sotheby's, arriving early. The sale was slow: the carpets knocked down at prices pulled from the audience as painfully as if they had been bidding for splinters. The prices of the furniture stumbled past reserves and collapsed in a heap. The room became hotter as the summer sun shone through the glass windows in the ceiling. The only highlight was a Stradivarius violin that sold for £8,000. After this lot, sold at ten minutes to one, nearly everybody left. The auctioneer was at last about to sell the icons when an Armenian entered the room. A look of horror came across Dick Temple's face. This Armenian was the only man in London who might know the true value of the icon that we hoped to buy. What should he do? Perhaps he might miss it. He approached this charming Armenian and did a deal. The icon came up for sale; we bid £200 and there were no other bids. That icon, a remarkable piece with a central painting of St Nicholas, and his life in cartoon strips around its edges, was sold for a considerable profit. It now sits in the British Museum.

David Wynne became a great success. He bought himself a large house on Wimbledon Common, as his family grew apace. Often I visited him to look at his work. Some days the studio was empty, with just the shadows of John Gielgud and the Beatles caught in bronze. At other times there were interesting people to meet. One afternoon that sticks in my memory Joan Baez was there. I have always enjoyed folk music and she was a considerable star at the time. She sat on a stool in a shiny red raincoat, played her guitar and sang and David worked. Gypsy Dave and the pop singer Donovan played billiards there; indeed Donovan wrote his hit 'Jennifer Juniper' in that billiard room. As we played, David turned to Donovan and said, 'Why not have one of the verses in French?' Donovan replied, 'I don't know any French.' So David wrote out the verse for him.

Donovan was a considerable character. He came once to a party in 1966 that I gave at my house near Henley-on-Thames. There were about a hundred guests and the party was held in a pavilion that I had built in my garden to house what at that time was an extensive art collection. The works, large painted sculptures in metal, wood and fibreglass, were stored away; the pavilion filled with tables and chairs; a discotheque set up in a darkened room at one end, in the centre of the discotheque a giant stuffed gorilla. The dancers coming from the bright lights took a minute or two before they could see this monstrous beast. The rest of the pavilion was decorated as if it were a zoo: cages were built against the wall and filled with foliage and stuffed animals. Donovan sang, from time to time, swigging Château Latour 1953 from the bottle – in fact from two bottles, one on each side of him ready for the moment when he had a free hand. All went well until the late hours of the early morning when the guests started to leave.

One guest remained, sitting in the hall waiting for his wife. Guests wandered to the front door and outside; they found their cars, engines roared competing with the dawn chorus as darkness turned to early light. The sun began to show, goodbyes were shouted cross the gravel of the drive, women held their dresses above the ankles as they tripped across the grass wet with morning dew. The air was clear, the temperature fresh – all the makings of a perfect summer's day were available that early morning. Still that lonely guest sat waiting for his wife. 'Would you like a drink?' 'No thank you,' was his reply. 'Would you like some breakfast?' 'No thank you,' was the reply. 'Where's your wife?' – I thought that perhaps a hint should be given that the proceedings were at an end. 'I don't know,' the morose guest replied.

I set off to look for her, thinking perhaps she might be ill. A number of people were staying that night, which is always a mistake if you want the other guests to leave a party at a reasonable hour. One of my house guests was an art dealer, Christopher Bibby. I found this poor man in some distress, believing that he had accidentally locked himself out of his bedroom. 'How did it happen?' I asked. 'I just crossed the passage and when I returned the bedroom door was locked.' Banging on the door, I shouted, 'Come out, come out.' And so she did. The lonely guest's wife appeared all bosoms and petticoats, her hair dishevelled, her make-up gone. Downstairs she scuttled and, seizing her husband by the arm, set out into the – by now – bright sunlight. Donovan followed a few minutes later, buttoning his clothes so that they barely fitted anywhere. 'Cheerio,' he said, and with a wave he was gone.

The collecting of paintings was for me like a paper chase, a hunt where every time I found the painting or the artist that I was seeking, that success led to other hunts. David Wynne led to Dudley Tooth's Gallery in Bruton Street, where I discovered the exciting, rich pictures of Matthew Smith; the search for Matthew Smith's work led me to Cork Street and the Redfern galleries, where I found the paintings of Jawlensky, the German Expressionist.

I just loved colour, I always have and I always will. As a child I played with the swatches of material that the dressmaker, Madeleine, whom my mother employed, used in her work. In the years after the war rationing was still the Socialist curse and so women like my mother employed dressmakers to copy clothes that they already owned. I would sit and watch Madeleine work in a back room of our London flat, all the while playing with the swatches, seeing how the colours changed from greens and greys through reds, yellows and browns to blues and on to black.

More importantly than the dead painters whom I discovered through David Wynne – Gaudier-Brzeska was another, David Wynne was passionate about his work – he introduced me to living artists. One such was the silversmith Gerald Benney, whose small London workshop David and I visited together. Some days later, Gerald Benney invited me to his new home, Beenham House, on the edge of the Chilterns between Reading and Newbury. I was a bit surprised to find that he had just moved into a vast mansion. We ate our lunch that day, just four of us, sitting at a card table in the middle of a room fifty feet long and twenty-five feet wide. The ceiling must have been twenty feet high. There was not another stick of furniture in the place. 'If you buy a really large house,' Gerald Benney informed me, 'it is usually really rather cheap.' Over the years, Gerald and Janet Benney turned Beenham into a place of beauty and at one stage there were a dozen silversmiths working there.

'Large furniture is also much cheaper than small furniture,' Gerald Benney also believed. A lot of his furniture, at the beginning at least, he made himself out of Formica blocks. There is even some furniture at Beenham that I designed, half a dozen pieces which, when I moved house, Gerald said he would like.

A tall man with a slightly distant professorial air, Gerald Benney is a genius at his trade. Janet Benney in those days had a neat waist and the most incredible bosoms that were the envy of many of her female contemporaries. A woman with incredible energy, she is a considerable poet and the driving force behind her husband's career. Janet cooked lunch for her family and the silversmiths, while entertaining with considerable style in the evenings and at weekends. It was in her house that I met Simon Hornby, later the Chairman of W.H. Smith, at that time heavily involved with the National Trust, and it was Simon Hornby who found me West Green.

The evening at the Benneys with Simon Hornby did not go well.

We were sitting waiting to go in to dinner when he turned to me and said in a loud voice – the sort of voice that causes silence in a crowded room – 'Do you enjoy gardening?' 'No,' I replied, for I was of the same view as Palladio that fields should nudge the foundations of a building. Simon Hornby looked at me without surprise and remarked, 'Cultured people all enjoy gardening.' I took this rather badly, for I regarded myself at the time as extremely cultured. 'Do you enjoy the work of Jackson Pollock?' I riposted.

Simon Hornby turned and talked about gardening to an elderly lady, who listened with rapt attention to his description of how convolvulus could be removed from the garden by putting its tentacles into a milk bottle filled with weedkiller. Some years later, Simon Hornby, hearing that I was interested in a country house, drew my attention to West Green, a National Trust property that needed restoring and had been on the market for some years. The advantage of this house, Simon Hornby pointed out to me, was that it had only the walls of an old and derelict garden. The National Trust were not intending to restore the gardens, so it should suit me fine. In the event, when I moved into West Green I became a manic gardener, spending enormous amounts of both time and money on its gardens, a victim of the urge to improve, to make a place that was once beautiful, not just beautiful again but yet more beautiful than ever before. I can, however, attest to the fact that Simon Hornby's system for stamping out the terrible and invasive convolvulus doesn't work, for I have tried it, to no effect. Simon Hornby is now the President of the Royal Horticultural Society.

Janet Benney threw herself into her husband's life, forcing him forward with the sheer power of her will. Janet was, I believe caught in that most awful of webs: the certain knowledge that you have great talent yourself, but an equally certain knowledge that your own talent has to be put to one side in order to organise the life of another, more talented, artist. Janet Benney was, like myself and my new house at West Green, in the grip of the strongest of human instincts, the desire to improve somebody or something. She knew with certainty when she first saw the great pile that was Beenham that she could turn that house into an exciting mansion. She knew that she could turn Gerald Benney into a truly great silversmith, not by telling him how to make silver, rather by creating the conditions in which he could make silver. Furthermore Janet Benney knew full well that there is no point in being able to make silver if you cannot sell the stuff. Gerald Benney was, and I suppose still is, not quite of this world. Immensely practical when it comes to sorting out a hinge or a fastening on a box, he is a romantic in his view of life and the people that inhabit this life, thinking only the best of people, and seeing only the events and the emotions that he wants to see.

Gerald is a natural teacher. In the early 1970s he left England, Janet and Beenham to live in India for some time to teach local craftsmen how to design goods that westerners might want to buy. He returned to England and became the Professor of Silversmith and Jewellery at the Royal College of Art. I was appointed a visiting examiner to Gerald's department. For two years I came and judged the students' work, much of which was very encouraging, and then lunched with the academic staff in their dining room. In the third year there was a girl who had done no work at all. Her work was neither bad nor sloppily executed, it just did not exist, so I failed her. I took the view that you cannot pass an exam if you do not do the work that the exam requires or, for that matter, any other work. That night I received a telephone call. Surely I had made a terrible mistake. Students at the Royal College do not fail exams; no student had ever failed an exam. This one had, I replied, and I was never asked to judge again. The girl, no doubt, has a sparkling certificate to say that she graduated from the Royal College of Art, London.

Janet Benney was knowledgeable in the matter of crafts; indeed, few knew so much about what was happening in the world of craft of the late 1960s and 1970s as she did. She introduced me both to John Makepiece and Andrew Grima and, at her suggestion, I bought from an exhibition a desk made by Makepiece. That pedestal desk, which I have long since sold, was a seminal piece of his work, totally covered in cow hide complete with hair, with a sloping top and ivory handles to its drawers. As write these words, I sit on a chair by Makepiece at a refectory table by Makepiece.

Andrew Grima I met after a lunch in London with Janet and Gerald. We lunched, I think, at the Etoile in 1965 and Janet told me about a bracelet that Andrew Grima wanted to make. Janet explained that he had a problem: no money, or at least, not enough to buy the stones that he needed. Andrew Grima's workshop was in Shaftesbury Avenue on the third floor. We travelled up the three floors cramped in a narrow lift, a face appeared at a small window in a heavily fortified office door. We were admitted and offered coffee, sketches were produced – careful coloured sketches, not the sketches that

Grima used to produce by the dozen while crossing the Atlantic in an aeroplane. Grima had a most productive mind in the years he worked in England; he was bursting with work. There was not a moment when he was idle; ideas came into his head in profusion, faster than he could note them down. He made notes and sketches with a ballpoint pen with the occasional name of a colour, or a stone, jotted in the margin.

Grima unwrapped the stones that were needed to make the bracelet. The whole work would cost £1,500 and I agreed to buy the piece. There was something quite different and totally courageous about Andrew Grima's work that attracted me. He gambled with every piece he made, missing vulgarity by a hair's breadth. That is what gave his jewellery its excitement. Every design took a risk, none of it fell into that deadly dull category of Good Taste. The bracelet won the De Beers International Diamond Award, making Grima the first British designer to win that award. Over the next few years I watched him prosper and move from a Shaftesbury Avenue attic to grand premises in Jermyn Street with a long frontage made by Bryan Kneil, the sculptor, of large slabs of slate held together with welded steel. The door was in cast aluminium by Geoffrey Clark. This shop front should have been preserved, for it was of considerable quality. However, those who decide these matters either did not know that it was there, or they did not care. A new tenant now has Grima's Jermyn Street shop and the important shop front is long gone.

I bought many pieces of his jewellery and soon had a large collection which, along with much else, went with my first wife. I have suffered fire and flood in my homes but none of these natural catastrophes was half as devastating to my property as the divorce from my first wife, Sarah Baron.

Andrew Grima was not a man to whom success came early, and for many years he laboured as a manufacturing jeweller. When he broke away from the tedium of manufacturing cheap and traditional jewellery, his talent was like a great explosion. It fitted the flamboyant and imaginative quality of his times and when those times changed Andrew Grima changed, and his wife changed. He moved to Switzerland, married a kinder, more sympathetic woman and now works at a slower, more considered pace.

A man who falls into the same class as Andrew Grima was Louis Osman, architect, jeweller and silversmith. He has built buildings, among the most notable of which is the convent tucked just back from Cavendish Square. The Benneys and I drove for an hour or two towards Banbury. In time we found Louis Osman's house, a priory, now the property of the National Trust. In those days it was a wreck, but a truly wonderful wreck. The owner of this house lived in the former Rhodesia, while Louis Osman squatted with his pack of Great Danes, herd of Fresian cattle and his family. Osman had created a collection of jewellery for the Australian Government, who were promoting the gold and the pearling industries. They provided both the pearls and gold for this jewellery; Dr Beers, to promote their product, provided the diamonds. This jewellery had not sold; Osman needed money to repay the sponsor. He did not seem, however, to be particularly worried about this matter. The house he lived in was stunning, derelict and chaotic, just as was Louis Osman's life. Nothing in that house was as it seemed. Nothing in Louis Osman's work either was as it seemed, the eye was tricked with every piece. About this time, Louis Osman had just received the commission to make the Coronation Crown of Prince Charles as Prince of Wales. Louis Osman was in a great state of excitement about this. The Crown he produced was controversial and brilliant. When, however, it was taken from its box on the day of the Coronation it fell apart, and had to be fixed together with Araldite. I bought the jewels that Louis Osman had made for the Australians but, like so much that I acquired in those days, unfortunately, I no longer have these pieces.

There can have been few periods in my life more exciting than the 1960s and early 1970s when the world discovered in London the great *mélange* of talent that spread from pop music to pop art, from the new school of sculptors to myriad fashion, jewellery and silver designers. These were the days of Terence Conran and Habitat, the heyday of Terence Donovan, David Bailey and Terence O'Neill, the photographers.

I never knew Terence Donovan in those day. More's the pity, for I greatly value the friendship that I had with him in the last years of his life. A physically vast man, he was restless in his talent, a photographer capable of brilliant work. His natural talent for the visual statement chafed at the restraints of photography and in his last years he became a considerable painter. The beauty of a friendship with Terence was that I could sit and eat a meal with him in a Chinese restaurant without the need for either of us to say a word. He was as at home dining at Le Gavroche as in a Transport Café, and was as at ease lunching with Margaret Thatcher, when she was

Prime Minister, as he was with the boy who helps him set up his cameras.

Terence was introduced to Margaret Thatcher by Gordon Reece during the early days of her career when she was a minister in Edward Heath's Government. It was Gordon Reece's idea that Terence should make the party politicals for television. At the 1974 election, when he photographed Margaret Thatcher, Terence recognised her talent; she impressed him then and that admiration for her lasted till he died. His are some of the best pictures that have ever been taken of her. I think because both are restless characters there was an empathy between them: she wanted the photo session over with, he wanted to finish it.

I enjoyed Terence Donovan's company because his approach to life was so straightforward. He had the art of taking what seem to be life's insurmountable problems and turning them into simple truths, cutting up a problem into parts, until each of those parts was of a size that could be understood and simply solved.

Once, a few years ago, I was sitting in a mood of deep depression in a hideaway that I had in the attics of Cork Street. The market for selling antiquities and curiosities had fallen about my feet; my business had in 1991 changed, along with the British economy, from an asset to a liability. Terence came to see me and we talked. I had bought a number of his photographs and only paid him for half – as for the rest, he said, keep them, they were a present. It was an act of generosity entirely characteristic of the man. I was, and still am, deeply grateful. What impressed me, however, more than Terence's generosity was that, having talked for an hour, he filled me with a spirit that I needed to fight back in a situation in which I had felt as if I was already destroyed. There was a quiet certainty about Terence Donovan, both physically for he did not make unnecessary gestures or movements, nor did he pace a room or fidget in a chair, and mentally, a certainty in his attitudes, a fortitude in his decisions. He once told me that he came from a very poor background and had made provision for a return to the district and the life that he came from. That, he said, was his greatest weapon, the greatest reason why he could conduct his life, confident and secure in the knowledge that he could not be harmed. My life has been crammed with people of differing characters and I have only ever come across two others, both brothers, in fact twins, who have impressed me more than Terence Donovan.

I first met Frederick and David Barclay in the mid-1970s. I had been given an introduction to them by my father. I have spent many hours in their company and never cease to wonder at their insights into how people will behave. I have, over the years, become fascinated by their interest in what motivates people. Their conversation is wide-ranging. As they exchange views, bouncing ideas off each other, the intellectual level of debate can leave one exhausted by the early hours of the morning. They are two people with one brain, one brain in two parts, each part complementary to the other. Their interests include both business and politics, how those two crafts interact, and the likely outcome of that interaction. Medical science and economics fascinate them. In all our conversations with the welter of words runs a humour and a ready wit. A humour, however, that is touched with humanity, there is no sarcasm in their conversation, no savage knocks at the defects of others. Frederick and David Barclay must surely be amongst the best-informed businessmen I have met. They are natural entrepreneurs with a great feel for what will make a business succeed. Those who have worked with them will attest that they are deeply interested in the minute detail and highly efficient in regard to the financial running of their business and investments.

Busy as the two men are, they unfailingly make time to listen to the problems of others – in life it is often inconvenient to make yourself available to those who are having a hard time either personally or financially. David and Frederick Barclay are scrupulous in attending on those amongst their friends and workforce who are suffering distress.

Had David and Frederick been the sort of people who promoted themselves, then their generosity would have been legendary. I have sat for many years as a Trustee of their Charitable Foundation and have witnessed this generosity that is unknown to the world at large. That, however, is how these two brothers are, not secretive, just immensely private in how they earn their money and how they give it away. Coming from a poor background they founded their enormously successful business without so much as sixpence from their family.

My time spent with Frederick and David has been an education, for I have learned more from them about business than I ever learned while I was actively engaged in business itself. I have learned the use of courage in business and the importance of fear as a brake on enthusiasm, the principles of economics, how trends come and go and how it is people who make those trends come and go. I have watched and observed how they run their business with a ruthless adherence to honesty, not just the agreement, but the spirit of the agreement. I have been immensely lucky to be allowed access to their family and I greatly admire how their children, now young men and women, clearly love and respect both their father and their uncle. (It is an unusually united family.)

A man who was my friend from the late sixties to his death was Sydney Nolan. I first met him in London when he was brought by Gordon House into the bookshop I owned in Cork Street. A considerable painter who is a typographer by trade, Gordon had become my friend as we worked together on publishing books. At that time I had only a few titles to my credit, including a limited edition of Aesop's *Fables*, illustrated by Elizabeth Frink, and a volume of the poems of Basho, illustrated by Bill Turnbull. Perhaps illustrated is the wrong word, for Turnbull had designed this book, inserting sheets of acetate at strategic points, which as you turned the book's pages cast a shadow on the poems. The work was really very good and quite beautiful, but sold extremely badly.

The problem was that I had not the first idea of how to distribute books. I would have felt badly about this if, in the years that followed, I had not discovered that even well-known publishers fail in this respect. My solution was to open a bookshop and sell my own books to the public. It was to this shop that Sydney Nolan and Gordon House came, their purpose to see if I was interested in publishing Sydney Nolan's own poems.

The bookshop was laid out like a sitting room, with armchairs and sofas; the books that were sold were extremely eclectic. My first wife Sarah chose the contemporary poetry and novels and I, the twentieth-century second-hand and antique books. The shop specialised in fine eighteenth- and nineteenth-century botanical and natural history colour-plate books.

Sydney Nolan was very taken with the place and set about the stock with a wild enthusiasm, while Gordon House was diffident about the purpose of the visit. 'Sydney thinks that perhaps you don't like his work.' It was not surprising that Sydney Nolan should come to that conclusion because, at the time, I collected abstract colour sculptures, mostly by artists from the St Martin's School of Art. I also collected American Abstract Expressionists and the colour painters of the New York School. 'I have always liked Sydney's work, at least since I began collecting paintings.' Reassured, Nolan began to talk about his poems and how he would like the book containing those poems to look.

A month or so later, I was invited to his house in Deodar Road in Putney. His home backed onto a garden that ran to the bank of the Thames. Dinner was simple: I was given a steak; Sydney, I think, was given a lettuce leaf. I was given a bottle of fine claret, Sydney, a glass of water. Cynthia, Sydney's wife at the time, was a wiry and often acerbic woman. The only aspect of her character that demonstrated any softness at all was her fanatical enthusiasm for gardening. On this particular evening, however, Cynthia was charm itself. Dinner did not take long; our conversation was mostly about the Nolans' recent journey to China. Cynthia brought the proceedings to an abrupt halt by announcing that we would go upstairs 'for tea and cake', a common Australian habit in those days.

All the while we had been sitting at the dinner table, I had been mystified by sounds in the room above. From where I was sitting during the meal, I could see the foot of the staircase, and no one had gone up those stairs. We arrived back in the first-floor sitting room. It had been cleared of empty glasses, tidied, tea and cake had been laid out. I began to wonder if the tea and cake, along with the mysterious tidier, was kept in the room above, instead of the kitchen which adjoined the dining room. Some time later, I discovered that Sydney and Cynthia lived in not one house but two, side by side, which were connected, so a helper had been able to mount the stairs in the other house and, unseen, clear the sitting room and lay out the tea and cakes. The other peculiarity of their house was its telephone. It was for outgoing calls only; it was impossible to ring them at their home. Contact was made with Sydney Nolan by leaving a series of messages at places that he might visit or with people whom he might see that day.

Sydney fidgeted and waited until Cynthia suggested that he show me his paintings. The whole house was hung with his early work and one picture in particular caught my eye. It was a heron standing on a river bank in the bush, painted in about 1949. It was, however, not the wonderful pictures in the house that Cynthia referred to, rather a collection of oils on paper, kept in Sydney's studio at the top of their house.

We all set out for the studio and there I looked, for the first time, at well over 2,000 paintings, small paintings each about a foot square that, joined together, made up the large *Paradise Garden*. Later Nolan painted two more sets of these oils on paper, which made up a painting called *Shark* and after that an even larger painting, *Snake*. These three pictures were many feet long and half as many high. It was only years later that I saw a *Paradise Garden* all in one piece.

We, Sydney and I, along with Lord Clark and Sir Norman Read, then Director of the Tate Gallery, had made a trip to Dublin to see a retrospective of Nolan's work on show in Dublin's Agricultural Hall. There was no doubt in my mind after seeing that show, that Nolan was a great painter. Lord Clark had always held that view. Apart from Sydney's exhibition, we were shown around the Irish National Gallery by its then Director. Lord Clark would listen to a man talk about a particular painting, and then contradict him. This work was not by so and so and, as a consequence, rather a minor work, by another, or by his studio. Painting after painting was consigned to the dustbin of art history by the great Lord Clark. The embarrassment was growing to such a point that it was decided we would take lunch. We lunched at the Shelbourne Hotel, at least some of us did. Lady Clark had a headache and left; Cynthia got cross about something – no one, not even Sydney, was clear about what – so she left as well.

Lord Clark held the conversation at the table in an iron grip while Sydney got slowly drunk. I said not a word, and Norman Read spoke only occasionally. Then Lord Clark told a joke in German. I, understanding not a word of German, remarked that it was a shame to tell jokes in languages that the audience could not understand. Norman Read, thoroughly fed up by this time, interjected that he understood German perfectly. The joke, he said, was not very funny and Lord Clark's German extremely bad. The party broke up and we all went our various ways.

I published Sydney's paintings and his poems, which mainly referred to his earlier years in Australia. Paying off old scores, their significance was clear to the people concerned but for the rest of us, they were just Sydney's poems. The book was a triumph, by which I mean that the book looked wonderful and still does. Unfortunately, it sold rather badly.

At the time that I had this bookshop, I was collecting catalogues of artists' shows. I bought large quantities of unsold catalogues from the London dealers and offered them for sale in my shop. Because I was deeply involved in the art world I was sent dozens of these catalogues. I filed them carefully, along with letters from artists to myself and to each other. In time, this collection of catalogues ended up in the Australian National Gallery, along with a small collection of Russian suprematist manifestos that I had put together. I also bought any correspondence that I could lay my hands on from nineteenth- or twentieth-century writers or painters. I advertised in *The Times* for these letters; I prowled around the premises of dealers in Paris, London and New York. The collection filled a whole barn at my home, West Green. West Green was a catalyst to my collecting; I believe that it was, at last, having the space to collect that set me free.

Alongside the chickens and the animals there, I had collections of farm implements, dairy and veterinary equipment, shepherds' crooks, garden tools, even nineteenth-century American rag dolls. And books by the dozen, then by the thousand: gardening books, art books, architectural books, first editions, back numbers of comics and magazines. I would have made any self-respecting magpie ashamed of himself, so compulsive was my collecting.

Then came the fire at West Green. I had spent the day in Sheffield and I was tired when I got home. Usually on a Friday night I would have gone to bed at about nine o'clock. That night was different. My second wife, Romilly, owned a food shop. A very grand and successful establishment in South Audley Street, it was called after her maiden name, Hobbs. We were in the habit of cooking at weekends, making Taramasalata, or various pâtés and pies for the shop's stock. This particular weekend I had bought Bath Chaps in Sheffield's meat market. The cheeks of a pig, they are a northern speciality which are not much found in the south. Bath Chaps need cooking for two hours or more, so I put them on the stove and fell asleep in front of a blazing log fire. Romilly slept as well. We were woken by the dog, Giorgio, barking. There was smoke in the room and I assumed that our chimney was smoking. The dog still barked. 'Do put the dog out,' I said to Romilly. The hall was filled with smoke; the house was completely on fire. We ran out onto the drive, wearing only our dressing gowns. Flames were coming out of the house's roof like fire from a Roman candle. The fire engines came, thirteen of them, and they pumped water from the nearby pond onto the fire. Despite the cold weather it was rather cosy standing there in our dressing gowns beside a roaring blaze. One hose squirted its water high over the burning house and Romilly and I, standing the other side, were soaked. The fire reached my cigar cupboard and the smell was truly delicious. Then it took hold of my gun cupboard, and the exploding ammunition sounded like a battle scene from Hollywood. Firemen came out of the smoke carrying objects and furniture. I remember a picture in which all the paint, melted by the flames, had run into an unrecognisable mess. A fireman stopped, for a moment, to ask where we wanted our mail the next morning – a strange question for a fireman to ask. The man raised his protective mask when I did not reply. 'I am your postman. I don't suppose that you recognise me in all this gear?' By this time, the television cameras had arrived and quite a crowd had gathered.

Romilly and I drove to London, dirty and damp, still wearing only our dressing gowns and no shoes. We wondered what the police would think should they stop our car at three o'clock in the morning. The next day, we went back and wandered through the burned wreckage of our home. The abiding memory I have of that morning is of thousands of blue-and-white shards, the fragments of my collection of blue-and-white porcelain, broken, shattered beyond repair amongst the cinders.

It was sad to have a home destroyed that Romilly and I loved, but it would have been a lot sadder had we gone to bed at our usual time that night, for the fire was caused by a gas explosion in a cavity of our bedroom wall. All that was left in that room was a few springs from our bed; we surely would have perished. Alison, my secretary, who later became Lady Wakeham, wife of John Wakeham, then Margaret Thatcher's Chief Whip, took charge. Romilly and I set out for Australia. Alison, God bless her, cleared up the mess.

Quinlan Terry was employed to rebuild a large part of the house and in one year we were back living there. More comfortable than before, it was as if the fire had never happened. My blue-and-white china was gone, along with most of my records and notes, all of my furniture, many of my paintings and my library of gardening books. The whole of my collection of 350 nineteenth-century American rag dolls was destroyed; just ashes remained. A tragedy to many people was, to an inveterate collector, the chance to collect again.

When we arrived in Australia, waiting for us was a collection of Sydney Nolan's paintings that had been stored in my attic at West Green. By chance, I had decided the week before the fire to send them back to Australia. I have always had the most amazing good luck, where fires and bombs are concerned.

I gave a dozen or so of Nolan's paintings to the Tate Gallery. For years, the Tate never hung them. Comparatively recently, they were taken out of store and shown, but only for a few months. The Art establishment were always slightly doubtful about Sydney's work. When he first showed in London, many people believed that he was an abstract painter, that it was impossible for landscapes to have the shapes and colours that he painted. Sydney Nolan understood the abstract quality of the Australian landscape; his colours were true to life. I used to buy his early work in Australia and swap it with him for his later pictures as he needed his early work as a reference from which to move forward.

One morning, I received a telephone call from Gordon House. Could I help Sydney? He sounded worried. Of course, I would help Sydney, but how? 'He needs somewhere to live and he wondered if he could move into the Dorchester.' This was a very busy time of the year and the Dorchester was full, but by lunchtime I had Sydney installed. He stayed for over a month, along with various friends and members of his family. Sydney, I understand, believed his stay to be free. I thought he would pay the bill and I had arranged a heavy discount for him. I never realised this misunderstanding until I read a book that purported to be written from a series of interviews that he had given. Sydney denied that this particular tale was true. I didn't really care either way, for it never came between us and Sydney always was a bit inclined to say the first thing that entered his head. Words were to Sydney like stones to be thrown at windows: he would wait to hear the tinkle of breaking glass.

It seemed Cynthia, as was her habit, had taken Sydney to have tea at Fortnum and Mason's tea shop. Sydney had always enjoyed cream buns and ate a great number of them while he stayed at the Dorchester. Cream buns in great quantities had no effect on his shape whatsoever as he remained slim as a hoe handle. Cynthia told Sydney that she had some shopping to do and that she would be back in a few minutes. Sydney sat there till closing time and then caught a taxi home to Putney. Cynthia had left the store by another entrance and booked into a nearby hotel, where she had committed suicide. The police were called, Cynthia identified, and Sydney contacted at home. It seemed that Sydney, in a state of great distress, was under the impression that he might be blamed for his wife's death. The next part of the story I will relate as Sydney Nolan told it to me: a young Australian couple had, by chance, knocked at the Nolans' door and

Cynthia had sold them the house for a derisory price. Sydney, when telling this tale, gave the impression that the couple had merely called to look at his paintings. Next Cynthia, according to Sydney, had sent all his pictures to an unnamed store and, when she died, he was totally at a loss as to the whereabouts of these pieces. If this is true, there must be a huge cache of Nolans stored somewhere in Britain. Who knows? But knowing Sydney, I have always doubted this tale.

Within a few months, Sydney was married again, this time to Mary Boyd, sister of Arthur Boyd the Australian painter, a woman who was as sweet as Cynthia was sour. My life moved on. I closed my bookshop in Cork Street, my stock all went to Christie's for auction, but not before I published another book illustrated by Sydney Nolan, *The Darkening Eclipse*, the poem of Ern Malley.

Ern Malley was a fake poet, a confidence trick played on the *avant-garde* art establishment in Australia. Two young Australian writers, McAuley and Stewart, were fed up with what they regarded as junk published by Australian *avant-garde* magazines and set out to show that work to be what they believed it was, totally phoney. With the help of a volume of Shakespeare and a rhyming dictionary, they wrote a number of modern poems and then attributed them to a poet of their imagination. The poems were sent to an *avant-garde* magazine *Angry Penguins*, edited by Max Harris and John Reed, which enthused about them. When Harris and Reed tried to contact the author of the poems, they were told that he was dead. No sooner had Harris and Reed published the dead poet's work than they were promptly prosecuted for obscenity. A trial was held, expert witnesses called for the defence, including Herbert Read and the American poet, Harry Roskolenko. The two young writers appeared and all Australia laughed at the putting down of the *avant-garde* movement. The problem with this whole episode is that the poems, while intended to be a joke, are truly brilliant. All these men did was prove that it is not the intention to write great words that matters, rather the result.

Often Sydney came to my antiques shop, which I had opened in the same building on Cork Street that had housed my bookshop. This new shop was indeed a cabinet of curiosities, containing everything from six-legged lambs to dinosaurs' eggs, from Renaissance bronzes to Roman silver, jewellery, weapons, mystic objects, ethnographical material, minerals, stuffed birds, skeletons, paintings and carvings. Things were packed in drawers, balanced on shelves and leaned against one another. The place was full of amazing objects; the chairs were comfortable; the wine good. Interesting people came and went, sometimes to shop, sometimes just to gossip.

Sydney bought antiques with the same enthusiasm that he bought books. The only difference was in the price. Soon he began to owe me large sums of money and I took his paintings to repay the debt. Sydney always insisted on buying. Even when I was not in my shop, he would charm my assistant into showing him the new stock and just take pieces of it home. 'We will settle the details later.' The details were never really settled. Sydney wanted to sell his pictures for the top retail price, so I sold him my antiques at the top retail price. It would not have made much difference to either of us if we had been more realistic about the relative value of our goods, but it helped the conceit of both of us to sell at unrealistic prices and so make unreal profits.

One morning, Sydney arrived carrying a plastic bag. On opening it he tipped the contents onto my table. Tiny slithers of silver tumbled everywhere. It was the remains of a very large and important Roman silver bowl, a wonderful object, that I had sold him some weeks before. 'What happened to this?' I asked. 'My cleaning lady dropped it and the bowl disintegrated. It gave her a bit of a shock.' It gave me a bit of a shock as well, for this bowl had cost Sydney Nolan, as far as I can remember, £250,000. You might expect a silver bowl to be a bit dented after you drop it, but not to disintegrate. Ancient silver is different, however; it is as fragile as glass. I remember a customer once picking up a Roman drinking bowl, its centre shaped like a breast. Romans held this bowl with their fingers on its rim and the thumb inside the breast. This is how my customer held this silver bowl and as he made an extravagant gesture, pretending to drink, his thumb popped through, its tip appearing where the nipple used to be. Was Sydney's bowl insured, I asked. 'No,' he replied. 'Was there anything that I could do about his problem?' 'No,' I replied.

Sydney was, in almost every respect, the most perfect of customers as he really loved the goods he bought. Always, he insisted on carrying them away with him, as if he could not bear to be parted from these objects. It was a strange experience, therefore, to visit his home in Wales and to be shown a room filled with parcels which had never been unpacked. I noticed amongst them parcels that contained books that I had sold him in the 1970s, still in their original wrapping, still unopened.

One afternoon, I had a visit from two smartly dressed gentlemen who informed me that they were from the Inland Revenue. They were investigating the affairs of Sir Sydney Nolan. We went into my back room and talked and these men required details of all the transactions I had conducted with Sydney. I willingly gave them this information. I did not see Sydney for some weeks after that, and the next time he came to my shop he was accompanied by his wife, Mary, and his accountant. They required the same information as the men from the Revenue. Sydney sat silent, Mary and the accountant did the talking.

I never saw Sydney again. I heard from friends that Mary went everywhere with him; I heard from friends that they could no longer see Sydney. I heard that he was sick, and then I heard that he had died. Sydney would, I believe, far rather die than live the life of a responsible human being. For Sydney was no such thing; indeed he had not the first idea of what responsibility meant and just as well that he had not, for the man was a genius. Technically brilliant, he could draw two different images at the same time whilst holding four coloured pencils in each hand. He had all the imagination of his Irish ancestors, but his creative energy was truly his own. When Sydney Nolan died a joy went out of my life, for I miss him and his company.

In the mid-1960s Stuart Devlin came to see me to ask advice as he had in mind setting up in Britain. An Australian, he had just finished designing the new Australian currency needed for the change from the pound to the dollar. Devlin was uncertain whether he would be better employed as a sculptor – his work was organic and when placed in the open air it deteriorated each year because the action of rain on its surface caused a chemical reaction. Or should he make his way as a silversmith? I advised that he did just that, as I did not believe disappearing sculpture would find a ready market in Britain, where, in the early 1960s, any works of art more adventurous than a painting by Augustus John were greeted with derision.

People visiting my house above Henley-on-Thames at that time, and seeing the work of Morris Louis, Rothko, Gotlieb and Kenneth Noland, would shudder with horror. As for the sculpture of Tony Caro and Bill Turnbull, they covered their eyes with dismay, asking when the builders were coming to finish fixing my boilers. Some of the more elderly guests sympathised with my father over his misfortune in having an idiot son who clearly was deranged enough to regard canvases with stripes and dots as art – let alone the heaps of scrap metal that he had lying about the place. I think that it was the battle to prove these people wrong that drove me on in my collecting. The more that I was told that I was wrong, the greater my determination to be proved right. Perhaps this is why I gave part of my collection of sculpture, some eighty pieces, to the Tate Gallery. This was the first of several large gifts to the Tate. They include a vast horlage by Dubuffet, a very large landscape by Graham Sutherland and a fountain by Naum Gabo, that now sits outside St Thomas's Hospital. In all, I believe that my gifts to the Tate were numerically more than those of any other individual except Turner.

I knew Naum Gabo, an impish man given to jokes. Possibly he was the only man to have held the positions of both Russian commissary and British knight. I used to go and visit him in his studios, where he showed me his vodka bottle. It was made of milk glass and was labelled in garish colours. 'People ask me where I get this wonderful vodka from. In fact I have had the bottle for years and I fill it with the vodka from Warrington. They can't tell the difference.' In his studio, Naum Gabo had only one painting, a work by Christopher Wood. A fine painting of *Fishing Boats at Treboule*, it seemed an odd choice for an artist interested in the most stylish and intricate abstract sculptures. Looking at some of Naum Gabo's drawings, I asked him how they came about. 'I see them in my mind and I just set about putting them on paper.' 'Do you build them up as you go, joining oblongs with lines where they are needed?' 'No,' he replied. 'I see them complete in my mind.' He talked about Russia and the revolution. His girlfriend had been Trotsky's sister, a woman who became Commissary for the arts. When the revolution started Naum Gabo was a student at Moscow University. He, like most of the students, was in favour of revolution. The professors of the University were strongly against it. When the going began to get rough, many of these professors fled to the West, leaving the students the run of the place. Gabo had been studying painting and sculpture under a very strict and traditional regime comprising endless life classes and suchlike. All of a sudden he could do what and go where he pleased. The science laboratories, he told me, had always fascinated him, so he used the equipment that was lying around to make sculpture. His first piece of that sculpture is in the Tate Gallery, a piece of wire that stands in the air fixed at one end only and just below the electric magnets which, when switched on, cause the wire to vibrate. The eye then sees the wire make the patterns that Naum Gabo uses in so many of his later works.

Trotsky's sister called all the artists together and explained, 'Henceforth, no artist will charge more than five kopecks for their work.' The reason for this was that such a price was within the pocket of a peasant. The artists were delighted, Gabo told me. Then, however, his girlfriend went on to say that no artist would be allowed to make a work of art that a peasant would not want to buy. 'But we have Russian dolls,' they cried, referring to the wooden dolls that fit inside each other, still a traditional product of Russia. 'They are for the peasants.' Trotsky's sister, however, could not be moved on this subject.

Gabo needed to make a protest. In Russia after the revolution there was no law directing what you could, or could not, print, just a restriction on the paper for printing it. Gabo, a commissary, had access to paper for 'proper reasons'. He and his friends realised that when they ordered a ream of paper and accounted for the number of its sheets, there was always one left over: the sheet that the paper had been wrapped in. This sheet of wrapping paper had been overlooked by the authorities. Gabo and his colleagues collected these wrapping sheets and printed and published their own manifestos. Soon afterwards Naum Gabo left Russia.

We gossiped for hours. Gabo explained to me the terrible mistake that the art historian, Herbert Read, had made. 'He saw my work,' and 'he recognised it for what it was, work of great importance, but what he did not realise was that there were those who copied my work – Barbara Hepworth and Henry Moore. They introduced strings and wires into their work as I did. Herbert Read was so impressed with the strings that he imagined that their work was as good as mine when in fact it was rubbish.'

Another artist whom I used to see often in the 1960s was Lynn Chadwick and I bought a considerable number of his drawings and sculptures. He and I used to lunch together in London, drinking gallons of wine and often finishing in the late afternoon. Chadwick is a fascinating man, who in his cups I found hilariously funny. On one occasion, I visited him at his house near Stroud. We had a drink midmorning and then set off to see his friends the Browns. Ralph Brown was a sculptor, a very good sculptor who has had far less success than he deserves. We looked at his sculpture for a while and then he and his beautiful wife Caroline returned with us to eat a late lunch cooked by Eva Chadwick. We drank Château Latour in its best vintages – several of them – and talked and drank until darkness came. I was due to take my wife, Sarah, to the theatre that night. The hours rolled on and I rang home to say that I would be late. How late, I did not realise. I have seldom enjoyed myself more. We sat and talked of art and artists, of life and objects of beauty; more food came and more drink. I returned to London very late and my wife was not best pleased. 'Food poisoning,' I muttered and with that fell into bed and passed out. In the morning it is a far better tactic to have no recall of nights such as those than it is to try to explain.

The Chadwicks' house was deeply mysterious – it would not have surprised me to find the magician, Merlin, living there. Lynn Chadwick had, like Gerald Benney, taken a great, in his case Gothic, pile, and turned it into his studios and home. Many of the empty rooms were filled with sculptures made in Formica. The master bathroom, while still Gothic, was modernist in feeling with a heated slab of terrazzo to lie on beside a sculptured bath. The rooms, all large, ran one into another. The gardens were wild and wonderful. The house sat on the edge of a craggy cliff, with the views from its windows on one side that looked over a sheer drop.

My wife, Sarah, did not like Lynn Chadwick for a number of reasons. He had on one occasion pinched her bottom and on another chased her around his dining room table with a bottle of wine under each arm. I explained that he was drunk and harmless and, not least, that he was totally safe because he would never have let two bottles of wine drop and go to waste. I do not blame either Lynn Chadwick or Sara. She just did not like artists very much and felt their presence in our home an intrusion, while I regarded it as a delight.

In those days I had several plan chests full of drawings and watercolours by Lynn Chadwick, Elizabeth Frink, John Hoyland, John Hilton, Patrick Heron and most of the young British painters and sculptors. These works cost me little and within a few years I had given them all away to friends who came to lunch or as gifts to celebrate birthdays and weddings.

My house at Fawley Green was a Georgian rectory. I am afraid, as I look back, that in my youthful ignorance I ruined the place. I had the idea that if I made it larger it would be better, when what I really should have done was make the house much smaller, restoring it to the original square Georgian building. The gardens of the house were non-existent. At the time I did not realise how much better they could have become just by the simple act of confining them, which could have been achieved by shutting out the views of seven different counties and designing the gardens so that a splendid view could be seen only through each of several strategically placed gaps in either a wall, a close-clipped hedge or through a bank of trees. However, in those days, gardening did not interest me and my priority was finding places to house the sculptures and paintings of my ever-increasing collections. The solution to me was an easy one: I just built on extra rooms and galleries.

When I had an enthusiasm for film, I turned a yard into a cinema. At the time my family's company was pulling down the Odeon, Marble Arch, so I bought the second-hand projectors for my private cinema. As for 35 millimetre films, Jack Isaacs, then the head projectionist at the Rank organisation, helped me to acquire them and taught me how to operate the projectors. My secretary at the time, Barbara Segal, an extremely intelligent and attractive woman, was a serious cinema buff and advised me on my choice of films. With her help I worked through the work of all the great directors, from Jean Renoir to Roman Polanski. I was particularly taken with the propaganda films of Leni Riefenstahl. The Japanese film makers interested me and I watched many Japanese films by an assortment of directors. I was hooked on MGM musicals and I believe that I watched all of them. Each weekend, I would sit through five different films. I became fascinated by the Serious Cinema. This was a new world to me and I consumed what it had to offer with an energetic relish.

Barbara Segal was also an enthusiastic theatregoer as well as a film and opera buff, so each week she booked me tickets to a play. It was Barbara Segal who introduced me to opera. *Madame Butterfly* was the first opera that I attended. After that I could not get enough opera, going to the ballet or opera several nights a week.

My house was filled with an eclectic mixture of eighteenth-century sporting paintings. I loved their naive quality. I collected at that time the early Staffordshire pottery by Obediah Sherrat and the Wood family, which sat shoulder to shoulder with pottery by Picasso. I must, I suppose, have had several hundred of his plates and jugs, a number of them unique pieces. Over the fireplace in the sitting room hung a collection of six small Renoirs. The first picture of any importance that I bought after John Heath took me to that gallery behind Marble Arch, was a Renoir about eighteen inches long and eight inches high, its subject a man sitting alone on the beach. It came from the Jacques O'Hana Gallery in 1963 and I paid £2,500 for it. I gave it to my mother. Six months later I bought again from Jacques O'Hana a charcoal drawing, about twelve inches square, by Picasso of his mother signed 'Pablo Luis Picasso' and dated 1898. A missed opportunity in the 1960s was when, having lunched well at Felix's Restaurant in Cannes, I visited the gallery next door. They greeted me with enthusiasm and took me into the back room, where I was offered a complete set of Picasso etchings, perhaps his most famous work – *The Vollard Suite*. They asked £12,000 for this great work but I did not have the money to buy them. I had, at that time, hit on the idea of approaching a company that organised hire purchase arrangements for people who wanted to buy motor cars. Why not, I asked them, hire purchase for people who want to buy paintings? They thought this was a great idea and so did I. At the time that *The Vollard Suite* became available, however, I was at the end of my already extended credit.

Picasso used to lunch in Felix's Restaurant and I saw him there on many occasions. Once in the winter he came in wearing a deerstalker hat. I left the restaurant before him and as I walked out I could so easily have stolen his deerstalker from the hook where it hung. Something stopped me. I hesitated, looked and walked on. I wish that I had stolen that hat. I would have offered to buy it, but Picasso would not have sold it and Felix would not have forgiven me for insulting his most famous customer. I left the hat hanging there and went about my life, occasionally wondering what happened to it. Is that hat still lurking in some second-hand shop without anyone realising its important history?

In my house above Henley in the mid-1960s most of the furnishings were eighteenth-century English, but my dining-room table and chairs were by Eero Sorensen; in my drawing room hung paintings by the Sartorius family; in my dining room stood a sculpture by Philip King. There were drawings by Sickert hanging in that home and works by a French Primitive painter whose name I forget – he earned his living working at the gasworks in Nice and painted in his spare time.

I have always had an enthusiasm for the primitive, whether it be in ethnic sculpture, furniture or painting. In 1962, travelling in the

Caribbean with my parents, we stopped at Haiti – at that time not the most friendly of places. We visited the Olafson Hotel, made famous by Graham Greene in his book *The Comedians*. The swimming pool of the Olafson Hotel was empty; the corpse that Graham Greene described lying on its bottom, long gone.

The rooms of this enchanting tropical hotel were hung with paintings by Haitian primitives, vibrant pictures with improbable colours in juxtaposition, their imagery so different from the savage nature of Haiti. The artists depicted scenes of country life – the markets, religious episodes – and even when they painted wild animals in an imaginary jungle, the animals smiled. I was soon put in touch with the dealer and bought 300 of these paintings. They were only a few pounds each. The dealer promised to deliver the pictures, already crated, long before we sailed. The hours went by and no crate came. The time for sailing drew perilously near, so I set out by taxi to the dealer's house. What had happened, I wondered? I had no need to wonder, for what had happened was obvious as soon as I entered the house. The crate that held the paintings was too large to pass through either doorways or windows. The ship sailed. A year or two later the paintings arrived in London.

The Sartorius family of painters were rather different from the Haitians. Working in the eighteenth and early nineteenth century this family painted horses and dogs, cats and cows. Their paintings of famous racehorses fetched the most money, not because they were better paintings but purely because the British prefer racing to collecting pictures. David Wynne once told me that when he was commissioned to do a portrait of a horseman's wife, it really did not matter whether the result looked like her or not; but when commissioned to make a portrait of a horseman's horse, just alter the conformation of that animal a fraction and all hell would break out.

These paintings by members of the Sartorius family can have borne little resemblance to their subjects, unless those subjects were horribly deformed. The paintings were, in fact, wonderful examples of the use of large flat areas of colour. The people and the animals that were the subjects were used only to make an abstract pattern, giving the pictures a tremendous power.

Identifying the work of the Sartorius family was not as simple as it seemed. I collected over a hundred of what I believed to be their paintings, discovering, when I had them all collected together, stylistic differences that led me to the conclusion that paintings apparently signed F.S., standing for Francis Sartorius, were in fact signed T.S., standing for Thomas Stringer. As these paintings rose in price, dealers – some less scrupulous than others – began to tinker with the work of the Sartorius family. For instance, hunting scenes that depicted the kill, in which the fox is held high above the huntsman's head as hounds jump up to bite the poor creature, savage scenes worth little, came back on the market with the fox gone and the huntsman's hands now lowered patting the dogs' heads. The hungry looks of the dogs' faces have disappeared and they are now the gentlest of creatures. The price for these rearranged pictures has thus grown by considerable proportions, the only snag being that the customer is unaware of the changes that have taken place.

At the time that I was buying paintings by the Sartorius family, I advertised in *The Times* for collectors who owned them. I had a reply from a lady who lived in St John's Wood. Arriving at the address that I had been given, I was greeted by a stunning redhead, her hair hanging down her back, her jeans squeezing the most elegant of legs. I was most taken with this young woman. She showed me her painting and at a glance I knew it to be a fake – an interesting fake by a well-known faker who copied the work of J.N. Sartorius during the early years of the century when the artist's prices were amongst the highest paid for English paintings. The lady made me a cup of tea; I was lulled into a sense of security that turned out to be false. 'What do you make of my picture?' Out of pure conceit, a desire to show off to this delightful creature, I replied, 'It is, I am afraid, no good to me. It is a fake, but take it back to the dealer that you bought it from and you will get your money back.' This creature of delight underwent a metamorphosis. In seconds she was a raging harridan. Her husband in the City was telephoned and I was told to speak to him. He called me a cheat, a liar and a series of names far more abusive than both of those.

This was on a Monday morning. On the Friday I went to spend the weekend with David Wolfson and his wife Susan. Arriving at about five o'clock, I was shown into the drawing room of their country house in Gloucestershire. Standing, a blazing fire between them, were this harridan of Monday morning and her abusive husband. I was introduced to them and they to me as Lesley and Edgar Astaire. We became friends and were so for a number of years. I don't know what happened to that fake painting, indeed, I never asked. Never ever criticise a person's pictures, or their children. In the matter of pictures or, for that matter, goods and chattels, when shown them and asked for an opinion, just smile and say of the object proffered to you, 'Very good of its kind, remarkably good of its kind.' And of the children, just mutter, 'Wonderful, wonderful, quite wonderful', as I have heard Willie (Lord) Whitelaw say on so many occasions when asked an opinion on the quality of a speaker at a political occasion that he had just attended.

It was in 1962 that I first met Leslie Waddington. He worked for his father and they were both assisted by Janet Myle. I had wandered off the street into the gallery and I bought a couple of sculptures by Elizabeth Frink and another sculpture by McWilliam. A few days later I returned the sculpture by McWilliam and Janet Myle, who had sold me the three works, willingly took it back. I learned later that Victor, Leslie Waddington's father, was furious with her. 'The man has bought the work, he must keep it.' Janet Myle replied, and Leslie Waddington supported her, 'He might be a big customer in time.' She was right. I did in a short time become, by the standards of the day, a considerable customer of theirs, but far more important than any of the transactions which passed between us is the friendship that developed between Leslie Waddington and myself.

Leslie Waddington has been a source of education as far as I am concerned. Son of an Irish art dealer from Dublin, his paternal grandfather was a Judaic scholar. Born of Yorkshire parents and brought up in the Church of England, he converted to the Jewish faith and emigrated to Southern Ireland. Leslie Waddington is, however, pure Irish with a Jewish overlay. As an art dealer, he has a touch of genius and was, at the time that I first met him, one of the few London art dealers to have any formal training for their job. He was educated in Dublin at the same school as Samuel Beckett, whom he used to meet regularly in Paris. I asked him what they talked about or whether, considering the nature of Beckett's plays, they talked at all. 'Oh well,' said Leslie Waddington, 'we spoke about our old school for a bit, and then Samuel Beckett just sat there farting and belching.'

As a young man Leslie Waddington taught French to the children of John Huston. He massacres the language with the same wild enthusiasm as he does English, never letting the lack of correct pronunciation stop him using a word. After a time at the Sorbonne studying art history and museology, working as a guide at the Louvre in his spare time, he joined his father in London's Cork Street.

Not long after I met Leslie, he parted from his father, who had the novel idea of splitting his art business fifty-fifty with his son. The father kept the debtors while the son took over responsibility for the creditors. Money was clearly needed by Leslie Waddington if he was to remain an art dealer. Leslie offered me the chance to buy half the business for £25,000. I was by this time a substantial client, buying paintings by John Hoyland, Patrick Heron and Milton Avery. With Elizabeth Frink, Leslie and I had an arrangement. I took every sculpture that she made for three years. I would pay £100 for each of them, plus whatever they cost to cast in bronze. This deal suited all of us. Elizabeth Frink, then comparatively unknown, received a steady income; Leslie was helped with the cost of casting her work and I was able to collect her sculpture at a bargain price. However, I already owed him £10,000, a prodigious sum in those days, and finding a further £25,000 was out of the question. Instead, Alex Bernstein had the foresight to back Leslie. He was, I may say, well-rewarded as a partner in one of the most active galleries during the art boom. The record year for profits was 1989, when the Waddington Gallery made £29 million.

It was not, however, as a businessman that Leslie Waddington really excelled – it is the sharpness of his eye that sets him apart. Often I would find him reading *Vogue* or *Harper's Bazaar*. Why did he read these magazines? 'Many of my customers are female. I must know about female clothes so that I can judge whether they are likely to buy expensive paintings and how good their taste is, so that I can offer them the right pictures.'

In the early days his taste was abstract; Heron, Hilton, Hitchens were among his stable as a dealer, as were Milton Avery and the Canadian, Jack Bush. In his home he hung the work of Morris Louis and Kenneth Noland. Leslie was early in his enthusiasm for the American Abstract Expressionists and he helped me put a considerable collection of their paintings together. It was from Leslie Waddington that I learned about Rothko, but from the Marlborough galleries that I bought my paintings.

In New York just after Mark Rothko's death, I visited the Marlborough Gallery. They offered me six paintings at what seemed bargain prices. I did not need, nor could I afford, these paintings, but I bought them nevertheless. Some months later the Rothko scandal broke in the press and I had a call from the New York District Attorney's Office. This officer of the law would be in London. Could we meet? Of course. I suggested tea at the Dorchester and the gentleman in question was very taken with the idea. It seemed that I had been sold these paintings at bargain prices to establish a false basis on which the whole estate could be valued. Would I come to New York and give evidence? Of course I would. I love New York and the thought of being there at the expense of that City's District Attorney's Office filled me with delight. Sadly, there was such a weight of evidence that they did not need my help.

The art dealers in London during the early 1960s were a pretty rum lot. Erica Brausen at the Hanover Gallery was a really tough woman. She handled Francis Bacon's work before he was persuaded to move to the Marlborough Gallery. A friend of David Wynne's, a painter, Peter Rogers, showed his work at the Hanover. He spent the whole of one day and the morning of the next hanging his show. When at last he was satisfied he went out to lunch, returning in time for the private view. On returning to the gallery, Rogers found that Erica Brausen had rehung the whole show. 'Bite my ear, Erica,' Peter Rogers requested. 'For heaven's sake, why?' Erica Brausen replied. 'Because when I get fucked about I like to get a bit of passion with it.' Peter Rogers married Andrew Wyeth's niece and left for California. A few years later, David Wynne and I recovered one of his paintings, a crucifixion. It had been too large for him to take with him and too expensive to store, so he had nailed it behind the closed shutters in the studio that he once rented.

The Hanover Gallery was financed by Michael Behrens, who was best known for running the Ionian Bank, a fringe bank that fell into trouble during the 1970s, at which time he closed the gallery. Behrens lived in a large late Georgian house overlooking the Thames opposite my parents' farm at Medmenham. In this house was a fine collection of De Stael's paintings, as well as many works by Balthus. The furniture, mostly eighteenth-century, was impeccable in its taste, each purchase made with the recommendation of the staff from the V&A Museum. Behrens was also a fastidious wine connoisseur. He did a lot of sniffing and puffing as he drank, with much swilling from one side of his mouth to another. He was a pompous sort of bloke, whose most redeeming feature was that he had been a close friend and patron of Gerald Benney and his wife Janet. I never cared for him, nor did he care for me. I put this down to jealousy, for he had a very competitive nature; or maybe it was just that I was jealous of him, his house and his art collection? I certainly was not jealous of his antics with wine.

Rex Nankiviel was another great figure of London's art world. He ran the Redfern Gallery and when I write 'ran' I mean ran. Nothing happened there without Rex Nankiviel's permission. I bought paintings by Jawlenski from him, works by Christopher Wood and a wonderful Sickert drawing of the Hotel Royal. Every art dealer, or for that matter, collector, always hopes to make a great killing. Rex Nankiviel made several, but the most notable of them was the exhibition of paintings by the French painter Soutine. Sixty paintings were exhibited; none was sold. Rex Nankiviel bought them all from the artist for, I suppose, no great sum of money. In time, Soutine's work began to sell for large amounts. With these paintings, as so often with works of art, the real profit is made from works that you cannot sell at the time that you buy them rather than the works that you can sell when you first show them.

I acquired from Rex Nankiviel several packets of letters written by Christopher Wood to his mother in the years before he committed suicide by jumping under a train at Salisbury station. They were wonderful letters and showed a great insight into a young man whom many of his contemporaries thought to be a genius. I recall one passage where Christopher Wood describes lunch with Picasso and Jean Cocteau: 'They must believe that I am a great painter,' Wood writes, 'otherwise why would they have lunch with me?' There were over three hundred of these immensely sad letters. They were, I am afraid, stolen from my office by a man, then a dealer in a small way, now highly successful in the London art world. Never underestimate the power that works of art and the ephemeral that surrounds them has over even honest individuals. Art has a strange effect on even the most rational of us. Leslie Waddington, for instance, was asked one afternoon by a lady of certain age, who had bought a number of paintings from him, whether she could see him in private. He showed her into his office and turned to close the door. Imagine his surprise when, on again facing the lady, he found her stark naked, with her mink coat laying at her feet.

After the crash of 1973 the construction industry was dead so I spent much time playing chess with Leslie Waddington. There was little else for us to do – no one was building anything, the whole of Britain seemed either on strike or forbidden to work by Edward

Heath's daft three-day week. Certainly no one was buying paintings. I could never beat Leslie at chess, although this, I must admit, says little for his skill because I am no chess player. Once, however, I did win and then only because a vast and immensely ugly woman burst into his office unannounced – it quite put the poor fellow off his stroke.

Not long afterwards, Sarah and I invited Leslie and his wife to dinner. Leslie did not turn up and the next day I discovered that he had been taken into hospital. A few days before this incident, I had dreamed that I had come into his gallery to find him lying in a pool of blood. I told him about the dream and then regretted mentioning it, for it really frightened him. Later, his staff told me that they had found him lying much as I had described from my dream.

I lived in those galleries of Cork Street, frequently visiting the Pilkington, Roland Browse and Delbanco and the Mercury Gallery. Amongst other artists, I bought the work of Alfred Wallis, an untutored primitive from St Ives. A local scrap collector, Wallis was encouraged by Ben Nicholson. He painted on pieces of cardboard at first, with house paint. I had over two hundred of these exciting paintings. They were, when I first collected them, only a few pounds each. Around that time, 1966, Leslie Waddington sold me a pair of découpés by Henri Matisse. They were four and a half feet square and cost £4,000 each. Matisse's cut-outs were not highly regarded then. These découpés were made as designs for scarves and commissioned by Asher. Madame Duthuit had written to Leslie Waddington, telling him that many of her father's cut-outs were ruined by restorers: they had stuck down the edges of the paper images, whereas her father had meant them to fly free 'like the wings of butterflies'. Madame Duthuit helped her father create these masterpieces as he lay in bed, his hands crippled with arthritis and rods tied to his wrists so that he could painfully point out just where the images were to be fixed. I was wildly enthusiastic about Matisse's sculptures. At this time not many people liked them. I bought several – they were about £20,000 each. Today they fetch millions and many people believe them to be amongst the master's best work.

Some of my collection I sold, the rest I gave away to the Tate Gallery, the Contemporary Arts Society and other institutions. Warwick University received paintings from my collection, important works by Patrick Heron, Roger Hilton, John Hoyland, Jack Bush and the American, Gene Davies. The Ashmolean Museum were given a gallery where they could show contemporary art. Other paintings I sold when I needed money to purchase new paintings or sculpture that I believed to be better.

It was the crash in 1973 that caused me to sell most of my collection. I was overextended and the market dropped. It was then that I sold the fine painting of the Baron de Roebeck by George Stubbs that I had bought a few years before. The Baron sat astride a rearing horse waving his top hat in the air, his dog galloping beside him. During the election campaign in 1987 I was having lunch with Grey Gowrie, Chairman of Sotheby's, his proprietor Alfred Taubman and Lord Young, then a Cabinet minister. 'How did the Stubbs sell in our New York rooms?' Taubman asked Grey Gowrie, for as far as I could tell no particular purpose. 'It fetched over two million dollars,' Grey Gowrie replied. 'I sold that picture once,' I interjected. Alfred Taubman turned towards me, half-interested. 'I sold that picture for £170,000.' Turning away, I have no doubt to hide his contempt, Taubman remarked, 'Well, you should have sold it with Sotheby's.' Unfortunately, I had.

The art market is endlessly fascinating, or at least it fascinates me. It is the way that prices rise from nowhere and drop again; the greed, the conceits, the way that buying and selling pictures bring out the worst traits in human nature; the way that artists can in youth have great success that dies with middle-age and comes again at death. I bought paintings and sculptures because I liked them and sold them again, mostly because I had to, in order to raise money. It is the hunt as much as the finding of a work of art that gives the pleasure. For me ownership is a secondary quality. I would as soon buy for someone else as buy for myself. I enjoyed the people whom I met, the visits to strange houses. The memories of that strange world and the Gods that inhabited it enchanted me. Almost without fail I bought too soon and sold before the market was ready. Leslie Waddington, walking with me in Venice in the early 1990s, suddenly began to talk of my collection. 'I found the inventory the other day. I revalued all the paintings. Can you guess what the total was? No, well it came to over £8 million.' These paintings were nearly all long gone before Leslie Waddington did his addition, and perhaps he felt that he should excuse my folly, because he added, 'But if you had kept them you would be a different sort of person.'

8

Down Under

As happens so often with many of the important changes of direction in my life, my association with Australia began by chance. At the beginning of February 1959 I stood on the deck of the *Oriana* as it drew into the dock at Fremantle. Migrants crowded the lower decks, looking for their relatives and friends on the quay, and a piper played. The trip from Southampton had been a long and exotic voyage, stopping at Naples and then passing through the Suez Canal. Travelling with us were close friends of my parents, Brigadier John Shearer and his wife, Mary.

As a young cavalry officer, John Shearer served in the Indian Army and during the First World War in the desert with Allenby. Between the wars he was without employment, so he took a job working on the shop floor of Fortnum and Mason. Before the next war began and he rejoined the army, Shearer had become Managing Director of the famous store. In the Second World War he was, for a time, the Head of British Military Intelligence in Egypt. Falling foul of Montgomery, who believed quite rightly that he was reporting directly to Churchill, he lost his job in the Middle East, but not before he had overseen the removal of Farouk from his throne. Shearer used to breakfast each day with Farouk's uncle. On this particular day he told Farouk's uncle that this nephew must resign his throne. The man protested. The café where they took their breakfast had a good view of the Palace, so Shearer merely waved his napkin and watched as a nearby tank blew a hole in the Palace gates. 'Now,' said John Shearer, 'will your nephew resign?'

John Shearer took it into his head that it might be fun if he and I took a taxi from Port Said via Cairo to Suez as the *Oriana* slowly travelled the Canal. It took us most of the day to find a taxi willing to make the trip, so we did not depart until late afternoon. The British were at the time immensely unpopular in Egypt, for it was only a year or so before that we had invaded the country during the ill-fated Suez crisis. Shearer was desperate to get into the desert, I just a passenger of his enthusiasm. Soon it was dark and our driver, who would have had trouble discovering the way to Cairo in daylight, was totally lost. One of the most irritating things in the world is when a driver is lost and he will not admit it. It is such a simple matter to stop and ask the way, but those who are lost so often become victim to a compulsion to drive on regardless. This driver had perfected that art, and the more lost he became, the faster he drove. Roundabouts meant nothing to him; roads were merely a rough guide as to the direction in which we might head. Egyptians settling down to their evening meal by the roadside were scattered; camels munching their cud were frightened to their feet and into the desert. The night was warm; the taxi stank of petrol and the journey to Cairo seemed endless. Shearer was not a bit daunted: his spirits were as high as mine were low. I felt the hostility of the driver, whereas Shearer was oblivious. 'What has happened to Sheik so and so?' he would ask and the driver would reply, 'He is in jail.' 'And Prince so and so?' 'In jail,' the driver replied again. 'And so and so?' 'He was hanged.' 'And his brother?' 'Shot.' There was no stopping Shearer as he questioned the driver, adding occasionally, 'So sad, he was a very good friend of mine.' It seemed that the worse the fate these poor individuals had suffered, the greater their friendship with him. In time we hit the outskirts of Cairo and headed for the Mina House Hotel. 'I was last here with Churchill,' John Shearer informed the driver, who belched.

It is no exaggeration to write that my bedroom had eight beds in it and Shearer's, twelve. The dining room at the Mina House in those days was a circular room with a domed ceiling about fifty feet above the heads of the diners. That night there were just two of them, Shearer and myself, and we ate the toughest guinea fowl I have ever come across. Tired by the journey, sickened by the food and frightened out of my wits by Shearer's resurrection of the names that all Egypt was trying to forget, I suggested that we go to bed. Not a bit of it. 'Princess someone or other is dancing at the Café de something or other.' We set off to watch the most famous belly dancer in the world – her belly covered by a silken veil. Nasser, it was explained to me, insisted on modesty amongst belly dancers. The place where this lady danced was packed with Russian officers smoking foul-smelling cigarettes and drinking copious quantities of vodka. Happily they took no notice of the two of us, an elderly British brigadier and a young boy just out of school. The belly dancer was fantastic. A lady then in her fifties, she was amazingly graceful, and I was much taken by the whole affair.

At dawn we stood and watched the Pyramids as they were struck by the first rays of the sun. There was not a soul in sight. We wandered in the bazaars, packed with Egyptians, and through the Cairo Museum, dust-filled and unguarded, a number of its cases open to anyone with a mind to steal their contents. There was not a single person to be seen.

Aden was the next port of call, an Arab town under British rule, untouched by a modern world. I was driven through narrow streets lined with buildings, squeezed against the walls of which Arabs took their evening meals. We were the guests of the Shell Company Representative, going ashore in his personal launch and taking coffee on the flat roof of his home. I collected guns at that time and he very kindly gave me a bundle of long Arab flintlock rifles. He was not to know the trouble that this generous gift was to give me at customs in Australia, America and finally Britain.

Then it was on to Colombo in Ceylon, where we took tea at the hotel where the British stayed during the Raj, black ravens waiting for scraps on its lawn. Colombo's streets were busy with red London buses, every window broken, their destination still marked as Waterloo or Piccadilly. Beggars were plentiful; traders' shops that sold fabrics sat shoulder to shoulder with the retailers of plastic household equipment.

My first sight of the most ancient continent in the world was the long, flat coastline of West Australia, and as the *Oriana* closed with that coastline, the Island of Rottnest which guards the entrance of the Swan River, and the port of Fremantle came into view. None of this, however, was very exciting and I had no idea then that I would fall in love with this great continent, with Western Australia, its landscape and its people.

A ship's officer came towards my father and with him a young man in military uniform, wearing a kilt. We were to take morning tea with the Governor of Western Australia. The young man took us quickly to his waiting car. The government driver saluted; customs officials stood aside. In those days the Swan River ran at the edge of the escarpment that is called Kings Park, several thousand acres of natural bush caught in the centre of a great urban sprawl, a park where all is wild except the occasional garden and avenues of ghost gums, each planted to commemorate the death of a West Australian soldier in one of the two World Wars. These were Australians who died fighting for the King. High in the afternoon breeze the black cockatoos curl and dive, shrieking and crying. The blackfellas in the north say that the different varieties of cockatoo call their own names; for me they are the unquiet spirits of men buried far from the home they loved. No war memorial can be more poignant than these great white gums, each bearing the name of men killed at Gallipoli, the Somme, North Africa, and the charge of the Australian Light Horse at Beersheba. Around these trees children play, and people whose grandparents had never heard of West Australia walk on Sunday afternoons.

The Governor, General Sir Gerald Gardner, was an old friend of John Shearer's. We took tea with him and talked about nothing in particular, for Perth was a country town where nothing particular ever happened. There was no talk of an exciting future; there was no talk about any future. We drove back up St George's Terrace, then lined with buildings two or three storeys high, at its end a red brick fortress built in the early years of the colony, blocking the view of Parliament House. Back along the road under the escarpment, to our left a squadron of small yachts sailed on the Swan River. At Fremantle we were aboard the *Oriana* and my father was serving dry Martinis in his suite. The young man in the kilt was, I suppose, not in the habit of dry Martinis, for he almost missed the sailing of our ship. There we were, four or five hours in Fremantle, just time to offload the migrants, just time to visit Perth, before we were off again to Melbourne and Sydney – cities with ladies who wore hats and long white gloves.

It might have been that I would never have returned to Australia, for on that trip I came across nothing that would draw me back, met no one with whom I fell in love, saw nothing so remarkable that I felt compelled to return. It could have been all over, but for one man and the fact that by chance my father was on holiday when that man telephoned him. He was Sir Halford Reddish, then the Chairman of Rugby Portland Cement. A customer of my family's, Sir Halford Reddish was living proof of how careful you need to be with your good clients. For many years, Sir Halford Reddish stayed at the Savoy

Hotel. He had a suite there which he kept permanently – permanently until the day when one of the Savoy's staff upset him. Instead of taking his lunch at the Savoy, as was Sir Halford's habit, he took it at the Dorchester on the day of his upset. 'Do you have any rooms?' he asked the waiter. The waiter told the head waiter, the head waiter told the manager. 'Certainly, sir. For how long do you wish to stay?' 'Permanently,' Sir Halford replied. After lunch he chose a room that he fancied, moved in that day and stayed until he died many years later. Sir Halford Reddish's chauffeur fetched the luggage from the Savoy.

It is not hard to imagine that when a call arrived at my family's office from Sir Halford Reddish, a considerable amount of trouble was taken to find someone to speak to him. 'Would you go to Australia?' Sir Halford Reddish asked. He had promised the new Minister for Economic Development in the West Australian Government that he would find a contractor in Britain who would be willing to take over the building of roads from the state's direct labour force. 'When should I leave?' I asked. 'At once,' Sir Harold Reddish replied. I left for Perth within days, after my family had wisely equipped me with a senior civil engineer to help assess the business prospects in Western Australia.

I arrived at Brisbane airport and then discovered just how far Perth is from the rest of the country. I flew via Sydney, Melbourne and Adelaide, stopping at each only for as long as it took to refuel. Perth had had a brand new terminal built the year before I arrived. They were in those days very proud of it, and it was as busy as anything. However, this was not because there was a great deal of air traffic coming and going from Perth – in fact there were very few aeroplanes using Perth airport – rather because the new terminal was the only place that you could buy a drink on a Sunday or, indeed, much of the rest of the time. The pubs or hotels, as they were called, were only open for extremely limited hours in Western Australia.

Since I had left England in a hurry without time for the necessary injections, I could not pass through the Far East, so I had travelled across America and then the Pacific, stopping almost everywhere. Looking back on that long and tedious flight that lasted over fifty hours, I can recall only the menus that Qantas offered to the first-class passengers. Not that I remember the food; rather it was the paintings by Australian artists on the menus' covers. One painting in particular caught my attention. Painted in 1948, it was called *The*

Dog and Duck Hotel. I had never heard of Sydney Nolan before I came across this painting.

At Perth airport I climbed from the aeroplane to be met by a government car and driver, drawn up under the wing of the aeroplane. Seated in the car were an elderly couple who turned out to be the State Manager of the National Bank, as it was then, and his wife. 'Do you play Bridge?' they asked in chorus. 'No,' my wife Sarah and I replied. 'Do you play golf?' the duet chimed. 'No,' I replied. 'We had been expecting a much older couple,' the bank manager's wife remarked, 'Oh dear.' I felt totally inadequate – no golf, no Bridge and too young. I have always had a dislike for golf and disinterest in Bridge. The bank manager and his wife were, in fact, very kind to me.

In Perth, however, the boom was on. The town was filled with Japanese buying iron ore, Americans buying cattle ranches, visitors from Britain buying land and Australians touting for investors who would gamble on growing cotton near the northern township of Kunanarra. It took but a few days for me to decide that there was little future in building roads in Western Australia. What was quite clear, however, was that Perth needed a new hotel, for the one that I was staying in was a disaster.

When I had arrived I had my suspicions, but I booked in nevertheless. The place was packed; I had been given a room only at the insistence of the West Australian Government. A key was handed to me and I made my way to that room. Sarah and I wanted something to drink, so I set about finding room service. I searched for a waiter and in time found a waitress, who reluctantly agreed to bring the drinks to our room. The room itself was narrow, with a proportionately small bathroom. The tin bath and basin were covered in white enamel stained with rust. The requested beverages arrived, a Coke in a bottle with a straw sticking out of its neck for Sarah, my tea in a cup. Sarah never, as far as I could tell, liked Australia, nor for that matter did she like Australians. Several times a year for the next ten years until we separated, more often than not I made the trip to Perth on my own, catching a plane that left England on a Friday night, arriving in Perth on the Monday morning, returning to England the following Friday, arriving back on a Sunday morning. On several of those trips I travelled with Sir Halford Reddish, which was a nerve-wracking experience. He would always book two seats and was insistent that no one sat beside him. What was more, he hated canned music. As he took his seat he would say to the air hostess, 'Please turn off the music.' She would reply, 'Excuse me, Sir Halford, I am afraid I did not catch what you said.' 'Would you please turn off the music, my dear?' 'I am afraid that I cannot do that, Sir Halford.' 'Please ask the chief steward to come and see me.' With the chief steward the dialogue would be repeated – and then again with the captain, after which the music would be turned off. This happened every time that we travelled together. Coward that I was, I would sit in the seat behind Sir Halford, pretending that I was travelling with someone else, which was not hard for he would not speak to anyone other than to the hostess from the moment that he got on the plane.

Sir Halford Reddish and my family bought the Adelphi Hotel and the block of flats behind it. The Adelphi overlooked the main street of Perth, St George's Terrace, while the block of flats, known as the Riviera Apartments, had a fine view of the Swan River and Kings Park. The idea was to knock down the Riviera flats and build a new hotel, the Parmelia, then knock down the Adelphi and build a multistorey office building. The scheme went like clockwork. In the period between the Parmelia opening and the Adelphi closing, when in Perth I took one of the four suites in the Adelphi. In time I grew fond of the hotel, and was really quite sad when we pulled it down. In the suite which I used as an office, there were plans everywhere and cups of tea were brought in series. Early on in the planning of the new hotel, the architect, Peter Arnie, my lawyer and close friend, John Adams, various real estate agents and myself were all huddled over a set of plans. One by one we began to realise that there was a stranger sitting at the table looking over our plans with us. As this realisation dawned on all concerned, the stranger, who was the maid who had just brought in another tray of tea, embarrassed no doubt by all these men looking at her, remarked, 'Well, I certainly won't know myself in this new place.' Then she added, 'Well, I don't know about you gentlemen, but I have a lot of work to get on with,' at which point she rose from the table and walked out of the room.

In order to make the purchase of both the hotel and the block of flats, we used a nominee. The vendor of the hotel was pleased with the price; the vendor of the flats, however, was distinctly put out on discovering the people who had really bought his property were wealthy foreigners. When he vacated the flats he stripped all the hot water heaters, light switches and anything else that he could detach from the building. When John Adams protested, the man said, 'Show me where it says hot water heaters in the contract.' 'The man' was a small-time property developer and the Riviera flats were the first property he owned in the City of Perth. His name: Alan Bond. His behaviour over my hot water heaters apparently became the standard for his business practice over the next twenty years as he rose to become the winner of the America's Cup and then a leader amongst West Australia's crop of failed tycoons.

The first time I met Alan Bond was shortly after the incident with the hot water heaters. For reasons that I have never been able to fathom, he believed that the men he had just cheated, namely Sir Halford Reddish and myself, might like to join him as his partners. I waited for Bond in the Adelphi's foyer, showed him to Sir Halford Reddish's suite, opened the door and showed him into the room. Alan Bond held out his hand for Sir Halford to ignore. 'Sir Halford,' said Bond, waving his unshaken hand, 'I would like to offer you the chance of becoming my partner.' 'No thank you, Mr Bond,' Sir Halford Reddish replied as I opened the door to show Bond out into the rather tatty corridor.

Few, if any, of Alan Bond's partners prospered from their association with that brilliant but basically twisted individual. The last time that I met Bond was at lunch with the industrialist and financier, David Davies. We lunched at Harry's Bar in London. Bond bemoaned the fact that he had missed at auction the one item that he really wanted from amongst the collection of jewels that belonged to the Duchess of Windsor. This jewel was a gold bracelet hung with enamel crosses, each cross commemorating, for the Duchess, a sad memory. 'There was another bracelet,' I told Bond, 'a bracelet of hearts, each given to remember a happy occasion.' 'Is it for sale?' were Bond's first words. 'Of course', and I pulled the bracelet from my pocket. The story would be so much better if Bond had gone on from triumph to triumph, instead of which his life fell about him like pine needles off a tired Christmas tree, and with him and his fellow tycoons fell the reputation of Western Australia. There is something pathetic about Alan Bond. He is a clever man. He did not need to be a crook; he just could not help himself. It was, I suppose, a way to show that he alone could beat the system. I believe that he got pleasure out of dishonesty.

As for Sir Halford Reddish, after increasing the profits of the Rugby Portland Cement Company every year for fifty years, he was forced to retire. He took this rather badly and shortly afterwards he died. I shall, however, never forget that peppery little man, for he was short in stature but long in vision. Despite suffering from terrible damage to his lungs by gas in the First World War, he was indomitable when he had an idea in his head that he pushed to fulfil. He was a man who devoted his life to his work, his wife and his collection of English antique silver in about that order.

I shall never forget travelling with him one day in the ancient and very slow lifts at the Adelphi Hotel. As we approached the lift a man in smart uniform, covered in gold braid, with a pair of wings surmounting his breast pocket, held open the lift door for us. 'Thank you,' said Sir Halford Reddish and then, after a pause, 'Qantas?' 'No sir,' came the reply. 'Admiral commanding the US Sixth Fleet.'

The Parmelia was a hotel of considerable character, furnished with decorative antiques and a fine collection of Australian paintings. The paintings were mostly bought from Rose Skinner, the dealer whom I met when, inspired by the reproduction of Sydney Nolan's painting on the Qantas menu, I set about finding examples of his work. This was not easy, for Nolan was at that time painting in England. Australian art dealers in 1965 were few and far between; in Perth Rose Skinner was the only one. In the end I tracked down one painting by Nolan, entitled *Ned Kelly at the Burning of Glengowan*, in Melbourne. It had been painted in 1955 and was about thirty-six inches by twenty-four. I took it home with me on the plane as hand luggage. Carried on and off the plane at each stop, of which there were a great many, this large package often took on a life of its own as I walked across the tarmac in a strong wind.

Rose Skinner held court in Perth, inviting to dinner anyone of note who visited the city. She was a small, birdlike lady, with a ready eye to a profit. Nolan claimed that she suffered from an incurable disease: paralysis of the right hand when faced with a chequebook. She lived with her husband Joe in a small house tucked behind Mount Street. Joe kept an eye on a block of flats that they owned and on his prize possession, the only avocado tree in Perth in the 1960s.

The West Australian Art Gallery bought a large painting by Sydney Nolan from Rose Skinner. Made up of eight panels and called *The Desert Storm*, it depicts the bright red landscape of the Pilbara with a purple storm cutting through, and is among Nolan's best. It was the sort of work that made collectors in England and America believe him to be an abstract painter. The art gallery trustees of the day viewed the painting and Rose told them in all honesty that it was a masterpiece. The deal was all set to go. Then there was a snag: the art gallery's wall was too short and the painting far too long. Rose Skinner had the answer: the painting came in panels, so why not take only seven of them? The gallery trustees agreed and for years the seven panels hung in their gallery. The eighth panel Rose sold to me for £220, never mentioning that it was the tail end of a much larger piece.

There were Nolans amongst the paintings we bought for the Parmelia, but by far the greatest number of paintings were by a young West Australian, Robert Juniper. One day in May, when the freshness of autumn was in the air, the landscape beginning to green again after the hot summer, the sky blue and the sun shining, Rose took me to the hills behind Perth to lunch with Juniper. He lived in a shack beside a small stream. We looked at his work in his studio and then sat down to lunch. On my plate was the smallest steak you have ever seen in your life or, at least, the smallest steak that I had ever seen in my life. This steak was then cut into three parts. Juniper, spotting how quickly I ate my piece, asked would I like a Yabbie? On being told that a Yabbie was a freshwater crayfish, I replied that I would love one. Juniper set the pot on his stove to boil and headed for the stream, returning after half an hour with a small crayfish. We sat in the sunshine, enjoyed a light breeze, drank local wine and coffee. We talked and the day fled by. It was all so very different from the Britain of the 1960s. Sitting in those hills with their forests and orange groves, lakes, streams and pastures, was as paradise compared to the trials and tribulations imposed on industry and individuals by Harold Wilson's new Labour Government. Given the exchange control, prohibitive taxation, strikes and, although the Government was not to blame, foul weather, I am, as I look back, surprised that I did not move then and there to Australia. I had, however, many excuses ready at hand; it was too easy for me to avoid taking the risk of moving to another country. My wife, Sarah, did not like the place; I had very young daughters, my home, my family, and I was British so it was incumbent on me to love Britain. Much later, it was the European Union, or Federation – something I greatly deplore – that made it possible for me to move abroad. I feel that the Union has changed Britain and further threatens to make Britain only a name for a place that once existed. I flirted with Australia. I never proposed to her, let alone married her. I don't regret it. The point is, in the words of Leslie Waddington, if I had moved to live in Western Australia, 'I would have been a different person.'

Again by chance, I met in Perth a man who was to become one of a small group of four or five people whom I number my closest friends. I do not make real friends easily, although I have many acquaintances that others might call friends. I had in London met the Agent General for Western Australia, an ex-West Australian Government minister, Gerry Wylde. He gave me an introduction to a lawyer friend of his in Perth, called Adams. I went one morning to the office of Mr Adams and asked to see him. Perth was like that then: you just turned up at somebody's office and they would see you; appointments seemed unnecessary. It was the same even with senior politicians. The whole place was extremely casual; there was no noticeable security nor, for that matter, any need of security. The Premier of Western Australia was about the equivalent of the Mayor of Nottingham, his budget then smaller than most large towns in Britain.

The population of Western Australia was something under half a million souls, the land mass of that state the size of Western Europe. The members of the state's parliament were tall men with wide shoulders, hands like coal scuttles and eyes that never flinched as they looked at you. Today, they are lawyers in shiny suits. The farmers have gone back to the land.

The receptionist, seeing before her a young man, assumed that I wanted the young Mr Adams, rather than the older and rather grander Mr Adams to whom I had an introduction. Young Mr Adams appeared and even he did not mention his father. I explained what I wanted done and John Adams explained that he could save my family a lot of tax if we made these purchases in a particular way. I did not really understand tax then, and I still do not understand it now, so I thought it better if John came to England to talk to experts. 'I am pretty busy,' he told me, but once in the street he ran all the way to the travel agent to get a ticket for the next day's flight. A month later John Adams joined the board of my family's Australian company and stayed there until 1990, when he left to become a Master of the Supreme Court of Western Australia.

In late March 1996, John died of cancer. I saw him in the last weeks of his life and spoke often to him and his wife on the telephone during that agonising period. He sat in his pyjamas on a sofa in his garden room, his ankles so swollen that he could not walk, the strength gone out of his fingers so that he could not write, but his brain, despite the drugs that he was taking, seemed clear as fresh spring water. Age seemed to have dropped from his face; there was a boyishness about him that I had not seen since the day, thirty-two years before, when we first met.

John Adams became far closer to me than many of my family. We spoke over thirty years to each other, if not daily, then certainly several times a week. When I was in Australia, John and I spent the majority of our time together. As young men we played when not working, going east with the excuse of getting counsel's opinion on some legal problem. In Melbourne we visited the night clubs. We partied and we gossiped and, like a pair of old crones, cackled at each other's jokes. We had the same sense of humour; we could read each other's moods. I think it is possible that I changed John's life, introducing him to art and artists. He changed mine, as he encouraged me in my enthusiasms, and steadied me in my follies. When I made mistakes, John mitigated their effect.

The two occasions when I sat and talked to John as he was dying were for me amongst the finest moments of my life. I have nothing but admiration for his wife Elizabeth as, over the months, her husband died before her eyes. There was no fake emotion, no drama for drama's sake, just that immensely rare quality that so many people imagine the world does not need in a modern age – dignity. Light as a child, thin and youthful, filled with intelligence, courageous and wracked with pain, suffering the malfunctions of his body with humour, no man could die better, no woman ease a death as patiently as did his wife.

My memories of John Adams are legion, but like so many memories of friendship, they are full of the jokes of fleeting moments, the joining of two people's sense of humour that, when written down, lose their energy. When in print the events that made us laugh become too laboured to seem humorous at all. The travels we made together, carrying a giant model of the new Parmelia Hotel and its attendant office block, visiting government office after government office, endlessly answering the question, 'Why would you want to build this hotel in Perth?' The answer was I had faith in Western Australia, I saw something in the economic climate that attracted me to the place. It was always the same, however: whether I spoke to civil servants or politicians, they all took the view that Western Australia is too far from anywhere to be of much use to anyone. It never occurred to the people in Eastern Australia that there are only New Zealanders and penguins between them and the South Pole, while the northern tip of Western Australia is but a hundred miles or so from Indonesia, one of the world's most populated countries with 180 million souls cramped on a series of 14,000 small islands. A thousand miles beyond are Singapore and Malaysia. West Australia is tangential to the world's wealthiest region on the Pacific Rim, while Sydney and Melbourne are 3,000 miles away. One day in a hundred, or two hundred, years' time, children born on Australia's northern coastline will wonder why the south of their continent was settled first. The world has changed and only now, thirty years later, do the official classes of Australia begin to accept that Northwest Australia is a useful part of their country, not least the spearhead of the continent's engagement with the rest of the world.

The model of the Parmelia had become the bane of my life. When I first brought it to Australia, the customs officers made me unpack it, which involved removing almost fifty brass screws that held the lid of its travelling box in place. Then they pronounced, 'This thing is made of wood. You can't bring it into Australia!' Happily John had met my aeroplane and I was able to say, 'Hold on a moment while I fetch my lawyer.' John persuaded them to allow the model into Australia provided we had it sprayed. Determined, however, to stop something coming into Australia, they picked on Sarah's fur coat. 'How long has that been dead?'

This box travelled with us from Canberra to Sydney, then to Melbourne and then back again to Canberra. Every time we showed the wretched thing, all its screws had to be undone. Every time we changed state, quarantine and health officials would ask, 'What's in that box?' And so we travelled from banks to borrow money to the government to ask permission to borrow money, and always we were asked the same question: 'Why would you want to build that hotel in Perth?'

Even when our travels around the capitals of the Australian states were over, the problems with the Parmelia Hotel persisted, for in Perth itself the officials did not believe that the badly needed hotel of international quality would ever be built. John and I walked across the road from the Adelphi to the licensing court. We had made application to transfer the licence from the Adelphi to the new hotel that we intended to build. 'There are no single rooms on these plans,' the judge pronounced. He was right, of course. 'You must have single rooms.' 'But, Your Honour, no new hotel has single rooms these days.' 'They do in Western Australia.' The judge then proceeded to tell us why this was the case. Looking straight at me, the crusty old fellow began: 'Just last week I was staying in a hotel at Port Hedland,' a northern boom town at the centre of major iron ore developments. 'I booked into my room and got into my bed. In the middle of the night I discovered three other men sleeping in my room. I had a terrible night and when I finally got to sleep again, I awoke to find one of them gone and with him my wallet. You, sir, will build your hotel with single rooms and they will be so small that you cannot put two beds in them.' Getting into his stride, the judge went on, 'You will also provide a reading room on each floor, where a fellow can get a bit of peace and quiet and not have to spend his time in a rowdy bar room.' It seemed to me as if nothing would stop him. 'What is more, the bedside lamps will be screwed down so that you can't take them away and sell them after I have inspected the rooms.' As for the licence, the judge had never heard of one that allows guests to drink when they please and banquets to continue after nine-thirty p.m. In the end, Charles Court, the Minister for Economic Development, and later the State Premier, had to sort the matter out. The judge had the final say: 'There's no such thing as "five stars" in Western Australia. We can only have four-star hotels and there are none of them.' It hardly seemed worth arguing about.

John Adams was the man who first took me to the town of Broome in Northwest Australia. The weather in Perth in the summer of 1979 was unusually hot. The power station workers had taken the opportunity of going on strike. The result: no air conditioning, and John and I decided to get out of town. I wanted to visit Kalgoorlie because I had heard there were large quantities of old farm equipment lying around the place. I collected such equipment at the time and was keen to discover a neglected source of rare pieces. 'Kalgoorlie,' opined John, 'is far too hot. Let's go to Broome. It's on the seaside.' I also collected seashells at the time, having been inspired by the collection of Paul Jones, the Australian botanical painter. John knew that if I travelled to a new town I would likely buy something. A cautious man, he preferred that the 'something' should be a small shell rather than a gargantuan piece of farm machinery. That day we lunched in Broome, the guests of the local chemist David Hutchinson and his wife Thea. I enjoyed the atmosphere of the town greatly.

In January 1981, the year after I had married Romilly Hobbs, we set off for Australia. I had determined to take Romilly to Broome and arrived there towards the end of the month. Again we had lunch with the Hutchinsons and their son, Tony, in the same Chinese restaurant. John and Liz Adams were with us, as were John Taylor, an architect, and his wife, Sue, as well as Michael Szell, a well-known London fabric designer.

At Wings restaurant, the food was wonderful and the place was empty, as Mrs Wing had opened her restaurant just for our visit. A woman of volatile moods, she was as likely to close when the town was full as to open when it was empty just for casual visitors. Mrs Wing also ran a Chinese takeaway from a hatch in the side of her restaurant's wall. This resulted in the guests who were sitting down being served drinks very quickly but their meal very slowly. Sir Robin Day, who visited Broome on my recommendation, called it, 'Same Day Service'. It was understandable, because an Australian waiting for takeaway food is likely to be less patient than one settled with a bottle of beer.

The town of Broome was empty; it was the wet season and the temperature was several degrees below that in Perth. There were no tourists and the locals were lounging in the sun on the beach; a beach that is amongst the most spectacular in the world, fifteen miles long with white sand edged on one side with the bluest ocean and on the other with the reddest rocks; a beach that is a delight to walk along, with the scent of the bush, the sound of the sea caressing sand and the sight of the sea eagles and ospreys curling in the air. In the town the gold rain and tulip trees bloomed, the frangipanis scented the air, and the flowers of the bush were bright.

After lunch Romilly went with the Taylors, the Adams and Thea Hutchinson to Cable Beach. I set out with Tony Hutchinson and Michael Szell. We drove around the dirt roads that were Broome streets. We looked at the old pearling masters' houses, with their wide verandas, sloping corrugated iron roofs and lattice walls, built on stumps so that the cool breezes could circulate under their floors. They stood amongst the mango trees, with bare earth around them. I was very taken by these houses, built by boat builders for men who sailed boats. One we came across had the sign '4 Sale' outside. We knocked on the door, first Michael, then myself. No answer. We called and then we shouted. Yes, the house was for sale. Her husband was at the hotel, but he would come in an hour. Could we come back?

I bought the house. We signed the contract, drawn up by the bank manager, in the bar of the Roebuck Hotel. John Adams checked it. 'What's this about a cinema?' he asked. 'Oh, you have bought that as well,' was the bank manager's reply. The Sun Pictures, now advertised as the oldest operating cinema in the world, became mine in this way. John had been right: I do tend to buy things when I visit towns for the first time.

The house was a wreck – smelly, tired, falling apart – but it was a lovely house and, standing restored amongst a grove of giant mangoes, it was wonderfully romantic. You could find that house described in a dozen Somerset Maugham novels. The Sun Pictures was really a spacious timber shed. Rows of deck chairs accommodate the customers and ceiling fans lazily move the hot night air of Broome during a film. Between the audience and the screen is a stretch of long grass. The local airport is behind the cinema and the planes of early evening flights out of Broome often appear over the top of the screen, the screech of the engines blocking out the film's soundtrack, the lights dazzling the audience.

I ran the cinema for a couple of years, then persuaded a chic young socialite, Lynn Page, to move from Sydney as its manager. She put on the largest festival of Kurosawa's films ever seen in Australia. This seemed appropriate, since Broome had strong connections with Japan. The town started with the pearling industry in 1882, and pearling is still the main reason for Broome's existence, although tourism is rapidly becoming the town's largest industry. The Japanese provided the divers in Broome in the days when the pearlers were more interested in the mother of pearl shell than the pearls themselves. Diving, at the turn of the century, was a dangerous business and as a result Broome has a considerable Japanese graveyard – in fact the largest outside Japan. The pearling industry has changed a lot in the last few years and few divers are used these days.

In the event, my season of Kurosawa films was a disaster as the few Japanese who still live in Broome went to the hotel rather than the cinema and no one else in town seemed interested in this esoteric programme. In time I sold the cinema to David Hutchinson's son,

Tony, a natural entrepreneur who has made a visit to The Sun
Pictures by Broome's tourists a cult activity. Strange things seem to
happen in Broome. When the fire station caught fire, the town's fire
engine was inside it. After the town's only bank robbery, the criminals
tried to escape on bicycles.

In the days I first lived in Broome, the general idea amongst the
town's entrepreneurs was to pull down the old pearlers' mansions
and build blocks of brick flats in their places. These mansions, like
the one that I owned, needed a lot of maintenance and many agreed
that they were not practical to live in. The unsealed dirt streets were
always dusty in the dry. The grass verges became red dust as well
and it was hard to tell the two apart. Few people bothered with
gardens, and so the gentle winds of Broome moved the dust straight
through the lattice walls into the houses. The days when the pearling
masters had a team of domestic staff to clean were long gone. Broome
was a neglected spot with only a dirt road into and the same dirt
road out of town. The days when the pearling masters wore wide
straw hats and white suits – each pearling master had twenty-four
of them made in London and sent by boat to be laundered in
Singapore – were long over.

Broome had been hit by the crash in the mother of pearl prices
when the plastic button was introduced in the 1930s. Then came
the war and the town was strafed by Japanese fighters. By chance,
the Japanese caught a number of Catalina flying boats refuelling in
Roebuck Bay. Over three hundred people, many of them women and
children, were killed. For years Broome slept. I arrived just as the
town began to stir. The tarmacked road that has been built around
Australia reached Broome the year after my first visit. Tourists began
to arrive, at first backpackers, and then the retired couples who
habitually drive around the continent. The population of Broome at
this time was about 3,000; now the town has about 14,000 inhabitants and during the tourist season it more than doubles its population.

Lynn Page stayed in Broome, becoming a leading local business-
woman and shire councillor. Broome is like that: people visit that
town and just forget to leave.

Opposite Wings Restaurant there used to be a shell shop owned by
Barry and Kerry Sharpe. Kerry Sharpe had a small collection of shells,
including one great rarity, a Western Australia Cowrie Rosselli. This
specimen was a shell of abnormal size. In the years that followed, on

my visits to Broome I used to spend a lot of time in their shop trying to buy this shell, but Kerry Sharpe would never sell. In time, the Sharpes became my friends. Kerry Sharpe was a strapping woman, good-looking but not outstandingly beautiful, earthy rather than pretty. Barry Sharpe was a burly fisherman who knew the Aboriginals well; the Bardi people were his friends. I travelled a lot in the Kimberleys with Barry, who was always interesting to talk with as he had ideas and a natural intelligence. Often Barry and Kerry would lunch with me as I sat under the giant mango tree in our garden. One day, Romilly and I sat and talked with the couple long into the afternoon. Barry had just returned from a Barramundi fishing trip somewhere near the Walcott Inlet, a distant and dangerous waterway with as many crocodiles as Barramundi. The fishing had been good; Barry was relaxed and in a fine mood; Kerry had enjoyed lunch. Romilly and I were setting off the next day for Perth. We were relaxed and, talking of many things, we laughed and joked.

There was in town another fisherman, who hired his boat for deep-sea fishing. He was a personable young fellow, who had persuaded Barry and Kerry to be his agents. I believe his business had gone well that season. The end of the year was coming, the weather was beginning to warm up and the tension that comes before the rain was building fast.

We, my wife and I, said goodbye to Kerry and Barry and, as planned, set out for Perth and then England. A week or two later, I had a telephone call from John Adams. Barry Sharpe had shot Kerry straight between the eyes with his pistol. Later there was a trial and I arranged for a good Perth lawyer to defend Barry, who was sentenced to three years in jail. He had pleaded guilty with mitigating circumstances. Kerry, he said, had been having an affair with the young charter fisherman, who had left town with Barry's money. He loved his wife, he claimed, and I believed him.

I visited Barry Sharpe several times while he was in jail. I would knock on the door at Broome prison, ask for him and be told that if I waited under the mango tree by the road 'Sharpey' would come and join me. 'What's it like in there?' I asked. 'Not bad,' he replied. To a tough bushie like Barry Sharpe, jail was no problem, for he knew how to look after himself. However, the laughter was gone from the man. When he was released on parole, he worked for me and I saw him quite often.

Barry told me that the part of the whole experience that really shattered him was when, on leaving jail, the police said to him, 'What do you want to do with the gun?' 'Why?' he asked. 'It's your property.' 'Keep it,' he replied. Barry lives in a remote village with his friends, the Bardi people. A man of the sea and river estuaries, a man of the outback and the bush, he seldom comes to town. Perhaps in time he may find happiness in the natural surroundings that he has chosen to make his home.

Northwest Australia seems civilised. They have television and telephones, but every once in a while the primitive nature of man breaks out. I have seen a gang of men kicking a fellow on the ground and when the police arrive to break it up, they all, including the fellow who had been on the ground, walk along together as if nothing had happened. Then, minutes later, when the police are gone, the same fellow is back on the ground and they are all kicking him again. What is so peculiar is that I would lay odds that none of them really knew why they were doing this.

Broome was a strange place in those days and the humour of the place was strange as well. The baker was having trouble with the Aboriginals breaking into his shop. In time, he caught one and swore at him roughly. 'You're only treating me like this,' the Aboriginal complained, 'because I am a black fellow.' 'Hold on,' said the baker, as he tipped a sack of flour all over the wretched man. 'You are a white fellow now,' the baker said as he hit him between the eyes.

It did not take long for me to find another fine old house in danger of being pulled down, so I bought the place and restored it. Later I formed the Broome Preservation Society to save these buildings, for it was clear to me but not, I am afraid, at that time to many others, that if Broome was truly to prosper in the new world of the 1980s and 1990s, then more people must come to live there and more people must come as tourists in order to provide work for the increase in population. The snag with this approach to life in a small town is that unless great care is taken, the need for constructing accommodation for both new residents and visitors destroys the very reason for tourists coming there in the first place. It is the atmosphere in Broome that is so valuable, an intangible but fragile asset, which could be destroyed by accident or simply by turning the town into just another hell of high-rise hotels and apartments edging the most beautiful beach in the world. Soon those who wanted to develop their land, but had historic buildings on that land, gave me their buildings.

I found other sites for these buildings, stuck them on the back of trucks, moved them and restored them. The people of Broome became used to the sight of pearlers' mansions moving around the town on the backs of lorries. I became fascinated by Broome and my vision for its future. My every move, my every investment was dominated by the desire to develop a tired old town into a modern tourist resort without destroying the soul of the place. In time the idea caught on that money could be made out of development in Broome. New developers came to town, supermarkets were built and shopping arcades. A town with previously one of the highest records of unemployment in Australia has become prosperous. In all schemes there are losers, and in Broome it is the old people who have lost. The town has changed beyond their recognition. Change, however, was inevitable; I just happened to realise what was going to happen because I had seen the same phenomena happen before in other places.

Drinking in the Pearlers' bar of the Roebuck Hotel in Broome, I listened to the local gossip. I had not long been a resident of Broome, and what I heard amazed me. The Crown, which is in fact the government of Australia, was giving away land – well, almost giving it away. All you had to do to receive a ten-acre block was to tell the government what you wanted to do with it. If no one else wanted the land for similar purpose then you paid AUS$10,000 and the land was yours. Well, almost yours, for you were contracted to develop the land: that is, fence it and put a shed on it. Then the government would give you the freehold and you could do what you liked with it.

The snag was that this land was at Cable Beach, six miles from town, adjacent to the magnificent beach but a long way from the population of Broome. That night at home I decided that I had better have some of this land. I qualified for a grant because I was a resident of Broome. What would I use this land for, I wondered? Well, I have always enjoyed keeping animals, so I would start a zoo. Getting the land was the easy part; the fight was with Western Australia's state bureaucracy to obtain a licence, the first of many fights that were to follow in the next twelve years.

At first I kept a dozen or so varieties of parrot, wild donkeys, dingoes, camels, buffalo and Banteng cattle, along with a bunch of assorted kangaroos and wallabies. That this would be enough to satisfy my urge to collect birds and animals was an impossible hope. The zoo grew: better cages for the birds were built on a scale that made them seem as if they were not in cages at all; spacious paddocks for the rare antelope that I imported from Britain, scimitar horned oryx, black buck, addax, as well as many other varieties of antelope. The climate of Broome was perfect for them and they bred well. My zoo was becoming an ark, where breeding stock of some of the world's rarest antelopes, along with Grevys zebra, water buck, gemsbuck and kudu could live in isolation away from disease and, more importantly, poachers and warfare.

My parrot collection expanded until I had almost all the Australian species and most of the varieties and subspecies of those parrots. A lake of about ten acres was built. As the country around Broome is dry for most of the year, with few waterholes, wild birds flocked to my zoo – I used to say that seventy per cent of my stock were volunteers. Even the kangaroos and wallabies tried to break in rather than break out. Raised walkways were built for the tourists so that they could cross the zoo without disturbing the animals.

By this time my zoo extended to about 150 acres. The tourist boom was on by 1989; we had about 35,000 visitors each year. Graham Taylor, my manager, had put together the best collection of parrots, cockatoos, macaws and water birds in Australia, and it was certainly equal to, if not better than, the bird collections of most European and American zoos. The other zoos of Australia were sending us their surplus stock; we had pygmy hippos who bred well with us. And we started a cheetah breeding programme. The thousands of trees that I arranged to have planted turned 150 acres of burned-out scrub into jungle, and my collection of native flowers expanded. The orchids of Australia grew well in my jungle – all was set for success. The surplus stock of rare birds, captive bred, was much in demand and there was talk of importing more birds from overseas to help strengthen Australia's breeding stock. No new exotic birds had arrived in Australia since the 1950s and the need for new blood was desperate. There was even talk of exporting captive bred birds – a course of action that would largely have stamped out the detestable practice of bird smuggling.

At Broome my zoo was well placed to export large quantities of captive bred birds. As I planned yet another expansion – a large complex to keep monkeys – I predicted 50,000 visitors that winter. In all this I was helped by John Knowles, the proprietor of Marwell

Zoo, one of the British pioneers in the conservation of endangered species, a man with a remarkable record of success in that field.

The Australian summer of 1989 was over. It had been wet, the trees and foliage of my zoo had grown well, all looked splendid. The winter, which is Broome's peak tourist season, looked as if it would produce a bumper crop of visitors. Then the Australian airline pilots went on strike. The winter season was lost. Instead of 50,000 visitors my zoo received a few hundred. Days went by and no one came to look at my birds and animals and, what was worse, there was no way to send the surplus birds that we bred for sale to the aviculturists of Eastern Australia. That year we successfully raised 700 endangered birds, plus many other common varieties. For the first time in Australia we had reared the tiny fig parrot, whose chick when it is hatched is about the size of a finger nail. At their moment of triumph Graham Taylor and Eddie, his assistant, were faced with a desperate situation that was neither their fault, nor within their capacity to correct. We struggled on borrowed money and then the crop of the pearl farm, in which I had a majority interest, failed. I borrowed more money and the next year the pearl harvest failed again. There was nothing left to do but to close the zoo.

Graham and Eddie did this as well as they had built it up. No bird nor animal was put down; all were placed either with other zoos or collectors. It was a great sadness to me to see the zoo that I had physically worked on in the early days, and certainly spent all my free moments planning, come to a close. Despite the fact that I would far rather have succeeded in what most people believed to be a mad venture, I do not regret for one moment the fact that I failed in doing what I set out to do, for my zoo helped change the attitude to zoos and captive animals all over Australia and the rare antelopes and zebras that I imported have become foundation stock whose progeny will breed in generations to come.

Broome has changed. I built a hotel on Cable Beach, but that hotel, the Cable Beach Club, is hidden amongst palm trees and white gums. It is a garden with a hotel in it. None of the buildings is taller than a palm tree, all are built in traditional materials, with corrugated iron roofs, ripple iron on the walls, lattice and timber, its rooms decorated with paintings by Aboriginals and carvings by Orientals. This hotel sits well with the multicultural nature of Broome. This nature is an asset beyond price in a world torn by racial tension.

Happily the town council of Broome has now caught on to the idea of keeping the best of the old and buildings of character are habitually preserved. Broome's new buildings pay homage to their environment. The streets are now sealed, many of them have kerbs, the verges have grass and trees proliferate throughout the township.

Governor Broome would not recognise the barren peninsula where he landed in 1882 and declared there would be a town bearing his name. That peninsula had one tree and only brackish water. There are changes in Broome, but Broome-time still exists. The lazy life is still there. You can walk down Cable Beach and not see a building and if you go there early in the morning you will not see another soul. The Humpback whales play in the sea off Cable Beach, lingering on their migration. The wading birds search for mussels in the gentle surf, eight million of them coming across the Australian coastline at Broome each January, tired after their flight from Russia. The birds of prey – eagles, ospreys, hawks and buzzards – still circle in the bright blue sky.

The rocks are still the same fiery red that they were the first day I set foot in Broome and the bush smells as sweet. The sand, washed twice a day by the thirty-foot tide, is still as clean and white as it was on my first visit. Many of the projects that I had in mind for Broome are unfinished, some not even started. Others have been taken up where I left off. If you don't set up a project properly at the beginning, it will not turn out right. Similarly, if you do set up a project right at the beginning, it is very hard for others to change the general thrust of that project as it goes along.

Broome was for me, I suppose, really a conceit. I was at the time when I first went there heavily involved in British politics and I found time for Broome because of the long summer recess. Instead of short trips I was able to stay three months on end and really get the feel of the place.

Not long after Margaret Thatcher became Prime Minister, I went to see her in Downing Street. She was, unusually, sitting in the Cabinet Room. I was shown in and offered the chair beside her. We were alone. 'You look a bit down today, Prime Minister,' I began. 'I am a bit down, Alistair,' she replied. 'Jim Prior has just defeated me in Cabinet over the employment legislation that we intend to bring in.' 'Don't worry about that,' I suggested, 'you will get what you want in time.'

Margaret Thatcher looked at me and those who know her well

would have recognised that strange look that she sometimes has – the look that an Old Testament prophet might have been expected to have when about to pronounce that some great catastrophe was about to descend on the people of Israel – a look far into the future. 'Alistair, you don't understand. Being Prime Minister is not just a job. I only want to be Prime Minister so that I can change things that I believe to be wrong and take actions that I believe to be right. If I can't do that then there is no point to it. Being Prime Minister is not just another job.' Years later, Margaret Thatcher again remarked to me on her role as Prime Minister: 'Being Prime Minister is about making decisions. Every day you are faced with a number of options, none of which are truly acceptable to you.'

My plans for Broome were a conceit, for I felt that I could have a beneficial effect on the lives of the people who lived in that town as I saw the future so clearly, I knew what was going to happen. What I had forgotten, however, is that those who try to lead do not really have an effect on the lives of others. The destiny of each of us lies in our own hands and whether we fulfil that destiny is entirely a case of whether we have the strength of character to break away from the disorderly human mass that moves in a particular direction. Each individual must choose whether to be victor or a victim. You can help people and you should, but how it all ends up with them is their own choice.

I have a concept of Northwest Australia, an area of almost a million square miles with only 29,000 people living in it. I believe that this wild and rugged land will one day be the heartland of Australian industry. One third of the world's diamonds come from there, eighty per cent of the world's pearls, clean, low-cholesterol beef roams the countryside, precious stones and gold are found there in vast quantities, minerals, silver, oil – are all there. But, more important than all this, there is water, great man-made lakes of it; Lake Argyll on the Orde river is eight times larger than Sydney Harbour. Another such lake is to be built on the Fitzroy river, making available agricultural land of high quality by controlling the flooding of the Fitzroy. Hydroelectric power now comes from Lake Argyll for the first time; other projects will follow. More electric power can be easily made available on many locations along the coast by using the flow of the huge tides in the north to generate it; some of the highest tides in the world are there. There are plans in profusion to take the water of the Northwest at great expense to the South. Why not bring the people of the South to the waters of the Northwest? If Australians do not occupy their land then, I believe, 180 million Indonesians living just across a strip of sea may well occupy it.

The tourists who come to Broome and the Kimberleys today are but the skirmishers of an economy. They are the reason to put in an infrastructure that will support the beginnings of industry; the endless abortive cycle of the chicken and the egg will have been broken. This is why Broome had to become a tourist town. Only by this happening can the Kimberleys, the oldest land on earth, become part of a modern world. There is no choice in the matter; that is going to happen. Let us hope that it happens gently and in a well-considered fashion, preserving what is good but at the same time bringing a new hope to the people who live in Northern Australia, who also deserve to profit from their land. It is possible for development to take place in an organised and civilised fashion, tourists and locals, industry and nature living together in comparative harmony. The alternative is the rape of the countryside, where the Kimberleys become just a money box for the strongest nation in that part of the world to take, to dig until they find what they seek, kill whatever they care to eat. I mention the diamonds, gold, jewels, silver, not because I want the Kimberleys to become one vast mine, but because if something else is not done then that is exactly what will happen.

I tried ten years ago to build an airport of international size outside Broome purely because the new generation of Jumbo jets, then in the making, had enough fuel aboard to fly non-stop from Europe to Australia, but only if they landed in Broome. I saw Broome becoming the hub for the Far East rather than Singapore. My idea was, in essence, not a commercial idea, although there were vast sums of money to be made from the venture, rather a social idea. It is normal in the Kimberleys for a child to grow up without access to the best education, which is available in the southern part of Australia. If parents wish their children to have a higher education, then their children must, on reaching a certain age, move away from home. When those children become adults and seek employment con-summate with their education, then they must, once again, leave home, often for ever. I dreamed of a Kimberleys where the native people could grow up, find a fine education locally, and then find employment where they can use the advantages of their education.

An international airport is the beginning of such a reality, providing a huge variety of jobs. Education would then follow in the way that

My great-grandfather, Sir Robert McAlpine, founder of my family's business.

Members of the McAlpine family at the time of the First World War. My father is second from the left and my grandfather third from the left.

My father, The Lord McAlpine of Moffat, Bt.

Myself aged three.

My mother in the 1950s with her long-haired dachshund, Russet.

From left to right: Mr Mann, my gardener, myself with a prize-winning African goose and Victor, Mr Mann's son-in-law, the cowman.

With Mrs Thatcher on the day of my appointment as Treasurer of the Conservative Party in 1975.

Romilly and myself in 1978.

West Green House, my home between 1973 and June 1990, when it was blown up by the IRA.

A monument designed by Quinlan Terry and built in 1976 to mark the socialist government's extortionate taxation policies.

With Romilly and Skye in 1989 on Cable Beach, Broome, Australia.

Walking with a brolga crane at my zoo in Broome, Australia.

With some of my parrots in Australia.

The arrival of the pearl harvest, Broome, Australia, in 1984. On my right, HRH Crown Prince Alexander of Yugoslavia and on my left, Snowy County, my partner in the pearl farm.

Our dining-room, Broome, Australia.

Interior of our house, Broome, Australia.

A signpost which we passed during our travels in the outback, Australia.

The late Sir Sidney Nolan with some of his paintings, Perth, Western Australia.

In my antiquities and
curiosities shop in Cork
Street, London.

Cartoon by JAK, given to
me by the staff of Sir Robert
McAlpine and Sons Ltd at the
time of my elevation to the
peerage in 1984.

An audience with the Pope, John Paul II, Rome.

Romilly and Skye in Venice, 1994.

The Thatchers and our daughter, Skye, 1994.

Photograph taken by my friend Terence Donovan in 1992 at my fiftieth birthday party. Left to right: Olga Polizzi, Gordon Reece and Margaret Thatcher.

Myself on a writing assignment in Italy, 1995.

it has followed the tourist boom in Broome, where departments of two universities have recently opened. The servicing of aeroplanes requires technicians of great skill in a variety of trades. The problem of what to do with the food grown in the immensely fertile soil of the region is solved: fly it in Jumbo jets to Malaysia, Singapore, Indonesia. Suddenly, Australia is truly in touch with the rest of the world. An international airport will happen, of that I am sure. My airport would have happened already. It was, however, stopped against the will of the local people, who were overwhelmingly in favour of this venture, by a small group of unimaginative and vindictive political activists who frightened a timorous Labor government in the South. A few local people, who cared more for their political careers than their neighbours' futures, who wished to keep the region poor with a native population who habitually voted Labor, who saw the opportunity to make names for themselves among their Labor colleagues in the South using this issue as a Soap Box, stopped my scheme. A state government who cared for their political careers were frightened by this group and saw no reason to help a community for which they cared not a jot. They withheld their consent, where both Federal and local authorities were keen to proceed.

The irony of the whole episode was that no one was asking the state for money to pay for anything more than the cost of the piece of paper that the signature of Mrs Henderson, the then Minister, was written on. My airport did not happen and at about the same time the airline pilots in Australia went on strike. Broome once again knew what is was to be isolated. Businesses failed, the price of land fell. The political activists who had long sought a fall in the price of land had what they wanted, and I suspect secretly hoped that land prices would stay that way in the future. But did the old inhabitants of Broome now have the chance to buy property at cheap prices as land and buildings became available in fire sales? Was there a glut of cheap housing for them on the market? Not a bit of it. They were hurt by that strike as badly as, or worse than, the developers. In time, the strike over, the markets rose again and those who had not left town began to recover their wealth. By now Broome was an open secret and speculators were active in the market.

Broome will grow and the bare branches of my dream are sprouting suckers. Broome has been saved from the high-rise buildings and the hard concrete walls of modern apartment blocks. Today the architecture of the town at least nods towards its history.

Whether it be in the outback of Australia, or in centres of population, Australia is a hard place. The only difference is that the harshness of both landscape and climate are obvious in the outback, while urban landscape has a veneer of civilisation that dupes the casual visitor into believing that all is easy. The people of Australia, whether they be urban or country, have learned to live in that hard country and in doing so have become as hard as Australia's ancient rocks themselves, as difficult to pin down as the shadow of a hurrying cloud on a plain lit by fierce sunlight. They have learned well that they survive only by taking every opportunity that presents itself as though there was never going to be another such opportunity. These people live and survive in Australia, a country where nearly every success is built upon a previous bankruptcy and where every Australian knows full well that his success may one day be a failure and just a stepping stone for the generation that follows.

9

Journeys through the Outback

In 1980, when I decided to live in Northern Australia at least three months of each year, I determined to find out more about the Australian people. For many years I had visited the cities of Australia and over that time I came to believe that I understood how the urban Australian thought. I was wrong, for I now believe that the roots of all Australian thinking lie in the bush. Outback Australians respect the bush as an enemy; urban Australians positively fear it. Indeed, they are terrified of it, so they try to turn it into a romantic phenomenon. In this way they attempt to come to terms with over eighty per cent of their continent. I do not mean when I write of the bush, the wild lands along the Hawksley river, not far from Sydney, nor the countryside around Perth, Melbourne and Adelaide. This I call the Sunday bush, a place for weekend picnics, pretty cattle and horses. Brisbane is different, but then Queensland and Queenslanders have always been different. When I speak of the bush I refer to the barley table lands, the Gulf country, the Kimberleys, the great deserts – the Stony Desert, Sandy Desert and Tamini Desert – a land where you are alone with yourself, a land where, if all goes well, you are as safe as if you sat sipping tea in a suburban sitting room, but if you make a mistake, or experience an example of what passes for bad luck, but is usually your own negligence, you die.

My first trips were by light aeroplane. Siggi Halter, the local charter pilot in Broome, flew me at first, all over the countryside from Broome to Darwin. We flew to the Bungle Bungles, a large mountain range only recently discovered, where we dodged between mountain caps. These mountains, like beehives of coiled straw from the last century but cast in rock, were boils on the ocean floor millions of years ago. Forced up by volcanic activity, they now form a curious mountain range, with waterfalls caught amongst them and palm trees growing where their roots can find water, making small rain forests amongst these mountains in the desert. We landed nearby and walked or clambered as best we could in the heat amongst the inhospitable rocks. There are now tourist facilities at the Bungles, but when I first went there it was a wild and savage place.

We flew up the Prince Regent river, a few feet above its surface. The crocodiles, some of an immense size, could be seen as they slept below the greenish water. Or did they sleep? The model, Ginger Meadows, met her death there some years later, attacked by these savage beasts. The saltwater crocodile is a mammal unchanged for forty million years, the finest killing machine God ever invented. I asked Siggi whether it was safe to fly so low. 'No worries,' he replied. 'I've done a lot of this in the jets of the German air force.' The jets of the German air force, I pondered, are equipped for low flying, whereas in a Cessna you do it by eye. We flew amongst the thousand islands of the Buccaneer Archipelago, landing on the Mitchell Plateau, on a remote airstrip put in during the war by the Americans. No one lives within a hundred miles of this spot.

Not only did I fly north towards Darwin with Siggi Halter, I made a number of memorable trips south to the Gorges at Witternoon. Siggi insisted on flying low up these gorges. The wings of his small aeroplane almost scraped the rocks of their sides, the end wall raced towards us at an impressive rate. Siggi pulled the nose of his aeroplane up and we trimmed the bush that grew along the gorge's rim.

I have also walked up these gorges, and it is a far more rewarding and, indeed, safer way of seeing what must be one of Australia's great wonders. Silent pools lie surrounded by great monoliths of rock, their surfaces engraved by the weather so that they resemble the Hindu temples of India. If ever a place had a right to be called 'sacred' it was these silent gorges. I felt the atmosphere was as busy with spirits as Oxford Street during the Christmas sales, yet I stood alone.

Once Siggi could not fly because he had gone to Perth on business, so his place was taken by a young girl. It was with some relief that I saw her at the aeroplane's controls; at least, I thought, she had not learned low flying in the German air force. My relief was short-lived, however as, first of all, the door of the aeroplane fell off as I tried to close it. Repaired, the door was shut and my fellow passenger Clodagh Waddington and I were strapped in our seats. Soon the plane was in the air. We turned over the sparkling white beach at Broome, Cable Beach, over the red rocks of Gantheaume Point and out across the deep blue waters of Roebuck Bay. Everything was as perfect as a travel brochure. That is how Northern Australia is, and that is what makes the place so terribly dangerous to the inexperienced traveller, for out of that perfect picture can come sudden disaster. There are rules for travelling in the outback and you break them at your peril.

Our pilot, while young and charming, was not an experienced traveller in the North and already a rule had been broken. We were on our way to see some of the world's most remarkable rock carvings, which are to be found on the heaps of rocks piled, sometimes a hundred feet high, amongst the spinifex of the desert two hundred miles inland from Port Hedland. Our pilot spotted the landing strip we sought. We landed and were met by a gentleman in a Land Rover. 'What were we doing here?' he asked? 'Didn't he know that we were coming?' 'No.' We explained that we were looking for rock carvings, only to be told that we had landed at the wrong place. In fact we were seventy miles from our destination. I should have been suspicious at this point and insisted that we return home. I was keen to see these carvings, however, so we carried on. When we found them they were miraculous: snakes thirty feet long and skeletons of fish, anatomically correct in every detail. These were like the X-ray Aboriginal bark paintings that had inspired Picasso, but carved in the hardest of rock. Any fish brought here would be rotten long before it arrived. Perhaps the Aboriginals transported the skeleton, but if so, why were they brought? Just so they could be used as models for carving? Perhaps the powers of these people's memory were so great that they could remember every detail of a skeleton while they walked two hundred miles before carving it.

Beside the carvings, which were thousands of years old, are hollows in rock worked smooth by women who ground spinifex seed to make bread. Spinifex came to Australia as seeds in the packs of the camels brought for transport in the desert, along with their Afghan drivers. Camels still roam this district in large herds.

On our return journey we stopped at Karratha for fuel. To travel from there to Broome in a light aeroplane usually takes about two hours. Two and a half hours later, it was dark and we were freezing cold: 'I am afraid the heater is not working,' the pilot informed us. Clodagh and I were by now a trifle nervous as two and a half hours became three. Looking behind us, I spotted a light in the far distance. I drew the pilot's attention to it and she changed course towards it. The light was, in fact, not a town but a bush fire raging across the empty outback, its front between fifty and a hundred miles long. Our pilot had been taking us away from the coastline without realising what she was doing and in time, I suppose, we would have run out of fuel. Another hour and the bright lights of Broome were ahead, but far to our left. They were not the lights of the town, which are distinctly muted, rather the lights that illuminated the town's tennis courts – luckily its citizens were playing in the cool of the night. It was a relief to finally land in Broome.

With my friend Barry Sharpe I visited Calumburu to see Father Chris, then the priest at the mission, now the Bishop of Broome. His appointment to this last post, in 1996, was greeted with great joy by the people of the Kimberleys. His diocese is an area of 780,000 square miles with only 29,000 souls living in it. Over 2,000 people turned up for the ceremony in Broome. In a service of great emotion, binding both native and Catholic ritual together, Father Chris became Bishop Saunders. The Aboriginal rite of smoking, or purification by smoke, so similar to the western concept of purification by incense, was practised. The people of each parish brought an offering, often a painting or sculpture, and many of the hymns were sung in the Aboriginal tongue. During one part of the service the haunting tone of the didgeridoo came from the back of the town hall, which had become a church for the occasion and was beautifully decorated with flowers and painted banners. It was an extraordinary ceremony: it lasted two and a half hours and every section of the community participated. In attendance were the papal nuncio, twelve bishops and a cardinal. Some fifty other priests also travelled thousands of miles to be present at this grand service in a small town. Never have I felt such a surge of unity amongst those present. The Church was demonstrating leadership at a time in Australia when leadership was neither expected by Australia's people nor accepted by them.

When I first visited Calumburu, the Church was pulling out of the missions and the government was taking over its temporal responsibilities. That the civil authorities did not carry out these responsibilities with the same dedication as the Church it was easy to see as I travelled around the missions of the Northwest. Now what was, is largely forgotten; what might have been is no longer considered. Change has come to the Kimberleys, the starting gun has been fired in the race for wealth. In 1980 Father McKelson was in charge at the mission of La Grange. He tried to interest those who lived there in agriculture; unfortunately, his efforts had little effect.

Father McKelson is a remarkable man, conversant with several Aboriginal languages. He understands much of their history and a great deal of their law. It was he who started the carving of stone heads and it was he who introduced me to the carvers who made these extraordinary heads. First of all, he introduced me to Big John Dodo, a Karadjeri man. To begin with, Big John Dodo made two human figures for the corroboree, then he made heads in mud. After that he carved them in wood and finally stone. Father McKelson showed me the head of Christ carved by John Dodo, which was placed above the altar in his church. I commissioned John Dodo to make heads for me, bought him the tools to work with, and paid him a proper price. Too often collectors and dealers in Aboriginal art believe that Aboriginals do not need much money. In the dealers' eyes the Aboriginals are a simple primitive people and they expect to have to pay little or nothing for their work. The government agency that marketed the work of Aboriginal painters and sculptors in Broome disapproved of my activities: they had told the Aboriginals to paint only pictures of a particular size, so that the painting would fit conveniently in tourists' suitcases.

Soon I had a whole team of carvers: Mattie Gilbert, Hughie Bent, Spider Cababita, Ian Gilbert, Donald Grey, Richard Hunter, Mandijalu, Johnson, Judson Grant, Mullardy, Mervyn Ngampukarti, Patsy Pindan, Joseph Roe, Philip Wilridge, Andy Yandoga and a stack of others who tried their hand at carving heads. The officials claimed that there was no tradition of carving stone in the Kimberleys and so I was perverting the culture of these people. This is like saying that there was no tradition of abstract art in Italy, so that those who encouraged the practitioners of that genre in the twentieth century were terribly wrong. Some of these heads are true masterpieces when judged alongside both Australian sculpture and the sculpture of other cultures which, incidentally, is how the work of Aboriginals or other native people should be judged. Other stone heads are merely curiosities.

The vogue for carving stone came to a halt when I started to spend less time in Broome, and no longer bought carved heads. I will be delighted if, in years to come when some enterprising dealer finds a cache of these stone carvings and their price spirals, those of the artists who are still alive can be found and persuaded to carve again.

The government had given the Aboriginal people television and they bought drink. The impact of television on the Aboriginal people of the Kimberleys has, as far as I know, never been seriously studied. It is not hard, however, to imagine its effect on a people who lived simply fishing and hunting, sometimes attempting agriculture, but seldom moving far from their place of birth, when they switched on their sets and found themselves faced, for example, with the violence and the crime of up-town Manhattan. This is a people resident more than a thousand miles from any city and often a hundred miles from a small town, a people of strict moral codes, discovering a whole new set of values courtesy of the Australian Broadcasting Corporation and the Hollywood films that they show. It is not that change was not happening, or that these people were not slowly adapting to modern lifestyles; it was the swiftness of the change. Plugging in a television and turning a knob, they were transported to another culture in another world. Often the Aboriginals were given too much help in some respects, and too little in others, the 'helping' in the 1980s becoming an industry for enthusiastic white civil servants. The Aboriginals were given advice on what sort of art their artists should produce – a menace to natural talent, resonant of the way that the Soviet Bloc treated its artists – yet this suppression of cultural development went unnoticed by the Australians in the city, who hung the work of Aboriginal Australians in a different part of their great galleries from the work of Australian artists of European descent.

How different the wise but kindly words of Father McKelson and his brothers were to all this. Much has changed since I first visited La Grange mission nearly seventeen years ago. The days when the Liberal Party in Western Australia fought against the right of Aboriginal Australians to vote and live as all other Australians, are long over; the days during election campaigns when diesel oil barrels were filled with cheap alcohol and tipped from low-flying planes in the hope that Aboriginals would find them and, after drinking their contents, be so drunk they would fail to vote. Some Aboriginals died as a result of the polluted wine they drank. The days of Stephen Hawke and Tom Stephens fighting for Aboriginal rights are over, but the battle can barely be considered to have been won. The fight goes on, for today the attack on minorities still exists, it is just perpetuated in a far subtler form. It is well that men like Tom Stephens, the member of the Upper House for the large part of the Northwest who really cares for the population of the Kimberleys, still carry on the fight against a bureaucracy working 1,500 miles away.

The reform of Aboriginal rights carried out by Paul Keating during his term as Prime Minister is, in my opinion, one of the most enlightened pieces of legislation in Australia's history. In brief, unallocated Crown land, in effect most of Northern Australia, becomes the property of those who live on it. Freehold land remains the property of those who own it. A dispute, however, arises over cattle stations – large areas of land that are, in Western Australia, often leased from the government. In principle if a developer, whether a hotelier or a miner or in any other trade, wishes to have property, that developer must deal with the Aboriginal owners. Should the owner of a cattle station wish to change the use of that station then, again, that owner must deal with the Aboriginal owners. The Aboriginal owners have the right to protect sacred sites, which may be strangely shaped rocks, or a place of particular beauty, or just a spot where legends have grown.

This legislation to many Australians seemed to be downright outrageous when Keating first introduced it. It is, however, remarkably similar to the system practised in Britain. In London, for instance, while you may own land, you have to ask permission to develop that land and often are obliged to give the local council what is called 'planning gain' to facilitate the permission that you seek. As far as sacred sites are concerned, it would be unthinkable to demolish Salisbury Cathedral to mine uranium. For that matter, the same stricture would apply to Stonehenge, despite the fact that it is a shrine from a largely forgotten religion. In the matter of strange stones, we in Britain crown our Monarch sitting on a stone, the Stone of Scone, that centuries ago travelled from the Middle East to Ireland, then to Scotland, brought there by my ancestors. It was later taken to London by the English and is now back in Edinburgh, for reasons that know no logic. No one finds this strange, yet in Australia it is hard for many people to understand the power that the Aboriginals believe to be contained in certain rocks. It would be unthinkable to destroy the sites of some of Britain's great battles. We preserve sunken ships lost in war as we believe that to disturb them is to disturb the souls of their sailors – so it is with the Aboriginals. Our roots are not so very different, it is just that our cultures have taken different courses.

Paddy Rowe, the man who keeps the Aboriginal law for his people, the tribe on whose land the town of Broome is situated, came to see me one afternoon. 'Perhaps,' he said, 'I might be interested to learn more about their culture? Perhaps I might wish to attend a ceremony?' It was arranged that I would wait beside the road out of Broome, nine miles from the town.

The night was unusually dark, the time about nine o'clock. As I waited, as if from nowhere an Aboriginal appeared. 'Follow me and do not step outside the path, for to do that is very dangerous.' I would die if I did that, I was told. Indeed, a teenage girl, who had ignored warnings that she should not ride her horse across the sacred ceremonial grounds, had died. A highly competent rider, she was thrown from her horse and her neck was broken.

We walked in silence for half an hour, coming to an open space in the scrub. A group of men were gathered, sitting or lying a few yards apart from each other in a semicircle. I was asked to sit down and as I did so, chanting began and figures painted with white markings appeared. They carried bundles of gum leaves, and more gum leaves were tied to their heads and bodies. Food was cooking nearby and the exclusively male audience ate and talked as they watched. There was a considerable amount of bodily noise as well. Two other white males had also been invited, a senior policeman and my zoo manager, Ross Gardiner. The women were camped a few hundred yards away, I could see them moving around their fires.

The effect of the dancing and chanting was hypnotic. As time went by both increased in their intensity, some members of the audience joined in and the rest fell silent. After two or three hours, Paddy Rowe came up to me and suggested that I might be tired and would like to return home. I took the hint and was shown back to the road and my car; the other two left at the same time. The Aboriginals had ceremonies to perform that were not for the eyes of strangers and these ceremonies will have continued all night, perhaps even for several days.

By chance, an acquaintance of mine, Maureen Zaramber, who sells ethnography in New York, was staying in Broome with her husband and an Indian travelling companion. I had agreed to go with Romilly and our house guests to lunch with them at their lodgings the day after the ceremony. The Indian travelling companion was to cook curry. The lunch went well enough and the curry seemed to be the real thing. That night, however, I was very sick and the next day so ill that, most unusually, I stayed in bed. The illness lasted several days. I was just recovering and pottering around in my garden when

Paddy Rowe appeared. I offered him tea and he sat down to gossip. 'I am glad you are all right again. I was worried that something might have gone wrong at the ceremony as both you and Ross Gardiner were taken ill.' He went on, 'We were preparing to have another ceremony to help you.' I would, however, still put money on my illness being caused by the curry, not the initiation ceremony.

I had over the years become very friendly with Roy Wiggin, an Aboriginal of the Bardi tribe from One Arm Point. Roy had a dream about an epic journey that his father made. He was determined to turn his dream into a corroboree. The Aboriginal corroboree is not a sacred or secret ceremony; its character is not too different from Italian nineteenth-century opera. These corroborees are often filled with tales of heroes, triumph and tragedy. A popular corroboree might be performed for many years; an unpopular corroboree would not make it past its first performance.

I arranged with Roy to put on a performance of his own corroboree. As so often with Roy, there was a problem. He had lost his totems and needed money to make more. I gave him the money and arranged that the performance should take place at six p.m. on a particular day. Dinner would be served to the performers afterwards.

The day arrived and Roy fussed about most of the afternoon looking for exactly the right place to hold the corroboree. About five p.m. Roy disappeared and an hour later my guests began to appear. We waited, darkness came, and we waited. A search party was sent for Roy and returned without success. I was about to call it a day, when a rusty truck bumped down the track to where we all waited.

Out of the truck got Roy and his somewhat reluctant group of performers. Bonfires were lit, the new totems were distributed to the actors, the band sat in a small circle, each with a pair of small sticks that they clicked together as an accompaniment to the singing. The show began, the dancers danced and singers sang, the stick clickers clicked their sticks. On and on it went, the rhythm and the colours quite beautiful. I was captured by the performance. The music for a corroboree is a little like contemporary opera, apparently muddled and discordant but wonderful when your ear gets used to it. The dance is a continuous repetition of a series of simple movements that mesmerise the audience. After three hours I called a halt. Dinner, a gigantic barbecue, was ready. Tables were laid out with plates heaped with steak, cutlets and sausages. To say that they vanished in a flash would be a terrible slur on the capacity of Roy Wiggin's people to demolish a large quantity of food in a particularly short time. In literally ten minutes, it was all over.

I enjoy corroborees and I encouraged Roy to make more totems. His first production contained several, the last over three hundred. These totems are made of wood with wool of different colours stretched between nails as a spider makes a web.

One day Roy said to me, 'Alistair, we have two things in common.' What they could be I was in some doubt about, for two people more different it would be hard to imagine. Roy is tall, fit and strong and is much at home in the wild land of Australia. His skin is the colour of a moonless sky. I am short, fat and extremely unfit. I am a stranger from a northern city, and my normally snow-white skin was, at that time, burned bright red. 'We both have Scots grandfathers and the Australians don't really care for either of us,' he said.

Paddy Rowe also put on corroborees for me, along with his friend Butcher Joe, a painter who sadly now is dead. They devised one where the totems were mostly worn. Headdresses of stick and linen cloth were made to represent the heads of the pelicans that lived on the coastline of Broome's peninsular, and flew inland to nest on the Billabongs in the wet season. Their corroboree also had soldiers in it, who carried stick swords and wore twisted rag and stick versions of cocked hats. The Aboriginals who played the parts of cattle in this corroboree wore masks with horns. It was the tale of an Aboriginal who left the cattle station where he worked to fight in the First World War. It was a much smaller affair than Roy Wiggin's great extravaganzas, but then Roy Wiggin and Paddy Rowe are as different from each other as I am to either of them.

I have made boat trips from Broome as well as flying, often going amongst the Humpback whales that migrate along the coast line. I used to go fishing, but after a while I had no desire to continue, for we caught too many fish, sometimes as many as sixty or seventy in a morning. Once, while we fished, my daughter Victoria held a line and read a book at the same time as she caught three large emperor fish. Later on, while we ate lunch, she swam in the picture-postcard sea beside our boat. Lunch finished, I threw my line over the side and caught a sizeable fish. After a considerable struggle I brought aboard a cod whose body must have been the size of Victoria's. I write 'must have been', for that body had been taken by a shark, and only the head was left.

One winter I travelled with three young archaeologists to a distant island near the end of the Montgomery Reef. The Montgomery Reef is about a hundred miles long at low tide and a hundred yards long at high tide. As the tide goes out you can land on the reef in a flat-bottomed boat. When the water has all cascaded over the edge of the coral, you can get out of your craft and walk about. Holes in the reef, about two dozen yards across, go down a thousand feet or more. At low tide they become fish traps: sharks are often seen chasing the trapped fish which, one after the other, are killed.

We set out on our journey from Cockatoo Island, a short flight from Broome, in a dinghy about twelve feet long powered by an outboard engine. We spent a blissful afternoon crossing the fifty or so miles of sea to our destination. Dolphins followed us, we saw sharks, humpback whales, turtles, dugongs and sea snakes. When we arrived at the island, which had recently been cleared by fire, we found the strange rock constructions we sought. They were circles made of rocks piled one on top of another and when I saw them their walls were about two feet high. Each circle had an entrance with a path leading towards the sea. They were, I was told, for collecting sea spirits. Even more remarkable, I believe, was a baobab tree of giant proportions in whose branches nestled a rock weighing several tons. It seemed as if the tree had grown under the rock and as it grew it had lifted the rock into the air.

Late that afternoon we walked several miles on the mainland through the bush to caves with rock paintings. These paintings, of what we might call spider men, were quite fresh as it appears that tribal elders had, even in this remote and apparently uninhabited part of Australia, looked after the caves and repainted the murals as they begin to fade.

In the whole day we saw not a single soul and so desolate was the place that it was unlikely there was anyone living within many miles. That night we built a high fire and ate the fish we had caught on the journey to the island. Then we slept on the sandy beach, placing our sleeping swags around the fire. I was worried about the large, man-eating crocodile that exist in Northern Australia, as my companions had told me that they had seen one when they camped there before. The scent of dead fish attracts crocodiles and despite the fact that we had buried the remains of our supper far down the beach, I still felt uneasy. I woke often during that night to put logs on the fire even though the night was steaming hot, for fire is meant to be a deterrent to crocodiles. Suddenly I felt pain in my feet. I awoke instantly and quickly jumped up, the pain increased, I fell on my back and kicked my legs in the air. There was no crocodile, but the soles of my shoes had caught alight as I had drawn closer to the fire for protection.

On the voyage home, there was a heavy, but warm mist and the sea turned from its azure blue to green. All around us was silence as our boat jumped down from a ridge in the sea caused by the tide race. There was not much conversation that morning as we headed back to Cockatoo Island, for we travelled through seas where wrecks and whirlpools abounded.

The year after we came to Broome, Romilly and I decided to drive by the inland route to Perth, which had three or four towns along its way, but precious little of what you might call road. As a companion, we took with us Oliver Ford, the Queen Mother's interior decorator. The journey would take three days, we were informed. We were also informed that such journeys were dangerous. However, we were self-confident, believing in the European fashion that if we could not see danger, what danger could possibly be there? The first day out, we drove along the main road to just short of Sanfire, four hundred miles from Broome, where we turned left into the bush. After about an hour of driving in the hot sun, seeing nothing but bush – not a parrot, not a kangaroo, not a motorcar, not another soul, animal or human – a group of emu ran across the road behind us. I spotted them and as we wished to take a closer look at these strange-looking birds, I swung our land cruiser around, off the track into the virgin bush after them. I drove for a quarter of an hour but, seeing nothing, I stopped and began to think about finding our way back to the road. The earth was hard; we had left no tracks; the bush that we had crashed through with such ease had sprung back as good as new; there were no broken branches, or none that we could see; it was as if we and our vehicle had been miraculously transported into that patch of bush, for there were no signs of how we arrived there.

To help us find our way out, I stood on the roof of the vehicle. I could see nothing but the top of the scrub that makes up the Australian bush. We were desperate. Obviously we needed to try something, so we formed a line, each in sight of the other, the first of us in sight of the vehicle. Then the three of us circumscribed an arch. After the fourth attempt, moving the vehicle back each time to the extremity of the arch, we hit the road and there, standing right in the middle of it, were the same bunch of emus.

That night we stayed at the Iron Clad Hotel in Marble Bar. More of a tin shed than a hotel, we slept badly and started early, so early that no one was up and the barman was asleep behind his bar. When roused, he told us to forget the bill and piss off, which we did in a hurry. That day we passed through Que, a deserted Victorian mining town, once a place of great wealth. Its fine buildings had crumbled, the wrought-iron bandstand in the main street had no paint left on it to peel, its metalwork burnished by the wind and dust. But Que was still a town of great romantic beauty, set in a landscape of deserted mines and rusting mining machinery. Several hundred miles later the road, such as it is, turns left at Nulangine and then on to Mount Newman. The next stop, Mount Newman, a mining town, was totally different. A town in a brown wasteland, it is as if someone had put a glass dome over the whole place, for it has green lawns, rows of detached houses, cars parked in their driveways. Trees lined Mount Newman's streets along with town plants in concrete planters. With its supermarkets and cinemas, air conditioning and ice-cream stalls, Mount Newman could have easily been removed in its entirety from suburban Perth.

We stayed that night at Meekatharra, a town about which Malcolm Fraser's wife made some disparaging remarks while campaigning with her husband, then the Prime Minister. These remarks were picked up by the local press and the poor woman had to return and make a public apology. Meekatharra is not much of a town, it has an airport and a railway station, the end of the line from Perth. It is a town for shipping cattle and sheep, a stop on the far edge of the wheat belt. The hotel was filled with farmers and cattlemen. Indeed almost the entire population of the town, a couple of hundred of them, was watching the football on television.

We booked in, and foolishly, I suppose, I asked what the rooms were like. The reply: 'Good enough for Mrs Fraser.' I was not much encouraged and I was right. Romilly, seeing a kettle on the fridge, decided to make a cup of tea. The kettle boiled over, the water ran down the back of the fridge, there was a flash and the lights went out. I set out for the hotel reception to ask that the fuses in our room be fixed, to find that there was outrage in the bar, a room the size of a couple of tennis courts. Angry men and women banged their tables and shouted at the barman. The whole hotel was dark, the television blank and the match, needless to say, at a crucial moment, cut off from those who were watching it. I slipped quietly back to our room.

That night we dined in the hotel and I bought a nugget of gold. They still sell nuggets at the bar in Meekatharra. The Aboriginals bring them in and swap them for beer. The nuggets go in the safe and the credit from the sale is marked up on the slate. I fell into conversation with the man who ran the place. 'Been here long?' I asked. 'Couple of weeks.' 'Been in the hotel business long?' I asked. 'Couple of weeks.' 'What did you do before?' 'Kept a station, 600,000 acres and 6,000 sheep'. 'Why are you here?' I asked. 'The bloke who owns the place wanted a holiday.' 'A friend of yours?' I asked. 'Never met him in my life.'

The local policeman was drinking there in preparation for a night of cleaning up the town. 'The one thing to remember about drunk Aboriginals when you arrest them, is to throw their dogs into the van first, then they follow. Put them in first and they all get out to catch their dogs.' 'Are they any real trouble?' I asked. 'Good as gold. When I've got them locked up I say, "Behave yourself and you can have your own grub, misbehave and you eat my wife's cooking."'

The night before's haul of drunks seldom stay in jail past midday, when they are taken before the magistrate, who says don't do it again. Of course, they do, for these drunken Aboriginals are not just a people lost between two cultures; they are the same as habitual drinkers the world over and equally unrepresentative of their race.

Next morning, we set out for Perth. The last eight hours of driving were pure paradise as September is the wild-flower season. Even Oliver Ford, a fanatical gardener well versed in the world's great gardens, had seen nothing like this. The bushes were heavy with flower, miles and miles of bright yellow, heavily scented wattle followed by a thousand or so acres of pink flowers, then blue flowers and so it went on, the flowers of each colour all growing together in vast quantities. We drove through country liberally sprinkled with Western Australia's thousands of different varieties of wild flowers.

Oliver Ford was probably the last man in London to be prosecuted for homosexuality. This had a devastating effect on him, as he had merely been obliging friends with a few introductions to acquaintances in the armed services. The judge quite rightly did not punish him. Ford's life changed after his conviction. He decided to take work only from a few clients, seldom travelled and used to return every night from London to his house near Bath. He was a great help to my family's business. Not only was he in charge of redecorating the Dorchester Hotel when renovation was needed, but each week he inspected all the suites to check that the furnishings had not been muddled up by careless housekeepers.

He also helped me by designing foyers for the buildings that I was putting up in Perth. I had hit on the idea of 'the Portable Foyer'. Instead of designing the foyers of office buildings so that they were all marble and brass, we used paint and plaster. Ford was a master at getting just the right colours to make the plaster look expensive, then I would hang often very valuable paintings on his beautifully finished walls. The furniture was always antique; the carpets, often copied from Aboriginal paintings, were woven in Thailand. The total cost of these buildings per square foot was about the same as the ones with the marble and brass foyers, but the scale and the feel of our foyers was domestic. The beauty of the whole scheme was that when we sold our buildings, we could move the pictures, the furniture and the carpets on to the next building that we were developing. No one has yet invented a convenient way of shifting marble and brass. In any case, these materials would quite reasonably be considered part of the building, whereas the decorations in our foyers were merely furnishings. Oliver Ford gave me the idea, for he used to make immensely beautiful gardens by acquiring wonderful tubs and planting them with shrubs and flowers. When he moved house, his garden moved with him.

Despite the rigours of a couple of nights in outback hotels and getting lost in the bush, even if it was only for an hour or two, Oliver Ford was game for another expedition. This time we were more cautious and took my partner in a pearl farm, Snowy County, and his mate, Charlie Diesel, with us as guides. Snowy County and I, over the years, remained good friends as well as partners. A more decent and, in the true sense, honourable man than Snowy County it would be hard to find. Any time spent in his company is pure pleasure. What does he talk about? Well, nothing really; he just gossips and tells tales that, written here, would seem so very simple. Humour for the writer is such a complex art, while the humour of the raconteur has a terrible simplicity, its effect depending so much on the circumstances in which a tale is told. Snowy County is the master of a far greater art than that of the writer, for Snowy County is a teller of tales.

We drove straight across Australia from Broome to Sydney, by road and dirt track to Hall's Creek and then past the Wolf's Crater, a great hole in the earth made by a giant meteorite, on down the Tamini Track. For me, the first night that we spent in the Tamini Desert was one of intense excitement. We did not bother with tents as we slept on swags, a roll of canvas that you lay on the ground. If the weather is wet or chilly, you just put half of it over your head and body. I always slept with my boots on and fully clothed because you can never be sure what will happen in the outback. I took a heavy calibre rifle with me, mostly in case we got lost and needed to shoot something to eat.

The stars on that first night in the desert were as I have never seen stars before: they started on one horizon and cluttered the night sky across to the other horizon. Amongst them there was an almost continuous parade of shooting stars. I was so excited I did not sleep more than a few minutes all night. Always an early riser, I woke before first light in the bush. Snowy County also seemed barely to sleep and was already dressed. We used to break sticks rather noisily in an attempt to wake the others. Failing this ploy, we would usually build up the fire, cough a bit, drop billy cans and then make tea.

At first light, I had the whole group awake. It was shortly after four-thirty. I liked to be underway by five and to get a good four hours' driving in before breakfast. On our trips I drove the Toyota Land cruiser with Romilly and other companions. Snowy County and Charlie Diesel took it in turns to drive a Toyota truck. The advantage of these two vehicles was that the parts were interchangeable. On the truck we carried sixty gallons of diesel, sixty gallons of water, and six spare tyres. Spare tyres are vital in the outback, for in rough and rocky country punctures are not uncommon. On our first trip together, Romilly had calculated the quantity of beer that Snowy County and Charlie Diesel would drink – about a can an hour each. After two days, they were not drinking anything like that amount; in fact, they had barely touched more than a couple of cans. Unfortunately, Romilly had in error bought non-alcoholic beer.

It rained that day and we bogged down several times. On the Tamini Track we helped tow a low loader, with a D8 Bulldozer on it, out of the red mud by hitching both our vehicles together. The Pindan, the earth of Northwestern Australia, in the sun is as hard as rock; in the wet it is like a quicksand. After driving for two hours, we reached Rabbit Flats, where there had been trouble between the local Aboriginals and the owner of the filling station-cum-hotel. The hotel owner was a surly sort of bloke and we had to wait outside his stockade of corrugated iron, topped with barbed wire, until he felt like opening to sell us diesel. That morning, as we left our camp, I had seen footprints around where we slept. They were bare footprints and none of us had been barefoot so I can only assume that some Aboriginals had taken a look at us during the night. Every once in a while a small tribe of these Aboriginals, who have never seen white people before, turn up.

Just past Rabbit Flats, we passed an Aboriginal standing silent and still beside the road. In one hand he held a dead goanna, in the other a spear and a boomerang. He did not move as we passed. It was as if we did not exist. This was his land; he could live where we would surely die and he clearly knew that. It was to him as if we were a party of tourists on a cultural tour, while we rather grandly called ourselves travellers because we travelled from one place to another.

At Alice Springs, we encountered a traffic light. It is hard for someone who has not just had the experience of coming out after any time in the bush to understand how we felt about that traffic light. There is a sadness that strikes the traveller who moves from the remote regions to apparent civilisation, a sense of loss. The foyer of the Sheraton Hotel in Alice Springs had a heavy carpet of white wool. Who was so foolish to put that carpet there, I will never know, but I am certain that there was never such a demonstration of its incongruity as when Oliver Ford, Snowy County, Charlie Diesel, Romilly, my father-in-law Tom Hobbs and myself entered that brand new hotel and walked across their carpet. We were covered, head to toe, in bright red mud. We were shown to our rooms and a moment later there was a knock on the door. It was a maid delivering, unsolicited, a huge pile of clean towels.

Next day, we set out for the Diamantina river. We passed through flood country and saw how an inoffensive little stream could become a raging torrent that left the carcasses of cattle high in branches of trees to dry in the wind and sun. That night we camped on the Diamantina's banks. Along the road we passed through Boulia with its population of 287 souls, the capital of the Channel Country and home to the mysterious Minmin Light. Asking the shire foreman about the state of the roads from there to Quilpie, we were given an invaluable insight into the nature of Australian local politics. 'They are really good as far as the shire president's house, after that I wouldn't give much for your chances on them.' In the Channel Country, steam engines were scattered across the landscape, perfectly preserved by the dry air. Green grass edged the channels that carried artesian water and slowly the plain became farmland and we came upon Hungerford. It is a village from another century, deserted or so we thought until we entered the pub and found a hundred or so of the inhabitants drinking.

Quilpie smelt strongly of sulphur. It is the centre of opal mining and the area depends on artesian bores and where you have artesian water you can smell sulphur. We decided to take breakfast in the local hotel.

'What are you doing here?' the waitress asked. 'I rather thought that we might take breakfast,' I replied. 'We don't serve breakfast after nine o'clock.' 'Well, it's only eight forty-five.' 'You couldn't eat it in a quarter of an hour.' I suppose we were the only travellers to pass that day, perhaps that week. We took breakfast at the place down the road, recommended by the filling station attendant. That place belonged to his aunt and there was a parrot there in a cage with a note that said, 'Don't put your fingers in the parrot's cage, that is if you want to keep all of them.'

After crossing the Simpson Desert, with its rolling sand dunes that stretched for miles and miles, the landscape became friendlier.

The drive from Burke to Sydney was boring, the weather wet and cold. Midmorning, we stopped to visit the zoo at Dubo then carried on to the Blue Mountains, which I did not care a lot for: I am a desert man, not a man of the mountains. I have always suffered from vertigo; I really dislike mountains and I abhor panoramic views. Too much all at once is never good, has always been my thinking.

Snowy County, Charlie Diesel, Romilly and I travelled far and wide in Australia, through the Kimberleys, swimming in the gorges, in billabongs, surrounded by Pandanis palms and fed by waterfalls from mountain streams, their waters as clear as if they had been distilled, cold in the scorching hot sun. Often our party stood naked below these falls, the cold fresh water cascading off our bodies. We drove in our convoy of two vehicles, twisting along rocky tracks, across mountain ranges, across the rivers of Arnhem Land. Sometimes the water covered our feet as we drove from one side of these rivers to the other. On one trip we crossed 130 rivers and streams in a hundred-mile journey.

In Arnhem Land we visited an Aboriginal leader who lived at

Ramingin. We arrived at the village and made enquiries about this elder. The village was at the back of beyond, not far from the eastern coast of Arnhem Land. Travel there is restricted and you need a permit to enter the area. These permits are hard to obtain and, as a consequence, few Europeans travel that way. After a considerable amount of discussion we were told that the man whom we sought was in Geneva. I thought it was incongruous that I should come all this way to meet an Aboriginal leader whom I could have seen in Europe with far greater ease. We drove through the forest of Arnhem Land, occasionally disturbing herds of buffalo. Beside the track, if you could really call it that, stood an Aboriginal hunter, this time with a repeating shotgun and a pack of dogs. He stood, one leg cocked, carrying his gun as if it was a spear. The dogs yapped as they chased after our trucks. We came across hidden waterholes surrounded by high Pandanis palms, brightly coloured water lilies flowering on the pitch black surface of their waters.

We drove through the Gulf Country, stopping at Borroloola, the ugliest of fly-blown towns with the prettiest name in all Australia; at Normanton, where there is a short length of railway going nowhere, right across the Barkly Table Lands, across plains and pastures, with flocks of parrots rising in front of our convoy, changing colours as in flight they changed direction. We came across eagles feeding on the carcasses of sheep and cattle. At an Aboriginal mission on the borders of Queensland we found a priest dressed in a smartly pressed beige linen suit, a white dog collar stiff at his neck and on his head a smart straw hat with a ribbon that matched his suit. About thirty years old, he opened his mouth to speak to us, revealing a fine set of expensive gold teeth. How different he was from the priests of the Kimberleys, who work in trousers, open shirts and have only a small gold cross on the collar to tell you of their vocation. He did not invite us to stop; rather he indicated that we best hurry on for we should not be there in the first place. In the Kimberleys we would have been invited to share whatever he was to have for tea and tea is really a meal in that part of Australia

I did not find the Queenslanders hospitable by nature; indeed they are often a surly, suspicious people. The country tracks are covered in dark grey bull dust, which the lead vehicle throws up in a great cloud that hangs in the air for hours. A day's driving through Queensland's bull dust and you are as grey as a cadaver. We came across a cattle truck, with the driver and his mate struggling to change a wheel. We stopped so Snowy County and Charlie Diesel could offer to help. When the job was finished and a new wheel in place, we asked where we could find fuel. 'None about here mate,' was the short reply. 'We're having trouble with one of our engines.' 'That happens,' was the short response. Later that day, just before dark, we arrived at a homestead, by chance the one where the truck that we had helped was parked. The people there were having a barbecue. It all seemed rather jolly, but no diesel, no help, no invitation to a meal was forthcoming. This is a different country from our state of Western Australia.

We drove across flat bush, coming on lakes where pelicans made a stately progress across their waters, ducks rested in large flocks, and parrots decorated the giant gums that surrounded these waterways, looking like white blossoms as they sat on the branches of the trees. The Brolga cranes in great flocks performed their intricate dance as we passed and bustards stalked beside the track, taking off like jumbo jets lumbering through the air. Seldom, however, did we see a kangaroo. Emus there were in plenty, and when we disturbed them, they charged off into the bush like a regiment of cavalry, their plumes straining in the wind of their passage.

Up one side of Cape York, through the Daintree rain forest, by ferry across the Daintree river, the going was hard. Badly built tracks, deep ruts and mud slides had made travelling almost impossible past the mining country to Cape York, round again, and down the other side of the peninsula. At Katherine, in the Northern Territory, we stopped in the town for a meal. We entered a new shopping arcade, where we found a restaurant, decorated in pastel colours, air conditioned and Formica lined. It was too clean for us and too alien to the bush where we had spent our time.

The Catherine Gorge was filled with tourists, so we headed back into Arnhem Land. At the Ropper river we saw the crocodiles that live in Australia's northern rivers, lying silent on the river's banks. We slept one night on a track than ran beside an empty river. Never, when travelling in Australia, sleep for comfort on the sandy bottom of an empty river bed, for a rainstorm a hundred miles away can turn that river into a raging torrent. Neither, however, is it a good idea to sleep on a sandy track. We had not seen another vehicle for two days, but that night we were woken by a terrible racket, only getting out of the way just in time to see a saloon car drive past, headlights full on, ghetto-blaster blaring music. The car was carrying seven or eight Aboriginals. Where this car was going we had not the least idea, nor, for that matter, did we know how it got to the place where we slept. The next day, driving was much the same: every few miles another river. Always expect the unexpected in the Australian outback.

The National Park of Kakadu is still beautiful and well worth a visit but filled, I am afraid, with tourists these days. To truly enjoy the Australian outback, it needs to be seen with as few humans in it as possible. Far better than Kakadu is Fog Dam. It is only a half-hour drive from Darwin and it was once a rice farming project. Now Fog Dam is a deserted swamp, inhabited only by thousands of birds and saltwater crocodiles. The time to be there is before sun up. Drive onto the dam and wait for daylight. The sight that you will see is truly amazing; the songs of the birds a delight. Do not, however, get out of your car until daylight is well and truly established, for the first time I visited Fog Dam, I parked my car and walked in the dark along the wide track that runs atop the earth dam. Buffalo could be heard in the distance, the morning was fresh and this was paradise. Some time after daylight broke, as I walked back to my car, I noticed tracks. Stopping, I looked at them. They were fresh, pieces of wet reed were to be found amongst them. These were the tracks of saltwater crocodiles. I must have disturbed them as I walked and, unseen by me, they had slithered quietly into the lily-covered waters of the dam.

I had many guests who came to stay while I lived in Broome. I think that they often found difficulty in coming to terms with the difference between the safety of the township and the dangers of the bush. Albert Roux was amongst the most delightful of my visitors, cooking bouillabaisse for twenty-five guests, the soup made from the fish that he had caught that day. I sent Albert and his wife, Monique, on a trip into the outback with David and Lita Young. Lord Young was at the time Secretary of State for Trade and Industry. The culture shock of the bush threw them a little at first, but by the second night Albert was cooking crocodile steaks over a camp fire. They told me that they were delicious, and I can well believe that to have been the case.

Michael Heseltine and his wife Anne also visited Broome shortly after he walked out of Margaret Thatcher's Cabinet. I have always liked Michael personally, despite the fact that I do not agree with a single political idea that he has ever produced. I first met him, then one of Ted Heath's Ministers, in 1973 at a dinner party. He regaled the assembled company with his views on the economy: 'We have released millions into the economy and what have you businessmen done but borrow that money to develop property when you should have invested it in re-equipping your businesses.' Even then it struck me that Michael Heseltine was a man who felt that he could run everyone else's business far better than they.

Years later I observed him as a Cabinet Minister. Given the chance to run a ministry, and faced with making choices, he was apparently far from decisive. I watched him in Australia as he went about his birdwatching. He is so different from me, for he is a maker of sets, a checklist birdwatcher, a checklist collector, a checklist politician. For myself, if I find a thing of beauty, I want more of that same thing. I am not remotely interested in making sets that include the boring and the banal just because they happen to be part of that set. Nor, for that matter, am I inclined to avoid people who just happen to have views that contradict my own. My friends are my friends regardless of their political views. I find any other approach to politics to be totally uncivilised. People become my friends because they interest me. Indeed I even have friends who are so boring that they become interesting – they are my friends because I like them, not because I happen to agree with them or they with me.

I have not seen much of Michael Heseltine since that time in Australia. In time he drove Margaret Thatcher from office. I bear him no malice for what he did. Politics is a hard game and Heseltine was Thatcher's enemy. It was the treachery of those who failed to support her that brought her down.

Amongst the British politicians who stayed with me in Broome, the most delightful were Richard Ryder and his wife Caroline. Richard and Caroline I have known since I first went to work for Lady Thatcher. Richard was then her Political Secretary and Caroline, her Private Secretary. In my early days with the Conservative Party they were always kind and considerate to me and we became friends over those years and I am happy to say still remain so these days. Richard, a man of immense talent, deserves more from politics than he has so far received.

Michael and Anne Spicer came to visit me in Broome when he was Minister of Aviation. Jean Haines, a long-time resident of Broome and local representative of the West Australia press, was there to interview him. 'What questions would you like me to ask you?' she began. The poor man was speechless. How very different this was from the reception that he usually got from the press in Britain.

A number of West Australian politicians came to Broome during this period – if you did business in West Australia, or for that matter, Australia, it was important to know politicians. Even if you find that you can run your business without actually having to meet them, at least you must know about them and how they are likely to behave, for they are likely by their actions to have a far greater effect on your business than almost any other single factor. Entrepreneurs today are well advised to study the characters of the politicians and the civil servants in the country where they have interests. Today, so much of industry and finance is controlled by regulations. Politicians can enforce or relax them, invent new ones or abolish old ones just as they please, without going anywhere near the parliaments to which they have been elected.

Charles Court, as Premier of Western Australia, believed in capitalism and he believed in his state, and under his administration both flourished. Ray O'Conor, his successor, took the same view but achieved little. Brian Burke, the next Premier, the Leader of the Labor Party, believed in enlightened Socialism, a mixture of free and state enterprise, a partnership between the state and its entrepreneurs. For a time this seemed to work. Then the inevitable happened: the functionaries of the state began to behave like entrepreneurs, using the apparently bottomless resources of the state as a bank roll. Meanwhile, great Australian entrepreneurs, sighting gold to be mined amongst the incompetencies of the bureaucrats, set off to have the lion's share of that valuable substance. 'It was,' said one senior civil servant who had disapproved of the whole venture, 'as if they were taking grain from blind chucks [chickens].'

When the stock market crashed in 1987, the West Australian Government bailed out Robert Holmes à Court. This single move, I believe, brought about the virtual collapse of the West Australian commercial economy. Of course, that collapse did not happen overnight – the West Australian Government bought several city properties from Holmes à Court, at highly inflated prices. As a result, they were now in the property business competing against the market, with two important advantages. The first was access to the money contained in various state pension funds, and the second was their ability to move government tenants, at will, from the buildings of the commercial developer to their own developments. They took both of these actions and as a consequence, at the first sign of a downturn, the market in Perth City property collapsed. Brian Burke, by now the Australian Ambassador to Ireland and the Vatican, resigned and subsequently was prosecuted, not for setting in motion the plan that destroyed West Australia for a decade, rather for fraudulently and dishonestly obtaining money. He went to jail for a short period. Now he is again facing charges for stealing money from the Labor Party to buy stamps for his collection.

Peter Dowding, the Premier of Western Australia who succeeded Brian Burke, was a highly intelligent politician who did the best he could, but the cycle of disaster was too far advanced for him to be able to take the action that was needed to throw it off course. Dowding was deposed in a coup while attending the Davos Conference in 1989. Carmen Lawrence succeeded him, and almost immediately appointed a Royal Commission, which, at great length, looked into the whole affair of the state's dealings with individuals.

Robert Holmes à Court had died of a heart attack and was never able to enlighten those of us who took an interest in these matters as to the circumstances that surrounded his original deal with Brian Burke and the Western Australian Government. It has now become clear that he was bailed out by Brian Burke on not one but two occasions. He was without doubt in the thick of the whole débâcle that brought such disrepute on Western Australia. Woven into the story of the years between the Holmes à Court transaction in 1987 and the appointment of the Royal Commission in 1989 were the equally flamboyant figures of Alan Bond, Laurie Connell and Dallas Dempster. This trio were involved in a series of convoluted attempts to rescue Laurie Connell's merchant bank. The result of their efforts cost the government and a number of others a lot of money.

Carmen Lawrence conducted a policy of masterly inaction and, at the same time, suggested to the electorate that they should be 'feeling good' about the way that their state was being run. The electorate did not feel at all good about any of this and threw her Government from power at the first opportunity. After it was all over, I discussed the tragedy of the matter with Tom Stephens. He told of how he had called on Brian Burke to warn him that matters were getting out of hand. 'You and John Adams had made it quite clear to us what was happening; you suggested that I told Brian Burke.' I had forgotten this, but when Tom reminded me, I remembered how Brian Burke had behaved after that meeting. Within days, he had made a speech linking my name with that of Alan Bond and his pals. This was an attempt either to discredit me or to give them credibility. Either way, the speech achieved nothing, for I had only the most casual of social contacts with Bond since the day when Sir Halford Reddish dismissed him with such contempt.

Laurie Brereton came to Broome after I had been on a fishing trip with him, Bob Hawke, Peter Doyle and Michael Kalis. A fishing trip with Bob Hawke was something apart. We all stayed in Exmouth at the Norcape Lodge, which was a small number of transportable buildings, pretending to be a hotel, close by a large country hotel or pub. A large part of this hotel was the beer garden; the rest of it did not amount to much. Exmouth is a beautiful spot off the Ningaloo reef north of Port Hedland; the Norcape Lodge in 1988 belonged to the King family. The Kings are master fishermen: if there are fish to be caught the King family's boats will catch them.

The first night at Exmouth, we all walked over to the beer garden, where Bob Hawke began to work the crowd. I had spent much of my life among politicians, but I had never seen the like of this. Each one of those large, heat-sodden, sweaty individuals in that place was treated by their Prime Minister as if they were the only people in the world that he had wanted to meet. How he had ever managed to run Australia without each piece of advice that he was given that evening, he made seem a mystery. He listened to the person with whom he talked as though they were sitting locked away from this rowdy crowd, in the confines of his prime ministerial office; he kissed them, he hugged them, he shook their hands as if he never wanted to let them go. These could have been his long-lost relatives, so great was his delight at meeting people whom he had never met before. After an hour or so we repaired to the transportable where Peter Doyle, the proprietor of Doyle's Pier, Sydney's most famous fish restaurant, was cooking dinner. After dinner the Prime Minister made me sit up until the early hours of the morning watching England being beaten at cricket.

Early the next morning we set out to catch fish and we caught them in plenty. By magic, however, the fish were always on the prime ministerial line.

Laurie Brereton, one of my companions on that fishing trip, was a senior Cabinet Minister in the last Labour Government. I first knew him when he was a minister in the New South Wales State Government and even then it was clear that he was about to become an important Federal politician. He has a remarkable flair for divining what the people are thinking or, indeed, are likely to think in a year's time. It would be no surprise to me if, in time, Laurie Brereton became Australia's Prime Minister. Laurie Brereton's wife, Trish, is a remarkable woman who has been a counterbalance to Laurie himself, a foil to sharpen his instincts, a guard to mind his back and a brilliant advocate of his talents.

New South Wales has always been a breeding ground for Labor politicians. Graham Richardson, one of the sharpest political brains in the business, the numbers man who made Paul Keating, from the same state, Prime Minister; Neville Wran, once a highly successful Premier of New South Wales; and the current Premier, Bob Carr, are all outstanding politicians. Bob Hawke was really an outsider amongst these men, for he came from Western Australia. I know all of these people, but perhaps Laurie Brereton better than the rest. I talked with them when they were in power and strangely, for a right-wing Conservative, I found little between us to argue about.

In Australia, I am, I believe a Labor Republican, while in Britain I am a Conservative Monarchist. I find no problem with this apparent split in my personality. The monarchy is thoroughly good for Britain and should continue, if only for the reason that if the monarchy goes, we will have Ted Heath or Roy Jenkins or Norman St John Stevas as President and that would be intolerable. However, the monarchy does nothing for the Australians. Take the simple proposition of a state visit to Japan. The Queen goes there to sell Britain, and often her visit will be timed to coincide with our trade missions, for Japan is a market that all and sundry would like to break into. The Queen is the Queen not only of Britain and Australia but also many of the Commonwealth countries. She does not, however, promote Australian trade interests in Japan or anywhere else. The monarchy is a thing of the past in Australia; Australia will never truly be a nation while the monarchy lasts there. Britain, on the other hand, could cease to be a nation should the monarchy finish.

As for my pro-Labor tendency in Australia, in truth I would be in a quandary if I had to vote in that country as to how I should cast my vote. The two parties both embrace free enterprise; their policies are so close that, at times, it is hard to tell them apart. While I disagree with particular policies in Australia, I seldom disagree with the overall thrust of either party. A good deal of what Paul Keating achieved, I am sure John Howard, now Prime Minister, agrees with, for it was John Howard's efforts as Leader of a Conservative Opposition that largely set the agenda of politics that forced Paul Keating and his party to the right. I am equally sure that a great deal of what John Howard will now do, Paul Keating would like to have done.

I went to see Paul Keating shortly after Bob Hawke's government came to power. At that time, he was the National Treasurer (the equivalent of the British Chancellor of the Exchequer). We talked about many things but, in particular, I was interested to know what he would do about the stranglehold that the trade union movement had on Australian industry. 'I am going to tear the trade unions apart, tear them up,' Keating told me. Some years later, after he had been Prime Minister for some time and just won a general election, I was lunching with him so I took the opportunity to remind him of his words. 'Well,' he said, 'I almost did it but first Bob [Bob Hawke, the Prime Minister] stuffed it up and then Richo [Graham Richardson] stuffed it up. There was always someone stuffing it up.'

Paul Keating is the most civilised man, despite his reputation for vile parliamentary language, which I have to admit I find rather engaging. Of the Shadow Minister who took up a portfolio he had relinquished only a few months before, he said in Parliament House, 'He is like a dog returning to eat its own vomit.' 'Scumbag, vermin, pedant', are words that Keating used all the time in Parliament. Privately a highly civilised and cultured man, he turned parliamentary abuse into an art form.

On occasion, he lunched with me in my suite in the Sydney Intercontinental Hotel. He is amongst the most entertaining of people to sit down with to a meal, a considerable connoisseur of wine and food, a collector of antiques. French empire clocks were his speciality. I asked him how, on a prime ministerial salary, he could afford to buy what seemed rather expensive items. His reply: 'Some people buy antiques already in captivity from experts who know what they are selling. The antiques that I buy, I catch them wild.'

Keating was quite content to sit late into the afternoon explaining, in great detail, some point of government financial policy and then ring up later that evening to make sure that his explanation had been understood. I asked him if he had to spend much of his time being briefed by his civil servants on his country's economic policy, 'Good Lord no,' he replied. 'I brief them on policy.' Would that a few of the politicians who govern Britain should take a leaf out of Paul Keating's book.

I flew one Sunday to Canberra to take lunch with Keating. I was shown into The Lodge. It was the first time that I had been there, and I was surprised by the modesty of the place. In the sitting room, a room of entirely domestic scale, the walls were covered in bookcases; a complicated stereo system and piles of compact discs dominated the room, its furniture was comfortable, the curtains and coverings of the soft furnishings were dark. I sat and listened to classical music as I waited for the Prime Minister. I was offered a drink by a motherly lady, an employee of the state, the prime ministerial housekeeper. She told me that the Prime Minister would not be long.

I asked him about the incident with the Queen. 'I don't think I actually touched her, I was merely ushering her along as one might urge someone to pass through a door.' I never saw the point of all the criticism of him for that incident; his was a gesture typical of Australian informality.

Lunch was a light affair, the dining room modest with an air of suburban England. We could have been sitting in the home of a not very successful stockbroker just outside Ascot. We gossiped about politics. Keating did not rate John Major very highly, saying it was a tragedy that Britain was governed by a man with so little intellect. His civil servants had told him that they were amazed at Major's inability to grasp the point of a complex issue quickly. But mostly we spoke of art, antiques and our mutual friend Warren Anderson, a controversial character with a touch of genius, a man who, starting as a tractor driver, became one of the richest men in Australia with a string of elegant homes. A fanatical collector, he bought the best in almost every field, from American Colt revolvers to rare stuffed animals, glass, china, books and silver. I once acquired a copy of Audubon's great double Elephant folio *The Birds of America* from Warren Anderson. One evening at dinner he was showing me an important silver bowl by an eighteenth-century French maker. It slipped from his hand and rolled around the marble floor in ever decreasing circles until it finally came to rest, at which point the base and the top of the bowl parted company. Anderson picked up the two pieces, looked at them, tried to put them together and, failing, put them on a side table, returning to his seat without a word. The bowl in question had come from Sotheby's in Monaco and had cost several hundred thousand pounds.

Anderson, when he was a successful tractor driver, rented a filling station and café in the southern part of Western Australia. Business boomed. Cheryl, his wife, cooked and instead of beef, she put kangaroo meat into the hamburgers. The health inspector put a stop to this practice and the customers all complained: they preferred the kangaroo meat. One day, the representatives of his landlords turned up to say that they wished, for their own reasons, prematurely to terminate his lease. Anderson, a large and very strong man, told them to get lost, for he was doing very well with his filling station and café. The next morning, rather more of the landlord's men returned and gave Anderson a beating. By lunchtime, he and his wife were packed and on their way. 'It was the greatest piece of luck that ever happened to me, that beating,' Anderson told me. 'If they had not done that to me I would still be driving a tractor and filling trucks with petrol.'

Anderson left for Perth. Fame and fortune attended his efforts, although some might say that fame was not the right word to use about Anderson – infamous surely would be more appropriate. I disagree. Anderson deserves far more than that, for he is the very stuff of Australia. Times were hard for him in the last few years, but he has shown the guts that were needed to fight his way back to further fortunes. That is Australia, ever the lucky country, where success is regarded as luck, failure as your just desserts. Australians are mostly best described by Oscar Wilde's famous *bon mot*: 'Success is entirely due to luck, ask any failure.' Ask about any person who is not successful in Australia and they will authoritatively point out how the success of others is only luck. Then they will combine with their fellows to set out to pull down the successful, if for no better reason than to prove their theory. In Australia, it is called 'the tall poppy syndrome' – any poppy that grows taller than its fellows spoils the symmetry of the field and so must be cut down. It was the same with Paul Keating. Endlessly, the population of Australia spent its time trying to find reasons for his success, while ignoring the truth that he just was more talented than most and worked hard using his talents to great effect. It will be the same with John Howard, now he has risen from the ranks of his contemporaries. They will soon set about disparaging his reputation in an attempt to bring him down.

I have known John Howard for many years, first meeting him when he was in Malcolm Fraser's Government. He was, at the time, the National Treasurer. A thoughtful, sincere man, he has none of the flash and sparkle of Paul Keating, but in his determined way he will be a good and possibly a great Prime Minister of Australia. At least he has the wit to realise that the legislation put in place to resolve the problems between Aboriginal and white Australians is important, if their country is truly to prosper. Australia needs three ingredients added to her many advantages and the hard work of her people. These ingredients are: first, to be her own country, to cut the formal links with Britain; second, to take in a vast number of new citizens and third, to become part of the Far East, to stop pretending that her continent is positioned somewhere between London and Athens. All these things will happen, whether the majority of Australians want them or not. Far better that the steady hand of John Howard sets about achieving them peacefully, than they are forced on Australia by her neighbours.

10

From Art to Politics

The twists and turns of life never cease to amaze me. I could never have known when I set out to collect art that this would lead me to become involved in politics. Towards the end of the 1960s, word was beginning to get around the art world that I was a serious collector, the sort of collector for whom the art world is always on the lookout. Their interest was not alerted by either my knowledge or enthusiasm, rather by evidence that cash, in some quantity, was apparently available.

First I received a letter from Witney Straight, the Chairman of the Contemporary Arts Society. In those days the society was run by Pauline Vogelpoel, a glamorous South African whose debut into London's art world had been marked by a visit to a function at the Tate. As she walked up the steps of the museum, Sir John Rothenstein came tumbling down them. His fall was the result of a blow on the chin from the fist of Douglas Cooper, the truculent Australian, a friend of Picasso and a member of Sir John's staff at the Tate. The Contemporary Arts Society had none of that excitement about it; in fact, it was far closer to a sewing circle than an organisation at the sharp end of the contemporary art world.

Pauline Vogelpoel ruled the society with a Machiavellian charm, until someone tried to cause trouble, when she could be extremely fierce. Every year two members of the committee were allowed to spend £500 each of the society's money on works of art. Every five years or so, the works they bought were exhibited and various museum directors allowed to make their choice of the works available. Pauline decided who these two people should be. She claimed that there was a rota; I choose to believe that she made the choice herself, and herein lay her power. Once a month I attended the meetings of this amiable society, learned little about art and quite a lot about practical politics for Pauline Vogelpoel was a master at handling her committee.

In the 1960s when I was collecting English coloured sculpture, about the only other serious collector in that field was Stuart Mason. He was in charge of the Leicestershire Education Authority and was putting together a collection of art for display in their schools. Stuart retired, and expressed the desire to move to America, there to earn his living lecturing on art. Leslie Waddington and I both felt that Stuart's move to America would be a great loss to Britain, and so to avoid this I offered him a job.

At first, as curator of my collection of both paintings and sculpture, he arranged for it to be spread amongst many British institutions. However, pieces were put on display as far afield as Australia. Before I gave my collection of painted sculptures to the Tate, I had been engaged in discussions with Camden Council, who were looking for a premises to show this collection. A disused Territorial Army drill hall was found in Cheney Street and part of the collection was shown there, after the Tate show. The pieces were rotated through Cheney Street for some years until the Tate began to show other work there. I was delighted about this, for I have always been keen on the idea of outstations to museums. I find vast collections too large to really enjoy, much preferring to see only a few works at a time.

Stuart Mason soon became Director of the Institute of Contemporary Prints that I had started. There was, at that time, no national collection of prints. The Tate had a few, the V&A had quite a good collection, and yet more were housed at the British Museum. I gave my large collection of contemporary prints to the institute, as did Christopher and Rose Prater. Christopher Prater was perhaps the most brilliant technician making prints at that time. It was to his workshop that both the Marlborough and the Waddington galleries sent their artists when they commissioned work. I also arranged for both the Marlborough and the Waddington galleries to give one copy of each print that they produced. The institute was supported financially to some extent by the Sir Robert McAlpine Foundation. The aim had always been to hand over the collection to the Tate, but the cogs of bureaucracy turn slowly, and it was some years before the gallery managed to establish that it was to be the museum that would collect contemporary graphic art. It was, I am afraid, even longer before it had a budget to support a gift of the size we had in mind, with the necessary curator and other staff. In time, all these obstacles were overcome and several thousand prints were sent from the plan chests of the Institute of Contemporary Prints to the Tate Gallery. The lady who had been the curator of this collection moved with it, after considerable argument, for although she was perfectly well qualified by habit to attend the curatorial duties of the collection, the Tate argued that she did not have the necessary qualifications on paper to do the work.

It was not long before I found myself on a number of other committees, such as the management committee of the Royal Court theatre. This organisation was much more in the spirit of Douglas Cooper and the blow that he struck Sir John Rothenstein. The committee, or council, met at the headquarters of Marks & Spencer, as Eileen Blond and Lois Sieff were the driving force behind all that happened at the Royal Court in those days. The Chairman Greville Poke kept the peace, or tried to. The council members, about twenty in all, would sit around Marks & Spencer's board room table, in the centre of which, when we arrived, would be several plates piled high with Marks & Spencer's best sandwiches. No one fired a starting gun, the Chairman did not drop a flag or say 'go'. However, as if by some strange instinct that gripped all the members of that committee at the same time, they would set about the sandwiches. It was truly a massacre – the piles of sandwiches disappeared in moments. Then we got down to business. This usually involved a row at the Royal Court. While I was on the council the row, that ran and ran, was whether we should take over the running of the Old Vic. Albert Finney was for it; Lindsay Anderson was totally against the idea.

I knew Albert Finney quite well. He is a man of natural charm, a fine actor who is also an immensely amusing companion. Lindsay Anderson I know not at all, and what I saw of him I did not care for. These two argued and argued over the Old Vic. On one occasion, Albert leaned across the table and tried to seize Lindsay Anderson's handbag, shouting that Anderson had hidden a tape recorder in it. Greville Poke, a small, dapper and charming, if somewhat vague man, tried desperately to restore order. In the event Anderson won by default and the Royal Court did not expand its empire beyond Sloane Square.

My great friend in the theatre world was Patrick Ide. I had known Patrick for many years at the Garrick Club and he was a most entertaining man with whom to dine. He was the director of the Theatre Investment Fund, whose leading light was Peter Saunders, the producer of *The Mousetrap*. Contrary to popular belief, *The Mouse-trap* was not always a success. After the first year, returns had not been good and the investors wanted to close the show. Peter Saunders, to his credit, bought them all out and made a considerable fortune as a result.

I took over from Lord Goodman as Chairman of the Theatre Investment Fund. An organisation that raised money from the theatrical industry to equal a grant by the state, it had been set up in the days of Harold Wilson by Lord Goodman to help balance the adverse effects on commercial theatre of the state-subsidised theatre. The Theatre Investment Fund would put up the first ten per cent of the finance needed for shows that the committee believed had merit.

It was, in fact, our duty to lose all our money and I am happy to say that over a period of years we did just that. Seldom did we get a real winner, which I suppose is evidence to the fact, if any is needed, that investing in the theatre is a highly speculative business. The board of the Theatre Investment Fund was largely composed of the most able brains in show business; I was there merely to see fair play. Lord Goodman, when welcoming me to my first meeting, told me that I would most probably find the meetings of the Theatre Investment Fund more entertaining by far than the shows in which the fund invested.

Patrick Ide was a stocky man with a bald head and fluffy white beard. He had entered the theatre while still a child, working in variety. When he drank a little too much, he was much given to quoting Shakespeare in rather an extravagant manner. Patrick and I often played slosh on the billiard table at the Garrick, usually dining together afterwards.

Patrick retired from the Old Vic, where he was in charge of Public Relations, and took on the job of running the Theatre Investment Fund. He was extremely close to Peter Saunders when I joined them. Much later, Peter took me on one side and told me, with great horror in his voice, that Patrick was homosexual. I was a trifle surprised: not that Patrick was homosexual, rather that anyone who had spent their life in the theatre should find this in any way unusual or, indeed, worthy of special attention.

From that moment Peter Saunders took against Patrick and worked to have him removed from his job. I retired and Peter took over my position as Chairman. Patrick left the Theatre Investment Fund. His life seemed empty. Failed business ventures led to selling his country home; physically he deteriorated, drank more, told the same jokes with greater frequency, and then died. A gregarious and friendly man, with what most people would regard as a host of friends, he died alone in his flat off St Martin's Lane. It was several days before his body was found.

I was, for a period, on The Arts Council and I have never disliked anything so much. Norman St John Stevas, now Lord Fawsley, was leaned on by Margaret Thatcher and forced to appoint me. It was, he said, like appointing an atheist to the Bench of Bishops. He was right, of course, as I have always held the view that the whole of that organisation should be closed permanently. It seems to me a most expensive way of giving away money. I have always advocated that the great national companies and galleries be given their grants direct from the Treasury and that they should be given pretty much whatever they need, for you either want to have great national companies and galleries, or you do not. Keeping them perpetually short of money is achieving neither a real economy, nor the point of having these institutions in the first place. As for the *avant-garde* arts, I would simply give the cash, if it must be given, to local councils. They are just as capable of distributing it as the members of The Arts Council, for the backing of artistic talent is a lottery. To the funds that are distributed thus, could be added the money saved by abolishing The Arts Council. I think many people would be surprised at the size of the sum that would be raised by doing this.

Industry should be encouraged to help the arts in the regions where it operates, just as industries help politics and charity in those regions. It is good business sense to do this and needs no subsidies. As for individuals, there should be no tax incentive for them to buy art, as is the system in America, for one person's tax incentive is another person's tax increase. People should buy art because they like it, much as they go to football matches because they like football.

I do not approve of the Lottery. It is shaming that the arts in Britain can only be supported by the proceeds of gambling. The Lottery is destructive of small businesses, destructive of charities and, in effect, just another form of indirect taxation. I do not understand why Mr Major's government, who want to privatise any state organisation that comes into their sight and then lay their hands on the cash that they can realise from selling these organisations, should set up the National Lottery, which is likely to become one of the largest nationalised industries that has been seen in years. The whole idea is not only daft and dubious, but it will lead Britain's people straight back to a dependence on the handouts of the Nanny state, this time with the Nanny heavily disguised as the National Lottery. Its funds, however, will be controlled, albeit at second hand, by ministers and the taxpayer will still pay in the end.

I hated my time on The Arts Council, an organisation that had so little to do with the arts. The meetings were tedious, the Chairman Kenneth Robinson, a former Labour Minister of Health, was pedestrian. I found the staff both arrogant and idle. I was Chairman at meetings of the subcommittee of Theatrical Touring, and the two officials sitting either side of me used to pass notes to each other behind my back and then giggle girlishly, which I suppose was only to be expected from one of them, who was a girl. I ignored their rudeness for several meetings but then I decided to put a stop to it. I moved my chair back from the table. They did the same, and continued with their notes. I moved again, and so it went on. Children in kindergarten would have known better how to conduct themselves. There was something terribly childish about these officials, in their grand Piccadilly premises, tossing sweets to artists. They spoke of artists as 'clients' and of their work as 'product'.

It was never satisfactorily explained to me why the Touring Committee, which I chaired, should spend money on a tour of *Oklahoma*, for if one show did not need a subsidy it was that. At the same time as they enthused about Rodgers and Hammerstein's musical, the officials wanted to halt the touring of the Glyndebourne opera. I could not stop the former folly, but I did put a stop to the latter and Glyndebourne continued to tour.

A counterpoint to The Arts Council, on which I sat in 1981, was the Council of the Institute of Contemporary Arts, which I joined in 1972. Lindy Dufferin was on this council, along with Martin Landau, who was considered something of a financial whiz kid in those days. He is now a highly successful property developer, with a genius for putting ideas together with the necessary finance and then making the whole package a reality.

The ICA was an unruly place; everyone got on with their own ideas. The tensions that grew out of the disparate activities of a group of very different characters, produced a creative tension. I, in my way, helped the ICA by giving them a new theatre and when they needed to raise some cash I also bought their Visitors' Book, a wonderful volume signed by many people famous in the arts and illustrated with original watercolours by Picasso, Miro, Henry Moore and many others. In time, when financial circumstances were not as happy as usual, I offered the Visitors' Book for sale at Sotheby's. Roland Penrose was furious. Why, I can never really understand, for he had sold the book to me for far more than it was worth. Why should I not sell it on to someone else, and try, at least, to recover part of my money? I had never made any promises to Penrose and at the time I bought the book he needed the money at the ICA to put on a show that would enhance his reputation. When I offered the book for sale, I needed the money to give to my bank. In the end, after he had grumbled and grumbled about the sale, I suggested that we buy the book together and give it to the British Museum. We did just that, and there it sits. I suppose very few people even look at that book, which is a shame, because it records well the art scene in Britain from the late 1940s to the late 1960s.

Lord Kissin was Chairman of the ICA. I never understood why, as he appeared not to care a jot for art in any form except perhaps for rather dull brown seventeenth-century Dutch painting. Lord Kissin conducted these meetings as if a bad smell was permanently under his nose. Lindy Dufferin went her own sweet way. Dr Jonathan Miller attended some meetings. Piers Paul Read attended most meetings and, at least, tried to be helpful. A new director, Peter Cook, was appointed. A young and soon to be eminent architect, tall and scruffy, with wide eyes rimmed by green glasses, Cook at the ICA was a breath of fresh air. He soon did battle with Penrose and the vested interests, while Lord Kissin continued to bore us all to distraction.

Meetings continued long into the evening, but little was decided because the ICA was not a place where you could decide things. It was an abstract experience, where thoughts were thrown into the air and practical solutions were not of much interest to most people on the council. Lord Kissin had one recurring theme – where is the money coming from – while most of those present felt that this was his problem. Round and round we went, tugging on the problem as if it were a bone and we so many mongrels in a yard. However, no sooner did we find a source of money, than the show that we would put on offended those who offered the money, or the show that they would have us put on offended those who worked at the ICA putting on shows. The number of meetings increased. I must admit that I am not good at meetings. In my view, the outcome of a meeting should have been decided before everyone sits down. The point of a meeting is to achieve an end, not to demonstrate personal brilliance. Meetings are for listening at, not for speaking. Listen carefully and fix the details afterwards. So many people want to speak at meetings, prolonging arguments, starting new arguments by the injudicious use of an irrelevant fact. Endlessly these meetings go on. If one person speaks, a whole troupe of others speak, as they feel that they must play their part, show how clever they really are by saying words that would have been best left unsaid.

Lord Kissin, whatever his other advantages, was in my view a bad Chairman of the ICA. His habitual end to a meeting was to announce that he would speak to the Prime Minister or Lord Goodman. In time I became as fed up as everyone else seemed to be, so I told Lord Kissin that I was bored out of my mind by his meetings, which were taking up far too much of my time and serving little purpose, and I would resign. Peter Cook, hearing these words, decided to resign as well.

The two of us had breakfast the next day with Cedric Price. What to do about all this, was the topic of our conversation. The answer was simple: to start a new arts organisation. What was more, start one that needed no money. We did just that. Borrowing a garage in Holborn, begging for pieces of equipment, we were in business. Peter Cook was the director on a small salary; lecturers gave their time free; artists whom we exhibited, hung their own work. Peter organised a whole series of lectures with Cedric Price; Buckminster Fuller and David Hockney were amongst those who, literally, gave them. We charged a small entrance fee and Art Net thrived. Norman Reid even brought a delegation of museum directors from the Soviet Union, who were visiting the Tate, to lunch. Art Net prospered and those interest in art and architecture attended its lectures in droves.

Peter Cook was delighted with its success, but could not understand why Cedric and I insisted on closing the whole thing down after five years. We had decided, when we started Art Net, that institutions only have a limited period when they are at their most useful. After that, it is a lingering death. This was not going to happen to us. Succeed or fail, we would run Art Net for five years, not one day shorter nor one day longer. And that is exactly what happened.

While I was at the ICA I became friendly with Lindy Dufferin, whose husband, Sheridan Dufferin, was the partner of John Kasmin the art dealer. Lindy was determined that I should meet a friend of

hers, Geoffrey Rippon, who held the post of Minister for the Environment in Ted Heath's Government, who were currently in power.
Lindy brought Geoffrey Rippon round to my house in Hans Place.

I had built this house myself, on a block of land leased from the
Cadogan Estate. Designed by the architect George West, it stood five
storeys high and had a street frontage of over forty feet. On the
ground floor there was a dining room and the entrance to a double-
height library, and a kitchen that looked onto a garden. In the
basement there was a staff flat and a private cinema. The first floor
had the entrance to both the balcony of the library and a single
drawing room, that ran both the length and depth of the house. This
room was twenty or so feet in height. Its windows ran from floor to
ceiling, the curtains were made from white PVC, the floor from
London paving stones, the walls painted white. At both ends hung
works by Morris Louis, a green-and-blue veil some eighteen feet
long and eight feet high as you came in, and over the fireplace, an
orange veil eight feet by six. The furnishings were eighteenth-century
English.

Geoffrey Rippon sat in a wing chair, drank champagne and, as he
talked, picked canapés from the tray on the table beside him. I
watched, fascinated, as he licked the caviar from the canapé and
then fed the redundant toast to my French bulldogs. Rippon, enjoying
himself mightily, seemed convinced that I was made for politics. I,
for my part, had nothing much better to do at the time. I had already
found that being a builder can become immensely boring. Much as I
had tried to break my routine, I was restless and uneasy. Only much
later did I discover that this condition had more to do with my own
nature than with whatever I might, or might not, be doing at any
particular time. Rippon said that he would invite me to lunch – he
would call and let me known when and where. I thanked them and
they thanked me as they left. I thought no more about the whole
idea until I received a call from a secretary saying would I please join
Geoffrey Rippon for lunch at the Head Office of ICI. This seemed
strange, but then the whole idea seemed strange.

At ICI I was clearly expected and shown to a dining room, where
I was greeted by Peter Thring, ICI's government relations officer.
Already present were John Harris, now Lord Harris of Greenwich,
who, in those days, was a right-hand man to Roy Jenkins; Geoffrey
Rippon; Geoffrey Tucker, who worked in Conservative Central Office
in charge of communications, and William Rogers. We ate the sort

of lunch that you might expect as the guests of an executive of ICI, we gossiped for a while, and then the others started talking about Europe. It was as if they assumed that I knew what they were talking about. The name ELEC – short for European League for Economic Cooperation – kept cropping up. I had, in truth, not the first idea what the whole thing was about; Geoffrey Rippon had clearly forgotten to tell me an important part of this story. By the end of lunch I found that I had been appointed Treasurer of ELEC.

My first job, I was informed, was to arrange a breakfast where we could all meet. This was no problem. I booked the Penthouse Suite at the Dorchester for eight o'clock on the appointed date. The one matter I really know about is how to organise a good breakfast. A choice of kippers, sausages, kidneys, scrambled eggs, bacon and tomatoes was laid on, and when the motley crew arrived they tucked in much as the Council of the Royal Court had tucked into the Marks & Spencer sandwiches. Soon we were joined by Douglas Hurd; Anthony Royle, now Lord Fanshawe; Graham Dowson, then Chief Executive of the Rank Organisation; Roy Jenkins, who was in Opposition, and Peter Carrington, the Secretary of State for Defence. There was much talk of a Referendum. There was, and my memory is quite sure on this point, no mention of a Federal Europe. The issue was quite clear: on one side were those who believed in the European Common Market and on the other, those who did not. The chief enemy, however, and the subject that concerned those at that meeting, was a dislike of the European Movement and, in particular, Ernest Wisterage, the man who ran that organisation. Ernest Wisterage was something of a *bête noire* as far as the Labour members of the group were concerned. The group met from time to time at either the Dorchester or the Rank Organisation's headquarters in South Street. Very much later I found out that a branch of the security services, called, I believe something like IDA (whose offices were in the building opposite the Tate Gallery), run by a man who is a Conservative Member of Parliament and was then employed by the Foreign Office, had been financing previous breakfasts and lunches for this and other bodies. They were, it seemed, set up to combat left-wing opposition to Britain remaining in Europe. Lord Armstrong, when he found out about this organisation and its dubious activities, persuaded Ted Heath to close it down. Now ELEC had need of a sponsor for its meals. I was cast by Geoffrey Rippon in that role, and as a result I was made Treasurer of ELEC.

On one occasion, after a long discussion at breakfast, Peter Carrington was dispatched to see Ted Heath to persuade him to have the European Movement abolished. At the next breakfast meeting, Tony Royle gave them the sad news that Peter Carrington had been kept waiting by the Prime Minister and had gone off in a huff, his mission unaccomplished. Vic Feather attended occasionally and another trade unionist, Jack Kemp, who held a post in Brussels. He was an able man, as well as being extremely likeable. We gossiped about many things both before and after these meetings. Once, he told us about Harold Wilson and Barbara Castle's attempts to curb the trade unions with their plan 'In Place of Strife'. Vic Feather, Jack Kemp and others had met with Barbara Castle and the Prime Minister at No. 10 Downing Street and, after much argument, Barbara Castle backed down. On the way back to the TUC headquarters in a taxi, Vic Feather said, 'Jack lad, did we do good work today?' Jack was doubtful about the wisdom of their actions. He was right, of course, because some seven years after he told this tale, the Trade Union Movement ceased to exist as a force in British politics. Vic Feather replied, 'You are probably right, but we taught that bitch, Barbara Castle, a thing or two.' How ironic it is that the Trade Union Movement could have been saved by a woman, Barbara Castle, and instead was brought down by another, Margaret Thatcher, when one of the characteristics of trade unions leaders in the 1960s and 1970s was their intense dislike of women.

Although this group was put together by Geoffrey Rippon, the two men who really made it work were Geoffrey Tucker and John Harris. Harris, as the years have gone by, has come to look more and more like his mentor, Roy Jenkins, which if you think about it is quite a trick as Roy Jenkins is medium-height and fat, and John Harris was in those days tall and slim. Geoffrey Tucker, in neither physique nor manner in any way resembled his mentor, Edward Heath. Heath was always mean spirited; Tucker open and generous with both his time and his knowledge. He was, I suppose, the first Conservative Party spin doctor, the man who brought Gordon Reece, the doyen of that trade, to Central Office.

Tucker was about the only person who believed that Edward Heath had a prayer of a chance to win the 1970 election, and is credited by many with the strategies that helped Heath win. Heath treated Tucker shabbily, but then Heath treated most of those who helped him shabbily and, in part, it was his meanness in distributing credit and subsequently reward, that brought him down in 1975.

Heath is one of those people whose sense of humour worked thus: he would say something to you that was mildly offensive; if you laughed, he was being serious, but if you took offence he was joking and you lacked a sense of humour. An example of this was his encounter with Geoffrey Tucker in the corridor of Central Office. 'Good morning, Sir Geoffrey,' was his greeting. Now it was the time when letters to those about to receive honours were shortly to go out. This greeting can only have led Tucker to believe that he was to receive the knighthood he richly deserved. Sadly, nothing came. Heath clearly knew that nothing would come when he made his little joke. Geoffrey Tucker was ill-treated by his Party in the matter of his reward for the service that he gave them. Part of the problem, I imagine, was that Tucker, an immensely Machiavellian man, did not tell the politicians how much he had really done for them. Many lesser individuals did nothing else but tell the often gullible politicians incessantly what a help they had been when, in fact, they had done little other than stand and watch.

There is little justice in the world of politics and perhaps it is right that it should be so. Tucker is neither tall nor short, smokes cigars, is usually overweight and untidily dressed. He bustles a lot and uses the phrase, 'We must get him [or her] in the mix.' He is immensely clever, but takes care to hide the fact. He has, in his time, helped more people out of political trouble than even he would care to count. Amongst those, I number myself.

I had not been long involved with ELEC before I discovered that the people with whom I ate such hearty breakfasts were not the people who openly ran ELEC. ELEC was actually run by some fairly stuffy old economists, of whom the late Sir Roy Harrod was one. The organisation, whose branches spanned western Europe, had a life of its own; the British branch, of which I was the Treasurer, was merely the nest in which that giant cuckoo, Geoffrey Rippon, had decided to squat. ELEC's British branch was simply the vehicle that he had chosen to use in a fight to keep Britain in Europe. Never try to take over an organisation that has members, Geoffrey Rippon told me; always choose a near-defunct organisation where the members have nearly all left as the vehicle for your covert operations.

Life moved on. Edward Heath's Conservatives lost two elections, which was enough to make any party dissatisfied with its leader.

There was a leadership contest and Margaret Thatcher stood against Ted Heath. Telephoning her husband, Denis, she announced. 'I am going to stand as Leader.' 'Leader of what, dear?' Denis asked. When she explained, he merely remarked, 'If you lose, you know that it will be the end of your career, but I support you wholeheartedly in whatever you decide to do.' Margaret Thatcher won and it was, for her, the beginning of a new and far more important career. Harold Wilson had by this time become Prime Minister, won two elections and was confident enough to call a Referendum. Peace broke out between ELEC and the European Movement or at least peace of a sort.

A new organisation, Britain in Europe, was formed. Run by Sir Con O'Neill, its sole purpose was to win the Referendum that would keep Britain in the Common Market. Lord Drogheda was made the Treasurer of Britain in Europe. John Sainsbury and I, his deputies, represented the interests of the European Movement and ELEC respectively. At a breakfast meeting with John Sainsbury we resolved the financial differences between our two organisations by agreeing to split any surplus funds in proportion to our normal incomes. The meeting took only a few minutes. I have always liked John Sainsbury and believe that he is one of the few businessmen who have any idea of how politics works.

I had found my role in this organisation. I took little interest in politics and paid a lot of attention to seeing that everyone had what they needed most – money. I also managed to borrow office space, furniture, typewriters, copying machines and transport, the ingredients which, along with telephones, make campaigning possible.

John Selwyn Gummer was sent by Geoffrey Tucker to see me. He needed money to help a publishing venture: a guide to the advantages of Europe, or some such document, which was to be distributed in schools. It was the first time I had met John Gummer, who at that time was in the publishing business, and I was not impressed with his plan, for the Referendum campaign was to last but a few weeks and it would be a few years before the children whom Gummer sought to influence ever had a vote.

Tensions grew as the campaign progressed. Lord Drogheda called Con O'Neill 'a desiccated old fossil'. Nobody liked Ernest Wisterage – at least that's how it seemed. Sarah Hogg was brought in to perform in the TV party politicals, and very good she was too. It was just a shame that her career on television was not more successful, for then we might all have been spared her efforts at Downing Street in the first years of the 1990s.

Drogheda divided the fund raising into industries. I suggested that Jeffrey, now Lord, Sterling, then a bright young property developer, should raise money from that industry. Sterling told me at the time that he had agonised over whether to become a concert violinist or a financial genius. In the event, he opted for money rather than art. Drogheda took the view that Sterling was not very respectable and unsuitable for the job; I argued that he was the perfect man for the job. My view prevailed and Lord Drogheda obviously underwent a conversion at the hands of Sterling, for a couple of years later, he sat as Chairman on one of Sterling's boards and Sterling was appointed Treasurer to the Jubilee Celebrations Fund, which Drogheda chaired. It was all a great success and Sterling became Sir Jeffrey and then Lord Sterling and started on the path to fame, with a fortune already firmly under his belt.

While the campaign was in progress, the Prime Minister and the Leader of the Opposition had both agreed to stand aside from the fight. I felt, however, that Margaret Thatcher's position as Leader of the Conservative Party was being undermined by her absence from the campaign. She was nowhere to be seen; Ted Heath was every-where. This was his crusade and he was going to win it mightily. Graham Dowson was of the same view as myself, so we set off together to visit Willie Whitelaw to tell him of our fears. This action was an indication of our political naivety, for Willie Whitelaw had just taken a sorry beating at the hands of Margaret Thatcher in the second round of the leadership contest. Furthermore, she had made Willie Whitelaw look foolish.

Gordon Reece had decided that Margaret Thatcher must be pro-moted as a housewife, so he had her filmed doing the washing up. Willie Whitelaw had allowed himself to be persuaded to do the same. Now Margaret Thatcher with a dish cloth and dirty dishes was one thing; Willie Whitelaw, in an apron doing the dishes, quite another. When Graham Dowson and I visited Willie Whitelaw I am sure the prospect of Margaret Thatcher rotting in oblivion was, to him, a thoroughly attractive one. In any case, Whitelaw knew full well that if Margaret Thatcher had joined that campaign it would most probably have been for the other side. In the end, however, she did speak in favour of the 'Keep Britain in Europe' party.

Tucker and Harris were a brilliant team. Opinion formers were lobbied and the general view spread about that anyone who wanted Britain to come out of the Common Market was totally mad. Just look at Wedgwood Benn, they would say, he wants to come out of the Common Market and everyone knows that he is quite mad. The campaign gathered in excitement; the money rolled in; the joint stock banks, who normally avoid political donations, promised £3 million. Industry was solidly behind those who manipulated the affairs of the Keep Britain in Europe Campaign. Meetings took place every morning; pounds of sausages and kidneys were consumed along with bowls of scrambled eggs. Tony Royle and I became good friends, as I did with a number of those who worked on the campaign. Jock Bruce Gardyne and I became very close. Jock was helping the campaign's treasurers raise money. As polling day approached we were cock-a-hoop, and with some justice, for as the results came in it became apparent that we in the Keep Britain in Europe Campaign had turned public opinion from sixty per cent against us to sixty per cent in favour of keeping Britain in the Common Market.

We had won, and by what a margin. The excitement at the party at the Waldorf Hotel was immense. We knew the result by lunchtime and then it was all over, just empty glasses and dirty plates. For the first time I felt the down that comes after the high of a political campaign. ELEC, or those who really ran ELEC, met for breakfast. The grander figures mostly failed to turn up. Geoffrey Rippon and Tony Royle were concerned for Douglas Hurd, who had no job and only a parliamentarian's income. We resolved the matter by appointing him General Director of ELEC. Conferences were arranged and took place. Now, however, the whole political emphasis in the country had changed. Now it was a case of whether Margaret Thatcher would last as Leader of the Conservatives and how Harold Wilson would tackle the unions and the economy. I set out for the country, where I was building the garden at West Green.

I did not care too much about politics and it was the principle of Europe that had attracted me. In defence, the Common Market would strengthen NATO; in trade there would be free trade in Europe and, as for employment, I wanted there to be freedom to work where you wished within Europe, furthermore, to live wherever you would like in Europe. All of these were good points. I never believed that the Common Market would stop a European war, because I believed that any war in Europe would be against the Russians. As for the European Union stopping Germany from going to war again, I believe that is rubbish. Certainly I do not believe that Germany will start a war in Europe again – there is no need, for Germany has the population to contest Europe democratically. It is the German instinct for war played on a larger stage that worries me, that Germany will take the whole of Europe to war with someone else.

I never imagined that the proliferation of red tape from Brussels would take place, because I used to visit Brussels and had no concept of how that place would grow. As for a Federal Europe, in the whole of the campaign we had just fought I can remember the subject being mentioned only on a few occasions and then only to confirm that such an idea was out of the question. I had been tricked, but I did not realise then, so I was not worried.

I was restless in the country. My garden did not progress as quickly as I might have wished. The building work took longer than I had expected. In the spring of 1974, the weather was fine; in fact, it was unusually hot. Unexpectedly, I had the chance to go to China. My now ex-wife, Sarah, and I joined a party who were mostly young Communists and we set out for Peking via Moscow.

Moscow was hot, but even in the sunshine it was tired and dull. I was always being mistaken for a Russian – perhaps it was because my clothes did not fit. We visited an underground station, which was of a magnificence usually reserved for palaces. Luckily, many of the great modern paintings and the works of the Impressionists were on show in Moscow rather than in St Petersburg; they are a truly wonderful collection. We stayed in a giant and particularly uncomfortable hotel. At breakfast an American whom I sat next to noticed that I had not touched my fried egg, which I must record was a greenish colour. 'Eat that egg,' he commanded. 'Why? It's horrible,' I replied. 'Eat that egg. For goodness' sake, eat that egg or we'll get it back for lunch.' Meals took hours to come and were inedible when they arrived. We visited the Kremlin Palace, where I was deeply impressed with the contents, the circus, where I was not impressed at all, and Lenin's Tomb, where the best part was queuing to get in.

China was extraordinary. It was the tail end of the Cultural Revolution when we arrived, so our itinerary was changed from a trip around the southern provinces to a journey through the industrial north instead. We visited Darien where there was not a great deal of artistic merit; industrial China, however, was fascinating. All over the landscape was filled with brand new boilers and parts for bridges.

No one seemed to know what to do with them. The factories had been told to start manufacturing boilers and bridges and no one had told them to stop.

We travelled through what must surely be the longest, if narrowest, forest on earth. It was four trees wide, two on either side of the railway track. We could see nothing of what was going on beyond them as we passed. The train moved at nearly a walking pace and it was stiflingly hot. In our cabin we had four bunks, two occupied by an American, who worked for a large corporation, and his wife, the other two by Sarah and myself. I would switch on an electric fan fixed just inside the compartment's door and, as I fell asleep, a hand would come around the door jamb to switch it off again. This went on all night. The stations were crowded; everywhere there were military officials and police officers. 'There is no crime in China, no cripples, no homosexuals,' our guide told us. 'So what is that building over there with the barbed wire?' 'That is for traffic offenders.' To be a traffic offender in China must have been quite a trick, for almost the entire population at the time moved around on bicycles. Only officials had cars.

Shenyang, the ancient capital, was lovely, its palace a miniature but far older version of the Forbidden City. The contents of its museums, while of great quality, were sparse in number. 'Everything has been stolen and taken to Taiwan,' I was told, and when I found a museum that was closed: 'History is being corrected.' As for temples found in Nagel's excellent guide but not on our itinerary: 'They are closed.' 'Well, can I see them from the outside?' 'They do not exist.' When shown Nagel's guide, they commented, 'A foolish man wrote that book.' The Communists on our tour, who made up most of the twenty or so people who travelled with us, would sit down outside museums and refuse to go inside.

We visited collective farms; chemical factories where we were shown disabled veterans of the Korean War; a motor car factory, where my American sleeping car companion explained to me that the Chinese produced in a whole day the same number of cars that one of Henry Ford's factories produced in the first ten minutes of their working day. The factory was chaos. We visited schools where pupils sat opposite each other, practising acupuncture by sticking pins in their partners' limbs. We also visited a hospital where a man was being operated on with only a pin to reduce his pain. He screamed and screamed until, exhausted, he fell into a daze. We visited a dentist where they were pulling teeth after squeezing the top of the nose, which they assured us worked as a pain killer. There was no equipment for drilling and filling teeth: the dentist merely pulled them out or left them in as the fancy took him.

We visited the opera, which was wonderful, and a stadium where acrobats demonstrated gymnastics and juggled with large china pots. On a trip to a university, I asked to see the library, for I was interested to see what the students read in English. The answer: Agatha Christie. Had they any ancient books, I asked. The professor, who spoke perfect English, said that many books had been destroyed in the Cultural Revolution, but he had saved some before he was sent for three years to work on a farm. I asked him how he liked farm work; he said he hated it. His books were truly wonderful. I could not read a word of them, but just to see these examples of the earliest Chinese printing and to hold them in my hand was an experience in itself. I have always thought that there was more to a book than just its contents. For me a book must look and feel just right. I have often bought a book for the design of its cover or, indeed, the quality of the paper it is printed on. Faber and Faber's poetry books of the 1950s come, I think, as near perfect as it is possible to get.

The old librarian was pleased to see us and be able to practise his English. In fact, I had the impression that for most of our trip we were being used by the Chinese in this respect. In the streets of these northern towns, a white person was a rarity. You would walk along a deserted street and turn to face a crowd of a thousand or so Chinese, who had silently followed you, and they would suddenly break into applause. Each evening after dining, which took place at six o'clock, we had a compulsory showing of a propaganda film. I enjoyed these films, for I had over the last few years become interested in propaganda. They were all in the well-tried tradition of Leni Riefenstahl, with flags, children, healthy adults, the males stripped to the waist, the females clad to the chin. Music played an important part in these propaganda films. It was only in the late 1970s that the Conservative Party began to understand the value of music as a means of changing a mood. Harvey Thomas, fresh from organising the production of Billy Graham's Evangelist meetings, was hired by the Conservative Party to cheer up their public meetings. This he did with a vengeance, much to the disapproval of many of the members of the parliamentary party, who thought the whole thing vulgar. The fact of the matter is that it worked and, like it or not, Harvey Thomas is in no small measure responsible for the Conservatives' electoral success in 1979 and the 1980s.

Back in Peking, I managed to get away from the rest of the party and wandered into the Forbidden City, where I came across a small courtyard with a dozen large blue-and-white bowls divided into two lines. At each bowl stood two women in ancient costumes. They used a bamboo scoop to take the water from the bowls, raise it in the air and pour it back. In these bowls were the most wonderful goldfish with great bulging eyes and long tails that hung behind them like the train on a silk wedding dress. It felt as if these women and the goldfish they attended were left over from another century. Indeed, I believe that may well have been the case. As I searched for my way out, I passed a group of Mongolians from the Gobi Desert, also wearing the costumes of another age and carrying swords. These were not guards, rather tourists on a visit to the capital.

The last evening, we all ate together at one table. There had arisen amongst this disparate group a camaraderie brought about by the often uncomfortable conditions of our journey.

Our trip had been paid for before we set out from England, and the organiser had insisted that payment be in cash. The conversation that evening turned to each of us revealing our occupations, Chinese wine was flowing, the conversation was relaxed. One of us, a woman who had said very little on the whole trip, when asked, announced that she worked for the Inland Revenue. There was a silence. 'I conduct interviews with people who may not be paying their tax. I really enjoy my job, the interviews are great fun.' The tour organiser turned quite pale and retired to bed.

All the time that we were in China we were out of touch with the rest of the world and had not the first idea what was going on. The Chinese could not answer questions about anywhere other than China, and then not many questions on that. Our guides knew that we were to return to England through Russia. 'Tell the people of Russia that the Chinese people like them, we Chinese are friendly to the Russian people. Tell them that it is the Russian Government that we do not like.' Each day we were given the same message. As for Margaret Thatcher, we were told that the British people would never elect a woman who stole milk from children. They were referring to the 'Thatcher Milk Snatcher' slogan that the Labour Party was running at the time. In China, the action of taking milk from babies has a special significance: the oriental stomach does not easily digest cow's milk, so the ruling classes used to take peasant women who were nursing children and, having murdered the child, 'steal' the mother's milk to drink themselves. Again we were given this message almost every day until one morning, near the end of our journey. That morning, a copy of *The Times* was circulated on our bus. It contained a full report of Margaret Thatcher's Helsinki speech. In the time it took to deliver one speech, Margaret Thatcher had become the Iron Lady in Russia and a solid ally of the Chinese people in China.

My next visit to China was very different. On my marriage in 1980 to Romilly, who was born in Shanghai, I was determined to take her to visit her birthplace. I applied to the Chinese Embassy in London and my application was greeted with enthusiasm. I held, at that time, the position of Deputy Chairman of the Conservative Party. The Conservatives were in power; chairmen and their deputies were greeted with great honour in China. The Chinese did not understand the difference between being a Deputy Chairman in the Chinese political party and one in a British political party. Romilly and I were invited to visit China and when there we were given three guides to take us wherever we cared to go.

The Chinese had changed dramatically in their attitude to foreigners in the intervening seven years. We visited not only Shanghai but the hospital where Romilly was born; we also visited the house where her parents had lived. Romilly's father had been the manager of the Chartered Bank in Shanghai. When the Communists arrived, he had been kept there for a couple of years. When I explain that he later became the Treasurer of the Special Forces Club in London, it is not hard to understand why they kept him.

We visited Suchow and its beautiful gardens. I remember leaving Suchow and at the station, parked on a siding, was a train of flat trucks loaded with bee hives, the beekeepers sitting on top. When the train set off, the bees followed it, flying in a thick black cloud. I was told that they moved every few weeks in this way – the bees, their keepers and their hives – following the blossoming of China's flowers.

As we travelled, one guide would sit with Romilly and the other two either side of me. They asked dozens of questions about the Social Democrats, who had just left the Labour Party to set out on their own. I knew these people well, for they were the faction in the Labour Party who were involved with the fanatically pro-European ELEC. I had little interest in their new party for, unlike many at Central Office who secretly sympathised with their position, I did not believe that they were going anywhere: all that they had to offer the public was an unreasonable reasonableness. In any case, the only Conservative defector was a man of no consequence. Today, the times are different. A new party could catch the public's imagination and succeed where these people failed. I felt very strongly that their right place was in the Labour Party, fighting for moderation. The defection of these people led to eighteen years of Labour lost in Opposition. This was all a bit hard to explain to my Chinese guides, so in imitation of their practice, when faced with a difficult political question, I told them some other old rubbish. The next day, they asked the same question again, and again, I gave them the first answers that came into my head. I wanted to talk about gardens and travelling bees, monuments, great rivers and, in particular, a rare rose that I sought for my collection, a rose that is one of the four grandparents of all the roses that we see today, which lives scrambling up the banks of the Yangtze river. 'That is not what you said yesterday,' my guide would point out. 'It is all a matter of emphasis,' I replied.

Back in England, after my first journey to China, I was invited to a dinner party that my father had organised at the Dorchester. His other guests were the Neaves and the Thatchers. I sat next to Diana Neave and she told me of the troubles from which the Conservatives currently suffered. No money – in fact, an overdraft of £500,000 – and no treasurers as they had just resigned. She told me the names of the two gentlemen who had just resigned and one of them, at least, was meaningless to me. I recommended John Sainsbury for the job and, if he did not want it, then perhaps Lord Drogheda, who had raised money for Britain in Europe. It was, I assumed, not a very onerous position. A couple of half-days a week, I was told, were what was involved. That evening I had a long conversation with Diana Neave about many subjects. This dinner was on a Wednesday and Diana invited me to take tea with her in her flat the next day. I turned up at four o'clock; we drank tea and talked for two hours about general matters, such as what the Tories should do to win the next election. Subjects that generally take a deal of study in order to arrive at a sensible conclusion we discussed over a cup of tea, so great was my ignorance. It all seemed so simple.

That evening when I returned to the country and my garden, progress there seemed negligible. A heatwave was well under way and with that heatwave, a drought. It did not matter whether I was away or here the whole time, nothing seemed to happen with any speed, except amongst the new trees, which died one after another. Water as we could, nothing could save them. The fox was at my wildfowl, as the lack of water in the lake made the island where they slept vulnerable. On Friday morning I was out working amongst my animals, feeding chickens. I heard the bell beside the garden door of my house, which was rung wherever I was needed on the telephone. I returned to the house to be told that Richard Ryder had telephoned. 'Who is he?' I asked. No one knew but the matter was urgent. I rang a London number. A voice said that I had reached Mrs Thatcher's office. I asked for Richard Ryder. 'Can you come and see Mrs Thatcher at eleven o'clock on Monday in her house in Flood Street?' 'Certainly,' I replied.

That weekend I thought little about Mrs Thatcher and a lot about how to keep foxes away from my stock and how to get water to my trees. Dead stock and dead trees were much on my mind.

11

Politics 1979–84

The following Monday morning in July, I visited Margaret Thatcher at her home in Flood Street, a terraced house of no great size, built of brick in the 1950s. I walked past a policeman, continued up a few yards of unimposing garden path and rang her doorbell. I was considerably excited at being asked to visit the new Leader of the Opposition and I had assumed it was further to discuss Conservative fundraising. Who would be suitable candidates for the post of Party Treasurer? I mulled a few names over in my mind; my favourite for the post was still John Sainsbury.

The door was opened by Margaret Thatcher, who seemed somewhat flustered. The telephone was ringing and there was no one else in the house to answer it. She indicated to me to go upstairs to her sitting room while she answered the phone. I stood upstairs for a minute or two and then she appeared, offered me a drink and told me to sit down at the same time. I could not think of what I wanted to drink, and suggested that I was fine without one. She insisted. I took the path of least resistance and settled for a gin and tonic. The phone rang again; she answered it and after that hurried downstairs to mix the drinks. When she reappeared, bearing my drink, she explained that the Treasurers of the Conservative Party, the Lords Ashdown and Chelmer, had resigned and that the appointment of the Treasurer was hers to dispose of as she wished. She would have to speak to Lord Thorneycroft, Chairman of the Party, who was in hospital at the time, but only to inform him of her choice.

I listened to all this, not quite knowing where it was leading. She then said how grateful she was that I had agreed to take the job. I was a bit taken aback, for no one had offered it to me, but as she was clearly happy for me to do it, what could it possibly matter? After all, I had never been offered a serious job before.

I thought, afterwards, I should have said that I must ask my wife, my family, my business partners, but I am extremely glad that I did not say any such thing, for that was not Margaret Thatcher's style. I seized this opportunity as if it was the greatest offered to me in my whole life, and so it turned out. I did not know then that I was to work closely for fifteen years with a woman who was arguably the best peace-time prime minister that Britain has had this century. Had I prevaricated, Margaret Thatcher would, I think, have borne with me; I would, however, have been a different person if I had needed all that sort of reassurance, and of much less use to Margaret Thatcher.

'You will need an office.' 'Will I?' Why should I need an office? I had a perfectly good office already. 'An office in 32 Smith Square.' And she went on to explain that the Party was half a million pounds in debt. There was, she said, a Treasurer's staff already at Smith Square.

I had only one request. 'Could I employ Jock Bruce Gardyne, who has worked with me on raising funds for the Referendum Campaign?' 'Of course.' Jock was a man she greatly respected. 'It is a shame that he is no longer in Parliament. He must be put back there as quickly as possible.'

I walked down her garden path, brimming with excitement, 'Good-bye,' the policeman said, as I left through the small wrought iron gate. Security in the mid 1970s was not the problem that it is today, but that friendly-looking constable, in front of the Thatchers' house, was a deceptive figure. A cat burglar that year made the mistake of trying to rob the house. As he climbed across the roof, alarms went off and lights came on, and from nowhere armed police appeared and the wretched man put up his hands, shouting, 'It's all right, I am only a burglar.'

On the following Wednesday, I returned. I rang the doorbell, was let into the house and again shown upstairs. There was one small problem: both Chelmer and Ashdown had withdrawn their resignations. But not to worry, I was told, the Party would have three Treasurers.

'We will go in your car, Alistair.' At least, that was the idea until Margaret Thatcher caught sight of my smart new Mercedes Benz. We went to Smith Square in her old Rover, driven by its Government driver. My car was swiftly changed for a British-made Jaguar.

At Smith Square there was a reporter and a photographer. Margaret

Thatcher took me a few yards down the pavement and, as we turned to walk into 32 Smith Square, there was a photographer from the *Daily Telegraph*. She said quietly to me, 'Take your hand out of your pocket.' I did, and the result was that in the *Telegraph*'s photograph we seemed to be walking hand in hand.

Inside Smith Square there was an atmosphere of almost total hostility. The Chief Agent, Richard Webster, met us and we were shown to the internal conference room, a room that in those days was decorated with rather bad murals of London acting as backdrops to spokesmen when they gave press conferences. It was, as always, airless, hot and dingy.

Margaret Thatcher introduced me and asked me to say a few words to the departmental heads and the various vice-chairmen and chairwomen who were assembled. I mumbled some uninspired junk and Margaret Thatcher left. I did not see her again for some weeks, as she went to America.

On her return, I was asked to attend her offices in the House of Commons. I was, I must confess, nervous at having to report how I had got on, for I had really not 'got on' at all. She was friendly and asked a question or two. Encouraged, I launched into a dissertation on how Central Office was run and on how it might be run. Then came the real questioning. She was direct and extremely incisive. I, for my part, realised that I was deeply out of my depth. For the first time in my life I felt cold sweat running down my spine. I understood, then and there, that I, at least, could not bluff Margaret Thatcher with broad generalisations and smart but meaningless answers. Margaret Thatcher is not much taken with slick quotations, either. Many years later I quoted Jimmy Maxton, the Communist Member of Parliament, to her: 'You should not be in the bloody circus unless you can ride two horses at once.' I received the reply: 'Quite a trick if they are going in opposite directions.' This was a typical Thatcher reply to such a proposition. Having embarked on a course of action, she saw compromise as an about-turn; as her speech writer, Ronnie Miller, so aptly inserted in one of her most famous speeches: 'The lady is not for turning.'

On that first morning, Ashdown and Chelmer introduced themselves and took me upstairs to the Treasurers' quarters, an oblong room with two large, old-fashioned carved oak desks. Between them, in the middle of the room, was a small functional desk at which a copy typist might normally work. This desk was mine. I was not particularly disturbed by this attempt to show me my place, for I have seldom worked at a desk. I usually sit in a comfortable armchair or walk around, often taking telephone calls standing.

My desk had no telephone; the two larger desks and their rather grander owners, the Lords Ashdown and Chelmer, each had one. The three of us entered the office together and they went straight to sit behind their desks. I had little option but to do the same. 'We do everything together,' said Lord Chelmer. 'Even go to the lavatory together,' said Lord Ashdown, a man given to vulgar interjections. The telephone rang, Lord Ashdown answered it and then made a big production of passing the rather heavy and old-fashioned receiver to me. They told me about the duties of the Treasurer. The telephone rang. And again. It was for me. And it rang again. And again. And each time the calls were for me. Finally, Lord Ashdown instructed the switchboard not to put through any more calls.

Our duty, as far as Ashdown was concerned, lay mostly in the fact that we had to fight the Chairman, Lord Thorneycroft, and his Deputy, William Clark. In between, we might try to raise some money. Ashdown and Chelmer, I was given to understand from Ashdown, did most of the latter. There were people of little importance, however, who might give the Party money, and it would be helpful if I could deal with them.

Clearly I was not going to get on with Ashdown. He loved Harold Macmillan to the extent that he had bought a house in the country next door to the ageing ex-prime minister and he disliked Peter Thorneycroft because Thorneycroft had resigned as Chancellor from Macmillan's Government. Ashdown also hated Margaret Thatcher because she had replaced Ted Heath, about whom he would slobber with excitement.

Ashdown considered himself a pretty grand figure. He came from a most extraordinary family of humble origins, and was one of three brothers who all reached the House of Lords, albeit by different routes: one as a Liberal peer, another as a Labour peer (he was Harold Wilson's doctor) and the third, Ashdown himself, as Treasurer of the Conservative Party. I took little notice of Ashdown and his antics, apart from trying to thwart his attempt to stab me in the back or any part of my anatomy that I could not easily keep an eye on.

Chelmer, a reserved and cunning man, kept to himself his thoughts about Thatcher, Thorneycroft and myself. I would not have lasted a week but for several pieces of luck. The first was that in the Director of the Treasurers' Department, General Sir Brian Wyldbore-Smith, I found an ally. Brian Wyldbore-Smith is a man of considerable class and great ability and when it comes to getting money out of people, there are few to match him. He led a troop of exemplary men who worked, at that time, for salaries that were derisory. Central Office's view, when I arrived, was that these people were useless and should be removed. That view did not change, and after I left, Chris Patten set about removing them. I understood but never applauded the fact that, after the 1992 election in which, after all, there were two great losers, Chris Patten and Neil Kinnock, both men were appointed to important posts. The former became Governor of Hong Kong, the latter a Commissioner in Brussels. It was as if these individuals had accomplished a considerable triumph rather than suffered rejection by the electorate of Britain.

At first I fell for the idea that the generals and their staffs were useless but, after a couple of weeks, I began to see the sense in employing these fine people. Wyldbore-Smith and I became close friends and I have only the highest respect for the work that he did for both the Conservative Party and myself. His honesty and integrity were of the highest order and his judgement invaluable to the Conservative Party.

My views were not accepted by Christopher Patten, who was then the Director of the Research Department. Years later, on becoming Party Chairman, he made it his prime objective to streamline the party organisation and to get rid of both Wyldbore-Smith and Brigadier Sir Henry Lee, his right-hand man and the conscience of the Conservative fund raisers. Along with them, the Party lost many of the most able of a whole group of military men. 'Too old,' was Patten's paltry excuse. Old they may have been, but they were wise. Many of the Party's current scandals arise directly from the fact that they have never been replaced by men of similar calibre or experience.

Patten came to lunch with me shortly after I became Treasurer. I was living at the time in a suite in the Dorchester and usually lunched there. I can remember him tucking into a plate of oysters, his blond forelock falling forward, hiding both his face and the oyster that he was eating. You can always tell the character of a man when he eats oysters and I marked Patten down as greedy. Years later, in the 1992 general election, a cheer was heard to come from my house in Great College Street when Patten lost his seat. Lady Thatcher was dining in the house at the time. There were two televisions showing the Election results, one upstairs that only Thatcher and a few others watched, the other downstairs, where there were those who cheered Patten's defeat. Any Conservative Party Chairman who allows a large proportion of the shopkeepers in his constituency to go out of business without trying to see that something is done to change the economy of the country, deserves to lose his seat.

Ashdown and Chelmer were heavily engaged in the politics of the Conservative Party and were interested in questions like: who should become the Area Chairmen of the Wessex Area, or who should become the Chairman of the National Union Executive Committee (a post that, on the face of it, seems to be extremely powerful but has, in reality, only negative power and not a lot of that).

I carried no such baggage. Always an early riser, I was usually in Central Office by seven-thirty a.m. Often the only other occupant of the building at that hour was Shirley Oxenbury, the Chairman's secretary. I cannot write too highly about her. She has spent her career at Central Office seeing successive Chairmen reinvent the wheel. A new Chairman always feels that it is his duty to try to change the way things are done. In fact, Central Office is yet another bureaucracy that plods along most of the time and springs into life every five years to fight an election. Its staff are often poorly paid; many of those who work there are, in fact, volunteers or tantamount to volunteers. The trick of successful chairmanship is to lead Central Office, not to try to change the way the place is run. Central Office is not a business. It is a political machine and political machines are best driven by politicians. The concept of budgeting does not work in politics, as money must be spent irregularly and sometimes in great quantity to anticipate a political initiative by an opponent and, on other occasions, to create opportunities for your own politicians. Sometimes, however, the machine just ticks over. The problem with budgets is that the departments have an overwhelming desire to spend them. The allocation of money to a prefixed pattern takes away the politician's flexibility and ability to surprise an opponent.

After that first day in Central Office, I came to the conclusion that I would need friends. In the Treasurers' Department I had Brian Wyldbore-Smith and Henry Lee; Jock Bruce Gardyne joined us after a few weeks. Luckily he was a friend of William Clark, Thorneycroft's Deputy, who kept an iron hand on his Chairman's expenditure. Clark, however, was prepared to make an exception in the case of employing Jock. Clark and I always got along rather well, for we had similar political views and a mutual enemy in Ashdown. Clark's wife, a pleasant woman, believed that I looked just like her son. I was thirty-two years old at the time, the youngest Treasurer ever to have been appointed to the Party. I think it was pure fear about what I would do as sole Treasurer, a fear that sprang from knowledge of my background and youth, that caused the two elderly Treasurers to withdraw their resignations.

I spent the afternoon of the day I was appointed sitting in that same airless conference room of Smith Square at a meeting of the Conference Agenda Committee. In the evening I was taken to dine at Annabel's by Jeffrey Sterling. He was most careful to tell me that in taking on the job of Treasurer, I had made a terrible mistake. Margaret Thatcher, he said, would not last six months and the Labour Party were set for several terms.

As I left Annabel's, I met Marcia Falkender coming into the night club. 'Congratulations,' she said. 'If only you had told us that you were looking for a job, we would have found something for you.' I knew Marcia quite well by this stage.

Every week, on Wednesdays, I barely made it to Smith Square by the time that the weekly directors' meeting started at nine-thirty a.m. It was my habit to breakfast with George Weidenfeld, of whose publishing company I was then a director. I would have liked breakfast to start at eight o'clock, but he made certain never to appear from between his highly impressive bedroom doors until eight-thirty. George had a cup of coffee and a cigar; I always ate a plate of fried eggs and bacon, sitting on the edge of a large sofa with my plate on a low coffee table in front of me. I was bent almost double as I ate. Each week, George and I would spend a few minutes on publishing and then get down to serious political gossip.

On other days, I took breakfast with my intellectual gymnast Cedric Price, with whom I limbered up for a testing day at Central Office. We ate bacon sandwiches in his Store Street office, I drinking mugfuls of tea, while Cedric eased the joints of his ungainly body with a glass of brandy. When we did not meet in Cedric's White Room, we ate at the Fox and Anchor in Smithfield or the Connaught. The White Room, whose name completely describes it, is often called East Grinstead by Cedric. When he has telephone calls, his secretary need not lie, but only explain that she cannot put the call through as Mr Price is in East Grinstead. The White Room has no phone.

During the summer of 1975 I had a series of meetings with politicians and apparatchiks working in 32 Smith Square. Alec Todd, who was then Director of Communications at Central Office, was kindly and explained to me that it was important that I got to know the political commentators in the media. He brought Harry Boyne, the doyen of the Parliamentary Lobby, to lunch. A highly respected figure, Harry and I got on extremely well and he subsequently worked for me in the Treasurers' Department during the 1983 and 1987 elections, answering enquiries from the press on Party funding. As a result of Todd's introductions a number of pleasant pieces about me appeared in the newspapers. Arnold Ashdown was furious. He publicly reprimanded Todd and I was forbidden ever to speak to the press again.

Alec Todd continued to encourage me to meet as many journalists as possible, and in all the years I was Treasurer, I did exactly that. I was lucky in many respects, but particularly in the fact that I was a member of the Garrick Club, where most of the top political writers eat their lunch. I made, at that time, many of the friendships that I still enjoy today.

I have never understood the secrecy that is supposed to surround Conservative Party Treasurers. If asked a question, I would try my hardest to explain the answer as I saw it, not to complicate but rather to simplify the issue. Journalists could come and go from my office in 32 Smith Square whenever they wished. During the 1987 election, Peter Jenkins was drinking champagne in my office when, looking at the clock, he jumped up as if to leave in a hurry. 'Why must you leave?' I asked. 'I must meet my wife, Polly. She's waiting downstairs.' 'Bring her up for a drink,' I suggested. 'Don't you know that she is in charge of the Social Democrats' Campaign organisation?' I didn't see that this made the slightest bit of difference, so Polly Toynbee joined us. Looking back, however, I can see now that the Social Democrats might not have been happy to have their Chief Executive drinking champagne with the Conservative Party's Treasurer whilst an election campaign was being fought.

I always liked Peter Jenkins. He was a highly intelligent, if establishment-oriented individual, whose view of the world and Britain's place in it corresponded exactly with that of the Foreign Office. Margaret Thatcher turned all that on its head: foreign policy was no longer run according to rules of Peter Jenkins and the Foreign Office.

After Margaret Thatcher left Downing Street in 1991, one day at lunch with Stephen Fay and Peter Jenkins, I discovered the real gripe that Jenkins had against her. Margaret Thatcher had never invited him to Downing Street. Charles Powell, he claimed, had put his name on the guest list often enough, but Thatcher had crossed it off. I do not know if this was true or merely a kind way of explaining to his friend why he could not get him invited to Downing Street. Either way, Charles Powell should have kept his mouth shut, for his words made a powerful enemy for Margaret Thatcher. I much preferred Peter Jenkins when he talked about art than politics. His views on the former were far grander than his nit-picking approach to the latter, perhaps because he knew a lot less about art than politics.

The last time I saw Peter was in Venice. He was sitting alone in the Church of San Giorgio Maggiore and I invited him to lunch. He came to my house and we had a pleasant lunch, despite Alexander Hesketh taking him to task over some particularly wet view that he was promoting. After lunch, as he walked away, I had a strong feeling that something was wrong. 'Either Peter Jenkins has had a serious row with his wife or he is going to die,' I said to Hesketh. Within a few weeks Peter Jenkins was dead.

On my appointment as Treasurer, I had many letters. One of the most kindly was from John Peyton, a man not greatly known for his benevolent use of words, who wrote to offer me any political help that he might be able to give. (He once told me that he had perfected the art of rudeness and that it had, for him, become a formidable weapon.) As Treasurer of London Zoo, he sought my expertise on fundraising. I was involved with the zoo world at that time because of my zoo in Broome, but even if I had not been, I would still have helped John Peyton, for he was a close friend of my father's. London Zoo was in a terrible plight when John took over its treasurership and to help him in his task I introduced him to David and Frederick Barclay. John came to know the Barclays and, as a result, became Chairman of their Medical Foundation, a job he takes immensely seriously. He is meticulous in investigating every application for money and sometimes searches out applicants who have not even applied. His time at London Zoo was frustrated by the small-minded confusion of most of his colleagues. Some years later I joined him on the Zoo's board.

The problem with London Zoo was that it occupied cramped and old-fashioned premises in Regent's Park, while its country zoo at

Whipsnade had never been properly developed. My plan was to greatly reduce the scale of the Regent's Park Zoo, leaving only a zoological presence there such as you find in New York's Central Park, while greatly expanding the zoo at Whipsnade. Whipsnade has one unique factor: the Whipsnade Zoo Planning Act, which in effect makes the trustees of the zoo the planning authority for the thousand acres or so of land.

My plan called for the extending of the land at Whipsnade. The Barclays, whose generosity to Regent's Park Zoo had been enormous, offered to provide the necessary money to buy more land at Whipsnade, land which was for sale at the time. My plan was that the zoo be extended into a series of pavilions, each sponsored by an oil or chemical company, and each dedicated to some aspect of the natural world. Hotels would then be offered sites in the new zoo, and there would be conference centres and a rail link to London. Many of the animals would be kept within vast glass domes, under which the appropriate climate could be created. The zoo would be open day and night to those staying in its hotels. This would all be financed by selling space to the companies that sponsored the exhibits and the hotels that used the conference centre. Whipsnade would become an ecological Disneyland, where all the exhibits and experiences were genuine. The Board of London Zoo barely listened to this scheme, so bogged down were they with the detail of next week's wages and whether or not the grand Natural History Library should be kept or sold.

When I first came to Central Office, I had never been to a Party Conference before and that first conference of Margaret Thatcher's period of leadership was not an easy introduction to these ritual gatherings. Looking back on those years it is too simple a conclusion to come to that all went well in the beginning and that Margaret Thatcher dominated the Conservative Party. It would also be an erroneous conclusion. Factions within the Party fought like mad in 1975. Happily, we were in Opposition and the press took little interest. Edward Heath attended the conference, causing a considerable amount of tension, all of which was part of his general plan. He, like Jeffrey Sterling, believed that Margaret Thatcher would not last until Christmas.

It was thought by various advisers that Margaret Thatcher should go to Heath's suite for a drink for a semi-public reconciliation, a meeting which Willie Whitelaw was to arrange. Margaret Thatcher was all dressed up and waiting to go, but the call from Whitelaw never came. She waited and waited. Eventually Gordon Reece rang Heath's suite to speak to Whitelaw, who merely told him that the meeting was not on. Having sat waiting for a couple of hours, Margaret Thatcher was deeply upset. Tears filled her eyes, not at Heath's rejection of her attempts at peace, but at Whitelaw's casual attitude to the whole affair.

At that conference I can remember only too well the Chairwoman of the Tory Ladies' Committee. She was in floods of tears because she had been asked to present Margaret Thatcher with a giant teddy on the last day of the conference, which was Margaret Thatcher's birthday. 'I do not want to give anything to that woman,' she said as the Party's PR people tried to persuade her. Her reaction was common amongst Tory activists. All were deeply loyal to Ted Heath; then, when she was in Government, deeply loyal to Margaret Thatcher, and I am sure now deeply loyal to John Major. Traditional Tories hated Margaret Thatcher's hair, hated her voice, hated her accent and, indeed, many of them hated the whole idea of her. She was, like so many of them, a woman. Along with the feminists, they disliked her because she had achieved the leadership of the Tory Party whilst asking for no concessions as a female. As she embraced radical ideas, she was the very opposite of the sort of leader they wanted. In time, the Tory activists learned to love her. The feminists justified their position by pretending to themselves that really Margaret Thatcher was a man.

On the last morning of that conference, the Party hierarchy was gathered behind the stage, drinking coffee from delicate cups. Margaret Thatcher was missing; the Chief Agent was worried. Search parties were despatched in all directions. They found her where leaders ought to be found as battle preparations are made, amongst the troops. She was standing gossiping with a group of Tory women on the floor of the hall. Her speech that day was not the best she has ever made, but it was filled with power and it firmly established her as Leader of her party. Denis told me later that Margaret was fairly relaxed about that speech; he on the other hand was frightened as never before. 'As we drove from the hotel to the hall, I held her hand all the way. I was more frightened than when I was on the beaches at Anzio'. Jeffrey Sterling's friends, in the know, were now predicting that she might last till the spring.

My main and most important ally in Central Office was Peter Thorneycroft. He was extremely kind to me for many years and I believe that it was his early kindness that made our later falling out so bitter. I got to know him extremely well during the latter part of 1975. Once I had discovered that he was Willie Whitelaw's cousin, that they had been at school together and were extremely close, their lines of communication became clear to me. What Thorneycroft felt about me, at that time, I do not know, because he always played his cards close to his chest. I do know, however, that he regarded Arnold Ashdown as a perfect menace, and Eric Chelmer as someone he could well do without at Central Office.

It was great fun campaigning during the late 1970s with Peter Thorneycroft. He would address a gathering of businessmen and then I would collect their money. He was a brilliant orator. He spoke just from a series of headings as an *aide-mémoire* for a speech that he had written, corrected and learned by heart beforehand. 'The most invaluable asset that a speaker can have is a stutter,' Thorneycroft opined, as it alerts the audience. 'Stutter for a moment and they come alive. They sit wide awake expecting the old fellow to break down, they don't want to miss a moment of the speaker's humiliation.' I once watched Harold Macmillan use the same technique with a pair of glasses. He moved his head and his hand-held glasses closer and closer to his notes as if he could not see them; the audience waited with bated breath as disaster seemed inevitable.

In the 1970s Thorneycroft had two assistants, who have subsequently become well known in Conservative circles. The first was a sensitive young man called Alan Howarth; the second was Tristan Garel-Jones.

Howarth was pleasant and erudite, with a considerable knowledge of the arts. Many of my dealings with the Chairman's office were through him, as he was usually most helpful. He had political ambitions, but did not get selected for a winnable seat until 1983, by which time he had left Central Office, a victim of the fallout when Thorneycroft resigned. I was not sorry to see Howarth go from Central Office in 1981, for although he had loyally supported Thorneycroft when I had my disagreement with him, I always felt that Howarth's heart may well have been in Thorneycroft's camp but his eye was on my job as Deputy Chairman and that Thorneycroft had promised him this position. Margaret Thatcher had always had reservations about Alan Howarth. He was, she thought, not one of us. Howarth appeared right wing but there was a weakness in there; somewhere perhaps deep inside him was a puritanical disapproval of how the Conservatives went about their business. In any event, it took great courage for Howarth to cross the floor of the House, a practice that is regarded as the darkest treachery by boorish figures on both sides. I regard the fact that a person can change sides as the very essence of politics. For what are politics about if they are not about converting people, both the electorate and the elected, to your point of view? Alan Howarth left the Conservative benches in 1995? and joined the Labour Party.

Tristan Garel-Jones was the junior PA to Thorneycroft. No one really knew why he was there. No one, including Thorneycroft, knew what he was supposed to be doing. In fact, he did nothing except listen, and file words and actions away for later use. He liked to get himself involved with other people's business. For instance, Marcus Fox, now Chairman of the 1922 Committee, then in charge of Candidates at Conservative Central Office, had trouble with his secretary, a woman with whom he had fallen out and whom he wished to dismiss. Garel-Jones inveigled himself into the position of resolving the problem. Marcus Fox must surely still be in his debt for that invaluable help.

Asked what were his ambitions should he be elected to Parliament, Garel-Jones replied, 'I want to be in the Whips' Office, nothing more nothing less.' There were a few of us sitting drinking champagne in Central Office and it was late in the evening. 'Why on earth the Whips' Office?' Garel-Jones was asked. A staunch teetotaller, he replied, 'In the Whips' Office I can find out about other people's private lives.' The man meant what he said. In those days, I felt Garel-Jones was a cold fish and a dull fellow. However, he learned quickly and, buying a grand house that once belonged to Harold Macmillan, he set out to become a political host, gaining a great reputation as a wit and a fine fellow amongst the Westminster Lobby. Later believed by a number of people to be a moving force behind the dismissal of Margaret Thatcher, he now appears as a fanatical supporter of John Major. Garel-Jones is credited with giving much advice to Major, but anyone with a brain in their head, eyes in the front of it, and ears at its side will know that whoever it is that John Major is getting advice from, that person has landed the Prime Minister into a disproportionate amount of trouble.

Peter Thorneycroft told me that when Garel-Jones left to become a

Member of Parliament, it was a considerable relief to him, for 'Garel-Jones hasn't got a political idea in his head.' It is true that he did not display a natural bent for the 'stand up straight and give it to them as it really is' politics of Peter Thorneycroft. Incubated in the Whips' Office, Garel-Jones hatched in the Foreign Office. Fanatically pro the European Union, he thrived in the atmosphere of the Conservative Party of the 1990s, one of festering suspicion, personal attacks and cunning ploys. The stuff of oblique personal attack was to this man as manure is to a vegetable marrow.

Janet Young, on the other hand, who was also then working in Central Office, was completely different from Garel-Jones. Puritanical, straightforward, honest and immensely tiresome, this woman's influence permeated Central Office during the days of Opposition. She had no feel for the grandeur of politics on the national stage, not to mention the international stage. Attending a grand dinner in New York, as the representative of Margaret Thatcher, Janet Young turned to the guest on her left. 'And what do you do?' she asks. 'I'm in the media,' he replies. 'And what is your name?' 'Walter Cronkite.' Moving to the guest on her right, she repeats her first question and gets the answer, 'I am in newspapers.' So, innocently, Janet Young repeats the second question, which brings the reply, 'Rupert Murdoch.'

Janet Young was prone to accidents. During the 1979 election, the polls suddenly took a dip on the last Thursday before polling day. I noticed this phenomenon also in 1983 and in 1987. I used to keep a chart in my office that demonstrated that the trend seemed always to change on that day. In all three of those elections, the polls swung back within a day or two. I began calling the last Thursday before Polling Day 'Wobbly Thursday', because this sudden change for the worse threw panic into even the sternest of nerves. Janet Young was not amongst those with nerves that were made of stainless steel. She was inclined to be as panicky as a highly strung filly and when the going appeared to get tough, she was all over the place.

On that particular Thursday, Janet Young was on tour with Margaret Thatcher. They were sitting eating their dinner when the news came through of these bad opinion polls. 'Margaret,' said Janet, 'this is very serious indeed. You have no alternative but to bring Ted [Heath] into the campaign. You must promise him a senior seat in the Cabinet. If you do not, all is lost.'

Margaret Thatcher did not reply. She simply left the table and went to bed. By the next evening, the polls had changed again and the Conservative campaign was back on track.

Janet Young was incapable of understanding Margaret Thatcher, a woman who did not want power for power's sake, rather power to carry through reforms that she believed in, and those reforms could not have been carried through with Edward Heath sitting at the Cabinet table. Janet Young's solution to a non-existent problem was not a solution that Margaret Thatcher could even contemplate.

After a sojourn in the Foreign Office, where the civil servants tried to educate her as to the world's geography, Janet Young became Leader of the House of Lords. Having been Leader of the House of Lords for a while, she then lost her job in a reshuffle. Not surprisingly, she was pretty put out about this – people tend to get cross when they get the sack. Janet Young decided to complain to Lord Soames. 'I know just how you feel,' Christopher Soames replied. 'I felt just like that when you took my job.'

I was by now fully engaged in the business of raising money for the Conservatives. Daily I met a series of industrialists; each day I lunched with Jock Bruce Gardyne and a likely customer and sometimes a politician, more often than not a member of the Shadow Cabinet. I travelled the country, going to constituency meetings and fundraising dinners. In between all this, I attended meetings at 32 Smith Square.

I was also responsible for arranging industrial conferences, where the various members of the Shadow Cabinet could address several hundred industrialists at a time. One of these conferences was in Glasgow. As Jim Prior and Margaret Thatcher waited behind the scenes before the conference began, Jim Prior asked her if she had a cold. He had, he said, heard her on the radio that morning and she sounded very sexy. Margaret Thatcher smiled at him and innocently replied, 'I don't need a cold to be sexy, Jim.' Jim Prior flushed a bright red. I always liked him. I did not often agree with him, but he is an honest and largely straightforward man, who actually believes in what he says. There is no trace of opportunism in him. The members of John Major's Cabinet do not compare very favourably when put alongside the likes of Jim Prior.

The atmosphere in the Party was different in those days. Jim Prior was, I suppose, Margaret Thatcher's political enemy, yet when his research assistant Richard Needham was in need of money to supplement his income, I found no difficulty in passing some to him.

Margaret Thatcher was in favour of Jim Prior being well served.

By 1993, the Conservative Government had become so edgy that the same Richard Needham, while being entertained to dinner by Eve Pollard, the then Editor of the *Sunday Express*, looked across to the table where I sat (I was a columnist for the *Sunday Express* at the time) and said words to the effect that if I did not cease my criticism of the Government, then the executives of my family's construction company would find difficulty in being included on the overseas trips that he regularly made with British industrialists in search of business. This was a stupid and offensive threat to make to a writer, regardless of whether that writer's editor was present or not. That evening he had certainly become agitated because I was criticising the Government. Luckily Eve Pollard thought he must have been joking.

We came, after a summer offensive in 1978, to the election in May 1979. Thorneycroft was enthusiastic about the summer offensive. 'All the politicians are away. We can do what we like, take all the actions that need to be taken in order to win.' He was right, because whenever a poster or party political had been prepared before, various members of the Shadow Cabinet or their junior assistants usually found a reason for changing it. Consistently, for four years, we at Central Office bored the electorate to death with our carefully considered and scrupulously edited propaganda. Gordon Reece, who was close to despair over this, had advocated reducing party politicals to less than five minutes or even doing away with them altogether. In the summer of 1978 he introduced the firm of Saatchi and Saatchi to the Conservative Party. More importantly, he produced Tim Bell. He was like a breath of fresh air; his arguments were logical and well constructed, and the advertisements that his firm produced had humour in them as well as humanity, two qualities that the Conservative Party lacked in their presentations in 1975. Tim Bell had an immediate rapport with Margaret Thatcher. It was not that he could or did persuade her to do anything so much as he could present what she did do in the best possible light.

Margaret Thatcher took a strong personal interest in these advertisements. She would allow no distortion of the human form; caricatures were out. No use of the Union Jack was to be made that in any way demeaned the flag: a poster of a baby with a Union Jack as a nappy was scrapped. Nor was use to be made of nurses or doctors.

The poster campaign 'Labour Isn't Working', which Bell and

Saatchis produced, was brilliant. When it was launched, the poster so angered the Labour Party that they were vociferous in their complaints. The result was our poster made every front page of the next day's national newspapers, netting the Conservative Party millions of pounds' worth of free advertising. At that stage, I was the sole Treasurer – Ashdown had died and Chelmer retired almost a year after I had joined them – and I spent every penny of the Party's money on that campaign, plus quite a lot of money that we did not have. By October, I was sitting in the waiting room at Saatchi and Saatchi, working out what I would say to the two brothers about their account, for we had no money to pay them. The proposition was simple: 'Insist on payment now and you may damage the Party beyond repair; the Conservatives will lose the general election and your customers will most likely blame you. Sit on the debt and the Conservatives will win, and you two will get most of the credit. Fame and fortune lies ahead of you.' In the event, they did as I asked. Fame and fortune certainly did lie ahead of them and they thoroughly deserved every bit of it, for a more talented trio than the two Saatchis and Tim Bell, it would be hard to find.

Tim Bell and the two Saatchis changed the political mood in Britain. That summer, for the first time in many years, the Opposition went up in the polls and the Government down. I give all the credit to Tim Bell, Morris and Charles Saatchi, and Gordon Reece, as the politicians were away on their summer holidays.

Gordon Reece, during the days in Opposition, was the *bête noire* of Baroness Young, my predecessor as Deputy Chairman. She regarded me as outrageous and Gordon Reece as quite beyond the pale. At a particular meeting between Janet Young and myself at which Tristan Garel-Jones was present, she said: 'Look at this bill. It's Gordon Reece's expenses. It is completely out of the question.' 'Have you ever owned a Rolls-Royce, Janet? No, well if you had, you would realise that a Rolls-Royce uses a lot of petrol. Gordon Reece is a Rolls-Royce among publicists and he only runs on champagne.' My words found their way into the columns of the *Observer*.

Reece's expenses had always been an issue at Central Office. It was not that they were particularly high, for they weren't; it was just that he gave the impression of living a rather grand lifestyle. In fact, his lifestyle was rather modest. Much of the time, whilst we were in Opposition, he had lived in my spare room. Reece spent money on only three items: cigars, champagne and books, about equally.

Gordon Reece is a devout Catholic. He was educated at the same school as, indeed he was an exact contemporary of, Norman St John Stevas, a Greek boy, also a Catholic. I asked Gordon what he thought of the young Stevas. All he could remember, however, was that Norman St John Stevas, now Lord Fawsley, had reported Gordon to the headmaster, a most pious monk, for being, so Stevas claimed, an atheist. Nothing could have been further from the truth. Gordon Reece has always taken his religion most seriously. Two men so very different it is hard to find. The only thing they have in common apart from their religion is that both of them became eminent with the help of Margaret Thatcher.

There are few people as able at presenting the character of their clients in the best possible light as Gordon Reece. The strange thing about Reece is that many of his clients, who are captains of industry, must often wonder what he has done to earn his fee. The answer is simple: events just seem to run in their favour when Reece is retained. There are few people who have ever worked in Conservative Central Office who had such perfect qualifications for the job as its then Director of Communications. Usually such directors come from the worlds of advertising, public relations, the press or even television. Gordon Reece started work on a provincial newspaper in Liverpool, then worked for John Junor at the *Sunday Express*. Entering television, he was a floor manager where he worked with the playwright Ronnie Harwood. Harwood, at that time a young actor playing the part of a policeman, was most impressed when Gordon Reece told him he had the Queen's private telephone number. A discreet man even then, Reece would not give Harwood access to this closely guarded secret.

Then Reece was amongst the first to produce *News at Ten* for ITN, going on to produce religious broadcasting at the BBC. Working for EMI he was lent to Margaret Thatcher and is credited with changing the colour of Margaret Thatcher's hair. It is more likely, however, that she changed the colour of Reece's hair, turning it quite grey. He certainly introduced Margaret Thatcher to Laurence Olivier, who gave her advice on who would be best to teach her how to project her voice and convinced her of the need to take such lessons. Gordon Reece's relationship with Margaret Thatcher had been a long and close one.

What neither Reece nor Tim Bell did, however, was to help in formulating Margaret Thatcher's political strategy either while she was in power or Opposition. These men were both specialists in the art of presentation. Both amazingly creative, neither of them was particularly popular with the general run of officials at Central Office who found it, as Janet Young had found it, hard to see the point of such people. Nowadays, all is different. No self-respecting minister would ever be caught without a permanent spin doctor and even the wife of the Prime Minister has her own press office, which quotes as a justification for its existence the fact that Hillary Clinton has a whole wing at the White House to look after her image. These spin doctors are a living testament to the fact that you can have too much of a good thing. The Tory Party's fortunes seem to have declined in almost direct proportion to the number of spin doctors they now employ.

During the 1979 election campaign, an intermediary had passed a message to me that Marcia Falkender would like to give us some advice to help our cause. I was extremely excited by this proposition for no one, in those days, knew the psychology of the Labour Party better than Marcia Falkender. Indeed, seldom had there been a smarter political operator than Marcia Falkender. The meetings were arranged by an intermediary who was the Man of Business, so to speak, of a great British industrialist.

The meetings took place in a flat that belonged to this industrialist. I took Alan Howarth with me as he was conversant with the strategy and detailed planning of the Conservative Party's campaign. In fact, he had worked on it for years. On one occasion, I also took along Gordon Reece. These meetings were fascinating, for the level of contempt Marcia had for the people who ran the Labour Party was incredible. This was not surprising, for they had treated both her and Harold Wilson badly. In 1975, when Wilson won the election, his party refused even to pay Marcia's salary. It was an act of personal spite. Marcia Falkender was also very taken with the idea of having a woman prime minister in Britain.

During the election campaign, I was helped by an immensely tall but equally pleasant young man. We all called him Spider Man, as it was not hard to imagine his long arms and legs stretching as he climbed across the facade of 32 Smith Square. One day during the campaign, around midday I sent Spider Man up to Gordon Reece's office. 'Give Mr Reece my compliments and ask him if he would care to join the Treasurer in his quarters for a glass of champagne.' Spider Man entered Gordon's office, came to attention and performed an extended salute as he delivered my message verbatim. Michael Heseltine was sitting there, open mouthed, while all this went on. 'Here we are in Central Office and it's just like the First World War. We politicians have been out there fighting the battle of the Somme while you Central Office staff are living the life of Riley, with your smartly polished boots and champagne, way behind the lines.'

Working in Central Office during that election was a lot of fun – working anywhere is a lot of fun when you are winning. One Saturday, I was alone in my office during the campaigning, when I heard an explosion. Gordon Reece entered, looking grim. Airey Neave had been murdered. The call had just come through from the police.

The day that Airey Neave was blown apart by Irish terrorists was a turning point in British politics. Nothing was quite the same again. Airey and his wife, Diana, had been very kind to me and I was sad at his death. At his funeral the following week, the sun shone and we, all those of the long march, the name Denis Thatcher gave to the days in Opposition, with many of Airey's friends and relatives, came to bury him. Despite the sad occasion, there was a feeling of excitement: the moment that Airey had played such a part in bringing to fruition had almost come.

As time for an election drew nearer, Labour defeat became more certain. Geoffrey Tucker invited me to tea at The Ritz. He wanted to introduce me to Bernard Ingham, a Labour supporter and a civil servant. Bernard, Geoffrey suggested, would be the ideal man to manage the Press Office at No. 10 when Margaret Thatcher arrived there.

Callaghan put to one side his intention of having an autumn election and his party, like a herd of cows, entered the fenced cattle race that led to defeat. Their options were closed off. As the election approached, their room for manoeuvre shrank; they were being driven by Margaret Thatcher. Their last chance to break free gone, they struggled as they came towards the polls, mesmerised by the seeming inevitability of their defeat. The election of 1979 was, as I discovered later, much like any other election, except we, at the time, were doubtful as to whether the electorate would accept a woman as a prime minister.

They did, and by midnight on polling day, the Conservatives were steaming ahead. That night I gave a party in Smith Square for many of our financial supporters. The excitement there was tangible. Television trucks were everywhere with their heavy electric cables littering the ground; the crowd that gathered early in the evening were in a frenzy. One by one the lights went out at the Labour Party's headquarters across the square and soon Transport House was in complete darkness. Margaret Thatcher came, the crowds went mad and, unlike her predecessor Ted Heath, she was meticulous in saying thank you to her supporters. The next morning, I had breakfast at about seven a.m. with some of the Central Office staff and then returned to my London flat. By nine o'clock I was back in Central Office. I had not slept all night nor, I suppose, had many others.

It was as if the world had changed. Socialism was gone, and with it a whole attitude to life that we had come progressively to accept since the end of the war. The Chairman's floor of Central Office was a shambles. Shirley Oxenbury and I started to clean the place up. By ten o'clock Margaret Thatcher's office was full of enthusiastic supporters, most of whom had not been seen during the campaign, others whose enthusiasm had been missing a few years ago when it would perhaps have been more helpful. Margaret Thatcher came into Smith Square, where she was greeted by Peter Thorneycroft amid much cheering. The crowds still thronged the streets around Conservative Party headquarters. I sat in my office alone with a pot of tea, watching the television. Caroline Stephens (now Ryder) came in and suggested that I go next door and join Margaret Thatcher in her overcrowded office. I thanked her, but said I would stay where I was. Just before eleven o'clock Margaret Thatcher came into my office. 'I'm just off to the Palace, Alistair.' 'Good luck,' I replied. Nearly twelve years later, I shook her hand as she returned from Buckingham Palace to my home in Great College Street, having resigned. I was, I suppose, the last person to see her before she set out to start her time as Prime Minister and the first person to greet her when she returned, having completed that time.

I slept well that Friday night. Saturday night, however, was a different matter. I was restless. The names of the new Cabinet were on the news broadcast that morning and during the day junior appointments were to be announced. As a senior official of Central Office, I had been at the heart of the battle for four years. On that Friday, shadow ministers had disappeared from Central Office in order to materialise on television screens as real ministers responsible for running departments. The young men and women of the research department followed them, the vice-chairmen of the Party took up positions as junior ministers. It seemed as if there were only Thorneycroft and myself left. I felt the loneliness of a terrible anticlimax. At about six-thirty p.m. my telephone rang and it was Margaret Thatcher. 'I would like you to be Deputy Chairman, as well as Treasurer.' I became, I believe, the first person in the Party's history to hold both roles. I was the sole Treasurer and Deputy Chairman, a position of real power, I imagined, for I held control of all income and expenditure.

Thorneycroft rang later that evening. We were both invited to Chequers for lunch on Sunday along with the Cabinet. I drove Thorneycroft to Chequers. He had been there often; I never before. 'We don't need instructions. I know how to get there,' he said, but they had changed all the roads since Harold Macmillan's day.

The lunch went well and afterwards we sat and talked in the rose garden. 'Chequers weather,' said Peter Thorneycroft. 'The weather is always good when there are meetings at Chequers.' The new Prime Minister walked with a member of the Cabinet amongst the trees. The rest of us watched from the terrace, excited as schoolboys who have just arrived at senior school. When the Prime Minister had finished with a particular secretary of state, he was returned to the group and another taken in his place to walk among the roses. At the end of the rose garden stood the indoor swimming pool built for Edward Heath. It was empty and it stayed that way all the years that the Thatchers were at Chequers.

Margaret Thatcher loved Chequers and, more perhaps than the house itself, she grew fond of the people who worked there. Over the years I visited Chequers often and I found that the place under her hand grew more and more like a home. When Margaret Thatcher left Downing Street to hand her resignation to the Queen, the press photographers caught tears in her eyes. Many believed that she cried for loss of office; I knew that she cried for the friends she left behind at Chequers and at No. 10 Downing Street.

On the drive back to London, Peter Thorneycroft and I discussed two issues. The first: who should be Director of the Conservative Research Department. In Opposition, Peter Thorneycroft had had trouble with Chris Patten, who had become quite hysterical when David Wolfson was appointed Secretary to the Shadow Cabinet. It was not the loss of personal position that angered Patten, rather the loss of power to nudge the Shadow Cabinet's policy towards his own views. Thorneycroft had also decided to move the Conservative Research Department from their scholarly quarters in Old Queen

Street to more workable accommodation in 32 Smith Square, where their wild excesses of making their own policy could be smartly trodden on. Several names were mentioned, but the only one who could be relied upon as the tool to do the job was Alan Howarth.

This decision made, Peter Thorneycroft went on to explain his strategy. 'We will try to create a situation where all the political debate in the country is within the parameters of the Conservative Party's many differing shades of opinion. We will, by these means, become our own opposition, making the Labour Party's views of no consequence.'

That was exactly what happened. While Margaret Thatcher was Prime Minister there was no lack of argument within the Conservative Party, but no one lost the whip for their views. No one was cast out of the party for having different views from the government. In fact, Margaret Thatcher herself often used to refer to her own government as 'they', and she would regularly attack her own Cabinet. Her ministers were, on occasions, the cowboys cowering behind the covered wagons while Margaret Thatcher rode with the Indians. For nearly twelve years the Labour Party became a political irrelevance. Margaret Thatcher believed in argument and argued robustly with all who opposed her. She may well have labelled her opponents 'wets', but she never called them 'bastards' or 'traitors'. In fact, one of the most remarkable things about Margaret Thatcher is that in all the time that I have known her, while she may disagree with an individual profoundly, I have never heard her say a word to the personal detriment of even her most virulent enemies.

Only when John Major came to power and peace was declared in the Cabinet, did the civil war truly break out. John Major rather naively believed that he had been elected overwhelmingly to the Conservative Party's leadership and that, as a consequence, all those in the Party should, if they did not think as he thought, at least do as he said. The Cabinet of Chums soon became a hotbed of rebellion; if a knife was missing it could easily be found, for it would be sticking out of a colleague's back. The backbenches became uneasy; criticism became tantamount to rebellion; a vote against the Government treason; those who wrote or spoke in criticism of the Conservative Government became anathema to be cast into outer darkness.

It is strange how men, and perhaps more so their wives, make a point of saying how difficult Margaret Thatcher was when in power. I never found this, although I was not accustomed to working for people. She can also be remarkably tolerant of failure, both professionally and personally. The only scandal that, to my knowledge, she took any interest in was that of Norman Lamont, a junior minister in charge of Tourism, who, having taken a great fancy to the vivacious and extremely attractive widow Olga Polizzi, had taken to calling on her. He was doing just this when a former boyfriend of Olga's arrived to try and effect a reconciliation of their friendship, which had been terminated some weeks before. This man, Richard Connoly, a large but elegant Irishman, was furious to find Lamont in her house. Their row ended in a brawl and, trying desperately to escape, using his red dispatch box as protection, Lamont received a blow to the eye. The next day, he explained his swollen face by saying that he had walked into a filing cabinet. The press, however, were told another story. The minister had been seen hanging around Bayswater Road, shouting abuse at Connoly, who was apparently giving as good as he was getting.

Margaret Thatcher was intrigued by this story and asked me for the truth. I knew all those involved and told her the tale. Margaret Thatcher laughed and laughed. 'The whole thing is quite Gilbertian,' she remarked. When asked does Margaret Thatcher have a sense of humour, I always reply in the affirmative. When asked for an example of her humour, I reply that she always laughs at my jokes.

When ministers grumbled that Margaret Thatcher was tiresome and difficult, I used to compare her to a great diva, difficult off the stage, but pure magic when she came to grips with a great aria. In truth, there is something of the actress in Margaret Thatcher. She can not only formulate and drive policies through Parliament, but she can present these policies as well. In the end, the excuse that her colleagues used to bring her down was the Poll Tax. When, on 28 August 1974, Margaret Thatcher announced that she would abolish domestic rates, it was a promise that she intended to fulfil.

In the early days of power she set about implementing that promise. Peter Thorneycroft objected strongly – to abolish rates would remove the link between the electorate and the elected in local government. Without at least part of local government funding coming from the local taxpayer, there would be no control over spending and no sanction by the electorate on local authorities that spent money promoting lunatic projects. There must, Thorneycroft said, be a better way. It seemed that there was. Kenneth Baker invented it and it was called the Community Charge. The Labour Party called it 'the Poll

Tax' and it brought Margaret Thatcher down. The irony of it all was that the million people whose names were missing from the electoral roll, mostly it is believed so that they could avoid paying the Poll Tax, were the million missing votes that helped win John Major the 1992 election, giving him an abnormally high proportion of the popular vote but only a small majority by comparison with the majorities that Margaret Thatcher had managed to secure.

She had been right at the beginning. She should have stuck to abolishing local rates. Kenneth Baker, as Chairman, was responsible for the Party's defence of Poll Tax. I pointed out to him that we were spending stacks of money defending the Community Charge, but it was the Poll Tax that people believed to be unfair. Why did we not change the direction of our attack? 'That would be to lose the battle of semantics,' Baker informed me. The battle of semantics, indeed? What a real load of rubbish. I had come across a senior businessman who told me, with great sincerity, that he had no objection to the Community Charge, but found the Poll Tax detestable. We might well have lost Kenneth Baker's battle of semantics, but we could have won the war of the Poll Tax.

No sooner had we finished one election than we were into the next. The European election campaign was yet another first: we had never fought anything like it before. At the Candidates' Conference, a motley crew was assembled. Fred Catherwood, a man of considerable experience gained in both the CBI and industry, stood up and asked a daft question. Margaret Thatcher, her patience by this time growing thin, replied that if he did not know the answer himself he could not be a Conservative. The fact of the matter was that Sir Fred Catherwood was far more of a pro-European than a Conservative, as indeed were most of those who sat in that room and fought under the Party's banner.

Sir Frederick Warner was another of those Conservative candidates elected to European Parliament. It was only a few months before he summoned me to his office at what was then the merchant bank, Guinness Peat. I sat waiting for nearly twenty minutes as he discussed the positioning of a chandelier with his decorator on the telephone. Then he instructed me to speak to his constituency agent. His agent, he said, was intolerable. He expected Sir Frederick to turn up in his constituency. Did the man not know how busy he was in Brussels?

A week later, I was being interviewed by the BBC. The sound

technician asked me if I had a pacemaker in my heart as electronic devices upset his microphone. A few years before he had interviewed the British Ambassador in Japan, who also told him that he had no pacemaker. In that case, the technician told me, the Japanese had bugged his breakfast. That ambassador was Sir Frederick Warner.

While he was on holiday in the summer of 1980, the Conservative press ran a story that Peter Thorneycroft was to leave as Party Chairman. Lady Thorneycroft rang me in Central Office and asked what was I going to do about the story? Not much, I replied; there are always inaccurate stories about in August. She, I believe, formed the unfortunate impression that I was after her husband's job, which, I must record, was not the case then, or ever. The summer passed and the end of September came.

I was to be married in October just after the Party Conference and Romilly and I had decided to spend a few days at West Green. I did not wish to be disturbed. 'Tell them that I have gone to Australia,' I said to my office. Thorneycroft was thrown into a flat spin by all this. He tracked me down and insisted that he come to see me. I invited him to lunch and cooked him a roast chicken with yoghurt and chopped mint inserted under its skin. We drank a rather good claret and ate a pudding of autumnal fruits, a mixture of berries. Walking in the garden after lunch, Thorneycroft opened our conversation with the words, 'I think you should resign as Treasurer.' I did not reply, and his tone became rather vague. 'There are plenty of other jobs – the NSPCC need a new chairman. You could do that very well, and then there is always the Lords.' I was not best pleased with all this – the thought of resigning did not appeal to me. However, I did not know the strength of Thorneycroft's suggestion, so I avoided any direct reply.

By chance, Gordon Reece was dining with Romilly and me that night. 'Thorneycroft wants me to resign,' I told him. 'I think I may have been sacked.' Gordon Reece rang Margaret Thatcher, who insisted on speaking to me. 'When I sack you, you will know about it, but until then you stay as the Treasurer.' She was reassuringly robust.

My attempted dismissal in 1980 was to be the first move in an attempt to unseat Margaret Thatcher. Thorneycroft and those like him in the Party thought that she had done a good job winning the election and that now she was out of control. Francis Pym was the preferred choice. Many people in the Conservative Party believed that Francis Pym came from an ancient political family. He was, in fact, no descendant of the Cromwellian Pym. His political stock in trade was a reputation for being reasonable. He was a professional, nice man, the type of person who prospers in Britain, a man who gets nothing really wrong nor, for that matter, anything really right either. Believe it or not, Thorneycroft was coordinating his speeches with those of Pym. I imagine that he was giving Pym ideas for speeches as well.

The atmosphere at Central Office was most unpleasant. When the Party Conference came, Thorneycroft made a bad slip at the opening press conference, supporting the Vestey family, who had managed to arrange their affairs so as not to pay much tax, with words along the lines of 'Good luck to them. I wish that I could do that.' The *Sun* hit him with an attack on its front page, and for the rest of the week he had a rough time in the press. Meanwhile, I managed to arrange a deal concerning the freehold of 32 Smith Square that threw up a large surplus for the Party, which greatly strengthened my position. The Conference ended and Thorneycroft declared that peace had broken out between us.

The autumn of 1980 at Central Office was not a happy one for me. Thorneycroft's declaration of peace was merely a device to throw me off guard. Gordon Reece had left for California to work for Dr Hammer; Jock Bruce Gardyne was in Parliament and a junior minister. I had only Bryan Wyldebore Smith and Henry Lee to guard my back. War had once again broken out between the Treasurer and the Party Chairman. I wrote to Margaret Thatcher, resigning my position. She ignored the letter and never even referred to it. Thorneycroft was pressing for the appointment of another Treasurer. The time was not right for the Prime Minister to resist his demands, so Tom Boardman was appointed. In retrospect it is hard to see why he was chosen, or even why he took the position.

I was now involved in a considerable battle. Margaret Thatcher, however, told me to hang on and wait. All this time, the rebellion against her was gathering force.

The help of my friend Geoffrey Tucker was invaluable to me during this period, his advice of the highest quality. One morning he brought a young journalist on the *Sunday Times* to listen to my tale, Peter Stoddart, now editor of *The Times*. I left England the next day. Romilly and I were to spend a few days in Singapore before continuing our journey to Australia. The storm broke on that Sunday morning, when the *Sunday Times* carried a spread by Peter Stoddart. The gist of his article was that the young people in Central Office were being replaced by geriatrics. This idea caught the imagination of the press and most newspapers took up the story in one form or another. Thorneycroft was incandescent with rage. I was long gone to Australia.

In Australia, I had a call from Margaret Thatcher, who told me that there was no question of my leaving. Boardman was just not raising the money and I had to stay. When I returned, I operated out of my house in Great College Street. Some months passed and the battle had deteriorated to one of occasional sniping, until Thorneycroft made a fatal error.

Briefing the Sunday lobby, as indeed the Conservative Party Chairman does each week, he was pushing a speech by Francis Pym, a leading Wet. Thorneycroft was asked where did he sit? Was he wet or dry? Rather wittily, he replied, 'I am really a sort of rising damp.' Many more political careers have been destroyed by injudicious humour than downright incompetence. Thorneycroft was destroyed by his own humour. The press took his words to mean that he supported Pym rather than Thatcher.

By the end of the week, Thorneycroft had left for Venice. The Sunday papers were not kind to him. I was called to Downing Street and I was asked to be there at seven a.m. When I arrived I was shown into the Prime Minister's office. Ian Gow and Norman Tebbit were both there. Thorneycroft was to go. The question was who should replace him. 'Who would you like, Alistair?' the Prime Minister asked me. My reply was Tom King. She turned to Norman Tebbit, who suggested Cecil Parkinson. I had always admired Parkinson's manner and I readily agreed with Norman's choice. 'Right,' said the Prime Minister. 'Alistair, you go over to Central Office and take control. You are the Deputy Chairman. Ian, you go to Venice and tell Peter that he must resign.' My job was considerably easier than Ian Gow's. I returned to Central Office, where I had not been for some months. Its occupants, always alert to the detail of day-to-day events, had read the tea leaves in their cups that morning and I was treated extremely well.

Ian Gow, arriving in Venice, met Carla and Peter Thorneycroft, who immediately invited him to dine with them. He had no option but to accept. However, he found himself in the position of telling

Peter Thorneycroft that afternoon that he had been sacked and then having to sit through dinner that night with both Peter and Carla.

Thorneycroft gone and Parkinson appointed, a great face-saving operation was entered into. Parkinson was to arrive at Central Office and shake hands with Thorneycroft who would then retire in a blaze of glory. In as far as it went, the hand-shaking worked. I even shook hands with Thorneycroft. 'What are you doing here?' he snapped at me. Innocently, I replied, 'Saying goodbye to you.'

There was a black hole in the Party's finances. The old Chairman had gone, and with him Alan Howarth. A new Chairman was in place. There was, Margaret Thatcher said, little point in humiliating Peter Thorneycroft by producing these appalling accounts. The solution was easy: we gave up publishing accounts. After all, we had only started when Peter Thorneycroft became Chairman. Parkinson, however, was keen to publish them the next year, when they showed a surplus.

At the press conference held the day before the start of the 1981 Party Conference, Robin Day asked me a long, rambling and really rather amusing question about the absence of those accounts. I simply replied 'No.' Everyone laughed, and that was that. Accounts, however, have been a sore point between the Party and the press ever since. Personally, I do not think that we ever should have shown how we spent our money. The Conservative Central Office is not a charity dedicated to helping the sick and suffering, it is a fighting machine dedicated to winning elections. I believe it to be the height of folly to expose how such a machine manages its resources or, indeed, how large or how small these resources are at any one time.

As for my relationship with Peter Thorneycroft, our paths did not cross again until 1984 when I entered the House of Lords, at which time he wrote me a letter putting aside past disagreements. I learned a great lesson of politics through this combat with Peter Thorneycroft.

In politics, people seldom ally with each other on a basis of personal friendship – although politicians would claim that they do. Rather, the issues that they are involved with become the basis of their alliances and friendships. When the issues change, then the friendships change. It came as a great shock to find that one of the few men in the Conservative Party whom I liked immensely and greatly admired; indeed a man whom I believed liked me and enjoyed my company, should, because of changing circumstances, become a formidable enemy. In the gaining of total control in Central Office

before an assault was mounted on the leadership of Margaret Thatcher, I had become just a person to be removed.

Parkinson took over and brought Michael Spicer with him. Michael
Spicer took over my position of Deputy Chairman. Tom Boardman
went to become Chairman of NatWest Bank and Oulton Wade was
appointed as my colleague.

The war in the Falklands broke out. One of Cecil Parkinson's con-
tributions to British politics was the skill with which he handled his
relationship with Margaret Thatcher during that strange war. They
were as one when Cecil spoke, it was as if Margaret Thatcher had
spoken.

After the Falklands War, we were straight into another general
election. Parkinson behaved very strangely during the campaign –
he took to walking about his office and singing to himself. On the
face of it, this is not a particularly strange way to behave unless, of
course, other people are present. His wife Anne became more and
more tense as the campaign went on. It was amongst my responsibilities to try and jolly her along. Generally, the campaign was a
happy one – we were, after all, winning.

Towards the end of the campaign, Cecil Parkinson told me that he
had a problem. I had a feeling that all was not well and that his
problem was serious. It was not, I was sure, the sort of problem that
I needed to know about. Cecil is an outgoing sort of person, a natural
communicator of information. If Cecil was to tell me something in
confidence, I could be sure that I was not the only one whom he had
told. The secret was sure to get out and I did not want to be suspected
of leaking whatever it was that Cecil was so keen to tell me. Cecil
was both a popular and immensely able Chairman of the Party.

Cecil Parkinson does not intend to gossip or pass on remarks made
in confidence. It is a fault that he cannot help, telling people stories
that are interesting or funny. In truth, he trusts people more than
he should. At Cecil's first meeting at Central Office, Angela Hooper,
a very attractive woman, was sitting opposite him. Angela has a
slight facial twitch that makes it seem as if she is winking. It was not
long before Cecil was winking back. He is naturally friendly. After
the 1983 election, Cecil was to be the Foreign Secretary. However, it
all came to nothing and he went, instead, to the Department of Trade
and Industry. It was a shame, because a Foreign Secretary with

commercial experience was just what Britain needed. Instead, Geoffrey Howe, a lawyer, went to the Foreign Office.

In the summer of 1983, the Parkinson affair surfaced. The Prime Minister rang me in Australia to tell me that John Selwyn Gummer was to be appointed to the chairmanship of the Party. I barely knew this diminutive little fellow. All I could remember of him from when I first met him was that he had been something of an opportunist, and that when a bachelor he had a large girlfriend called Arianna Stassinopoulos. Gummer was totally different from Parkinson: where Parkinson was open and generous, Gummer was not. He was a politician not in the grand mould of Parkinson, Ridley or Tebbit.

When the Party Conference came in 1983 it was in Blackpool. Cecil Parkinson, instead of a hero, the winner of a great election victory, went to that conference as if he was a man on trial. Gummer distanced himself and took what could be regarded as the morally sound high ground. Making no attempt to save Parkinson, he left his colleague to the political wolves. The advantage was to himself. As Gummer's efforts at charming the Conservative Party were puny by comparison with those of Parkinson, it must have been a matter of some convenience to watch his predecessor come unstuck. It appeared that, as far as Gummer was concerned, Parkinson was about to receive just punishment from God for his adultery.

John Wakeham rallied the Whips. In all the years I have attended party conferences, I can't remember one where so many Whips took the trouble to come to Blackpool on the day before the Conference's opening, a day when normally nobody was about except the serried ranks of the press. Sadly, the Whips were not there to save Parkinson's career, rather to put an end to it. Michael Spicer set out to try and save him from having to make a ministerial resignation. Gummer took Spicer's actions extremely badly and began to regale him and myself – I was in Gummer's sitting room at the time – with a litany of all the awful things that Anne Parkinson had said about Spicer. As there was nothing that Anne Parkinson could say or do that would make Spicer dislike her more than he disliked John Selwyn Gummer, these words fell on deaf ears. As Michael Spicer and the Parkinsons were exceptionally close friends, I was shocked that John Selwyn Gummer should repeat the contents of what was obviously a desperate outburst by Anne Parkinson delivered in a private conversation at a time when she was under immense pressure. It was clear to me that the purpose of repeating that conversation was to alienate Michael Spicer from his friends, the Parkinsons.

Much later, when John Major came to power, I warned him, in print, that he should not put his trust in Gummer. 'He is,' I wrote, 'not the sort of person that you would risk going for a walk with in St James's Park, let alone the jungle.' Gummer has begun to wither on the ministerial vine. Force-feeding his small daughter with suspect hamburgers during a BSE scare, along with his general sanctimonious air will surely, in time, do for him.

The first evening of the conference, I gave a party as usual and Parkinson was there. He had made a good impression on the press. He was to speak at the conference the next day. The hall was electric with excitement; the organ tinkled; it was as if we waited for a wedding. This was going to be one of those moments that those habitués of party conferences wait for and discuss for years afterwards. Cecil made his entrance. There was polite clapping where there should have been ecstatic applause. This man had, after all, devised a strategy that had won for his audience an election. The speech was of average quality, perfectly respectable and, considering the circumstances, downright brilliant. At the end the applause was at first supportive, but the Chairman did not rise from his seat nor continue clapping. The Conservative activists took their cue from John Selwyn Gummer; his was the party line. It was not a wedding that they had waited for, but a trial and as they left they wondered at what time would be the hanging.

Again that evening I gave a party for the senior figures of the media. Cecil and Anne Parkinson came and Cecil almost enjoyed himself. I felt terribly sorry for Anne. It was getting late, so Anne took him to their room. Half an hour later, Anne appeared at my door in deep distress. *The Times* had rung through the text of Sarah Keays' letter that they would publish the next day. Anne, Shirley Oxenbury and I went up to Cecil's bedroom, a small room at the back of the hotel. There followed the most extraordinary human drama that I have ever witnessed. First, Robin Butler came with a message from the Prime Minister. Cecil was not to worry about *The Times* article; they would discuss it in the morning. Earlier, Margaret Thatcher had told Cecil that there was no need to resign, but advised him to reflect on the effect that carrying on might have on his family.

Cecil and Anne prepared for bed. Shirley Oxenbury and I offered to leave. They both insisted that we stay and, as they busied themselves changing into their night clothes, they kept up a dialogue, he expressing his love for her and the fear that she might leave. 'I love you, I could never manage without you,' he kept repeating. Anne rehashed and rerehashed the problems of the day. Their small room was walled with mirrors, the images of the two of them were everywhere I looked. Robin Butler had brought whisky and pills and soon both Anne and Cecil were asleep. We had arranged to meet early the next day in my sitting room for breakfast and a discussion. By then, however, it was all over. John Cole, the BBC's political editor, had rung Cecil shortly after five a.m. Unfortunately the hotel switchboard put him straight through. Cecil had told the BBC that he would resign. That morning was frantic. Michael Portillo, Cecil's PPS, looked after him as best he could. The telephone kept ringing; the press were going mad.

Cecil escaped to his home, which was by this time in a state of siege. I sat with Anthony Royle. We watched the morning's proceedings on television. I have seldom been so close to tears as I was that morning.

I was angry at what to me was a gross injustice and I was surprised at the vicious cat fight that had occurred among colleagues, the way they had set about Cecil Parkinson as though he was a wounded animal and they, the rest of the pack. Tired and fed up with politics, I had in mind to leave Central Office and find another occupation. Tony Royle, always a good friend and a sound person from whom to seek advice, gave me some without my asking. 'Forget it. This is how politics is really played. Put any idea of leaving out of your head.' I took his advice.

The conference finished that afternoon and tomorrow was another day. Parkinson did recover his career, but it was never the same. I visited him the day he took up his post as the Secretary of State for Energy. He sat at his desk in his Millbank office. He was signing papers, I drinking champagne. 'I am giving away thousands of pounds,' he said. I enquired what he meant. 'These are resignations from my directorships,' he said, pointing at the pile of letters. Parkinson was back on a ministerial salary.

I have often wondered if it was after dining with Michael Spicer and myself that Parkinson got himself into the trouble that finished his chances of being Britain's Prime Minister. Spicer and I used to say that if we had lingered longer over the wine or Cecil had turned right at Vauxhall Bridge instead of left, he might be living in No. 10 today. One of his secretaries had a more practical solution to the whole matter: 'If only Mr Parkinson had told us what he wanted, we would have been delighted to oblige and caused him no trouble at all.' Cecil Parkinson is a changed man, but who would not be changed after his experience?

Life and Gummer went on at Central Office. I had, from time to time, my bits of fun. Gordon Reece, who called in occasionally to give some advice between trips from America, used to sit and listen to Gummer. Gummer's idea of how to get the best advice was to give it to the one who was there to advise him. Gordon used to get a bit tired of Gummer's monologues, interrupted only by telephone calls from Gummer's wife to tell her husband of the latest antics of their small son.

Gummer believed this kind of thing to be hugely funny. It was almost impossible to have a meeting with him without interruption, followed by his telling the assembled company what had been said during that telephone call from his family. At last, Gordon Reece hit on an idea to speed up proceedings. He took out a big cigar, and gave me the pair to it. In ten minutes, you could hardly see your hand in front of your face. The meeting came to a smart end.

John Selwyn Gummer was far from being an inspirational Chairman.

The Christmas of 1983 I spent, as usual, with the Thatchers at Chequers. Romilly and I would arrive at about eleven a.m. on Christmas Day, after calling in to see my parents at their home near Henley-on-Thames. The Christmas Day lunch party was usually composed of the Thatchers, Mark and Carol, and Denis's sister, known as Auntie Joy, a delightfully down-to-earth character.

Romilly and I were house guests and a variety of other people came to different Christmas Day lunches over the nine years that we stayed at Chequers. Regular attendees were Tim and Virginia Bell, Ronnie Millar, Sir Jack and Lady Page, along with other people who were down on their luck or lived nearby. Gordon Reece was often there on Christmas Day. Lunch went well as it always did, for Margaret Thatcher had a talent for making her guests feel at home. A great log fire blazed in the Great Hall, a giant Christmas tree filled one part of this hall with its long drooping branches. Under them, were the Thatcher family presents.

There was always plenty to eat and drink and Margaret Thatcher was assiduous in seeing that you ate and drank it. Denis was the most genial of hosts and there was a party spirit about the place.

After a few drinks, it was into lunch, usually melon followed by turkey. A giant bird, the gift of the Smithfield traders, it was carried in by a chef, who then posed with the bird and the other staff for photographs. After that the Christmas pudding, a flaming ball topped with holly, which was carried hurriedly around the table. The wines were good and the food well cooked. Mince pies, brandy butter, Stilton – all were in abundance. Crackers were pulled, but the Prime Minister never put on a funny hat. Photographs were taken by many of those present.

Then Jack Page rose to read his poem, a poem that had been specially written for the occasion. At this point, coffee was served and the Prime Minister began to fidget, looking at her watch and moving uneasily in her chair. Jack Page's poems were in fact sagas that ran and ran. The danger approached of a collision between the words of the Queen due on the television at three p.m. and the tail end of the Page poem. The Prime Minister stood up and we all hurried to the White Study to watch the Queen making her Christmas speech.

The National Anthem played and we all stood to attention. The speech over, the Prime Minister announced a walk to the Bothy, where the police who guard Chequers have their base. We carried with us Christmas cake and other refreshments. Some time was spent talking to the police, who had missed their Christmas guarding us. Then we set out for a brisk walk down the drive to wish the staff who lived in the cottages at the Churchill Gate, Happy Christmas. One year, the weather was unusually warm but it changed suddenly to a rather cold Christmas Day. Romilly was without a coat, so she asked to borrow one from Carol. Instead of lending her a coat of her own, Carol lent Romilly one of her mother's that was hanging in the hall cupboard. We were about half way down the drive at a very exposed spot, when the detective who was walking with Romilly a yard or two in front of the Prime Minister said, 'It's wonderful that you are wearing the coat the PM wore to church this morning. You make a splendid decoy. It's a great help because we're having trouble with the security equipment today. It's not working properly.'

Back at the house, tea was served and then the guests headed for home. When all the guests had left, the staff were given the evening off. Romilly and I went to our room to change. We always occupied a suite on the first floor of Chequers, a large bedroom comfortably furnished and a smaller one adjoining it. Both rooms had their own bathrooms. The point of this layout was that in the days of male prime ministers, who liked to stay up all night, smoking and drinking and I suppose plotting, the male Cabinet member could return to his room without disturbing his wife. I remember Carla Thorneycroft, a frequent visitor to Chequers in Churchill's day, telling me that she always knew when Peter came to bed next door by the smell of cigar smoke.

Dinner on Christmas Night was a simple affair, usually the six or so of us staying in the house sat at a round table in a bay window of the dining room. A buffet was laid out: smoked salmon, cold turkey, cold beef, salads, fruit and Christmas cake. One year, there was a large tin of caviar which had been sent to the Prime Minister. Margaret Thatcher decided that this half-eaten tin should be put away in the fridge, so Romilly and the Prime Minister set out for the kitchens. After some trouble fumbling around in the dark, they found the light switch and finally the way to the kitchen. The fridge was on an industrial scale. Inside were half-eaten chickens and turkeys, mince pies and whole piles of fresh food. 'This will not do,' said the Prime Minister, who immediately set about sorting out the fridge and covering plates of food with clingfilm and silver foil. I laugh to think of the surprise the next day when the staff returned and found this transformation of the inside of the fridge.

Boxing Day lunch was usually a more formal affair than Christmas Day itself. I would spend the morning in the library, which for me was bliss: the collection of memorabilia kept in the library at Chequers is wonderful. Lunch on Boxing Day was usually a buffet affair served on round tables seating eight or ten people, set up in the Great Hall. The guests were a mixture of politicians and industrialists.

Often both the politicians and industrialists grumbled at being asked to leave their own houses on Boxing Day, but they came anyway. There are in London a group of people who flit around power as honey bees around lavender, collecting a little more power for themselves at each encounter. I suspect it will be just the same when power changes from Conservative to Labour, as it was when power changed from Thatcher to Major. There is no room for either sentiment or principle in the lives of the overly ambitious. I felt certain that there would have been a telephone call to Downing Street if an invitation to any of these people was delayed in the post.

It is a matter of some amusement to observe how many of Britain's older industrialists are now strong supporters of John Major but were in fact equally enthusiastic about Denis Healey and Harold Wilson, not to mention Harold Lever. During a dinner at the Ritz in Paris with Harold Lever, then a member of a Labour Cabinet, I asked him why he had joined the Labour Party for he was no more a socialist than I am. 'I felt that Labour was more likely to win and be in power.' He was right, of course. There are, I suspect, members of John Major's Conservative Cabinet who made the opposite choice for the same reason.

John Major was often at Chequers, pretending to be a pair of curtains. He made no impact on anyone there, he was just a figure in a crowd. 'Why,' I was asked, 'was John Major the man that Margaret Thatcher wished to succeed her?' The answer I gave was simple: she was merely trying to humiliate Geoffrey Howe, who was impatient for his turn. As every foot soldier carries a field marshal's baton in his pack, so every member of a Cabinet believes that they will one day be Prime Minister, regardless of how ludicrous that idea might seem to the rest of us. Geoffrey Howe, squeezed between advancing age and a colleague who intended to go on as Prime Minister, became desperate as power and possibility edged further from his grasp. Margaret Thatcher's chief grumble about Geoffrey Howe, apart from the eccentric behaviour of his wife, Elspeth, who spent an evening in a cardboard box in Charing Cross Road, was his sheer reasonableness – it made him quite intolerable. I used to watch as Geoffrey irritated Margaret Thatcher beyond belief. It was the small things that upset her. For a start, he always spoke very quietly and she could not hear what he had to say. Then, as Foreign Secretary he used to recite, at great length, in Cabinet the tales of his travels. For instance he would begin, 'And then we came to Malaysia ...' This drove his Prime Minister beyond the point of boredom. Finally, the great misunderstanding occurred when, in order to appoint John Major as Foreign Secretary, she had to dismiss Geoffrey Howe. 'Geoffrey,' the Prime Minister began, 'I have to move John [Major] to the Foreign Office.' Geoffrey Howe replied, 'Wonderful, he will be a great help to me.' The misunderstanding had to be explained and Geoffrey Howe went. He waited, then made a speech resigning his position as Deputy Prime Minister that is credited with bringing down the Prime Minister.

I doubt myself that Margaret Thatcher was the victim of Howe's spite, rather the victim of the ambitions of her colleagues who, not for the first time, plotted and planned against her in order to install one of their own in her position. The mathematics of it all were so easy: if she had won the next election, it would have been at least another seven years before any of them had a turn (for that is how they saw it) at being Prime Minister. Their case against her was equally simple: she is unpopular but she has been unpopular before. However, this time will be her fourth test at the polls. No other Prime Minister had ever before won three elections consecutively; the chances of Margaret Thatcher winning a fourth election must be extremely slim.

Howe used his position to build up a power base with British political writers. Chevening is a fine country house in Kent and was available to the Foreign Secretary. The Foreign Secretary could, when entertaining foreigners, invite British guests to stay as well. The Howes, for example, invited an ambassador and, amongst the other guests, British journalists. They soon became popular and powerful political hosts. Perhaps this explains why the Howes squabbled over such a petty matter as which house they could have when Howe lost his job as Foreign Secretary. Although promoted to Deputy Prime Minister, he must have been unhappy that he had lost his power base at Chevening with the press. It is a commentary on the minute scale of Geoffrey Howe's character compared to the gigantic size of his ego that he could take offence at being promoted from Foreign Secretary to Deputy Prime Minister. The truth was that nothing less than the position of Prime Minister would do.

Before the Madrid European Council in June 1989, both Nigel Lawson and Geoffrey Howe gave Margaret Thatcher an ultimatum. At that European Council she outsmarted them. However, they did not resign as they had threatened, as a result of which she no longer had much respect for them. In the event, Nigel Lawson went in October with, given the circumstances, incredibly good grace. Geoffrey Howe lingered on for an entire year and then left after a period of immensely petty bickering. In his going he committed what he may have believed to be an act of supreme patriotism. However, many other people saw the manner of his going as an act of total treachery.

1984 was a hard year for the Government, with the start of the miners' strike and two national dock strikes. These were the manifestation of the last twitchings of the Trade Union Movement in the Thatcher era. The Party languished in the doldrums of the opinion polls. It always seems the case that, in the last twenty years, a person of consequence and ability is appointed the Party Chairman to win elections. In between elections, however, the party makes do with a Chairman of little ability and in the case of John Selwyn Gummer, a man at that time of no political consequence.

I spent most of the summer of 1984 in Australia, returning for the Party Conference. This conference started no differently from most other conferences. Gummer was, as usual, insufferable. This time he had arranged a ceremonial visit by Robert Maxwell to his hotel suite. Maxwell arrived, accompanied by a phalanx of assistants and photographers from his various newspapers. Some of us felt that the Chairman of the Conservative Party should not be receiving a man of Maxwell's background so publicly. Gummer, however, loved publicity. I thought that this whole episode was a mistake. Events, however, saved Gummer from later embarrassment. The IRA bomb took the news headline.

That night I gave a party in my suite. Luckily I did not have the room normally allocated to the Treasurer, in the centre of the hotel, rather I had been given a suite to one side of it. It was a suite with three bedrooms and a large sitting room, but only one bathroom. By happy chance one of the hotel's fire escapes was out through my bathroom window. My party seemed to go better than usual that night: there was an air of excitement about, as if everyone knew what was to happen. More people than usual came to the party and it went on until the early hours of the morning.

I remember talking to Margaret Tebbit. She was infuriated by the conversation that had taken place earlier that day. An agent had reprimanded her for the behaviour of her son. I have no idea what the boy had done, nor for that matter why the agent should be so presumptuous as to raise the matter with the boy's mother, who was, after all, the wife of a member of the Cabinet. Margaret was disgusted, hurt and angry. If their children were to become victims of party officials Norman should leave politics.

My suite was packed with journalists and politicians, businessmen and party officials. It was nearly two-thirty a.m. before the party ended. Richard Ryder had gone to bed in one of my spare rooms, Michael Spicer was preparing to sleep in the other. Shirley Oxenbury, Alex Mennell and Jan Fitzalan Howard were helping me tidy up the sitting room. I had, when I was Deputy Chairman, got into the habit of going around the ground floor of the conference hotel just to see that all was quiet. I set out to do this at about two-thirty a.m.

On the stairs I met Anthony Berry returning from walking his two dogs. We gossiped for a while. I had always liked Tony Berry, a generally sensible man, far from brilliant but solid on the backbenches. In the normal course of events, Tony Berry would not have had a room in the centre of the Grand Hotel, except for two coincidences. had been involved in a charge of drink driving. As he was a popular man in some personal distress, the officials concerned went out of their way to help him. By chance, Lord King was vacating his room early as he had to return to London on business, and could not stay for the last day of the conference, while Tony Berry only wanted to be there on the last day. Tony Berry was given Lord King's rooms. What was meant as an act of kindness cost Tony Berry his life. What was an irritating problem causing Lord King to return to London, saved his life. Tony Berry, for the first time, slept on the other side of his bed – the side nearest the door. This happened because his wife, Sarah, had gone to bed while her husband walked their dogs. She believed that she would be disturbed when he returned if she slept in her usual place. Of all the couples sleeping in the centre of the Grand Hotel, the husband or wife who slept on the same side of their bed as Tony Berry, was either killed or terribly injured.

After I had talked with Tony Berry, I wished him goodnight and, feeling tired, I decided not to go downstairs as was my normal habit. I returned to my room and went to bed. It takes me no time to prepare for bed: off with my clothes, a quick session in the bathroom, into bed and straight to sleep. I am an easy sleeper: I can fall asleep at a dinner table if need be; my problem is not sleeping but keeping awake.

I awoke on hearing a loud explosion. My bed was covered in plaster, the room full of dust. I switched on the lights and they worked perfectly. I looked out of the window to see the floodlights illuminating a huge cloud of dust.

My first thoughts were of immense relief. Those of us close to the leadership of the Party had suspected that something of this sort would happen sooner or later. Now the attack had been made and I had survived. The trick after a bomb blast is to get out as soon as possible. However, the trick after a fire is first to put on your clothes. I had already been involved in two fires so I knew this and dressed in a flash. First I looked out into the hotel's passage, a part of which seemed to have disappeared. I gathered together Richard Ryder, who was totally dazed having been in a deep sleep, and Michael Spicer, who had been in the bath. Out through the bathroom window we went, intending to go down the fire escape. Coming up that fire escape, however, were a group of hysterical Spanish women. We managed to turn around this stampeding herd of Spaniards and sent them all in the right direction. Out in the street, I ran around the hotel to the front. I was among the first to get there. When I arrived the street was deserted except for the police.

At first sight, the Grand Hotel stood there as if nothing had happened to it. Its façade was illuminated by yellow floodlights, a cloud of yellow dust hanging in the air. Then I could see that right in the centre of the hotel's façade was a hole starting at the second floor and extending upwards for several storeys. Out of the hotel came the most terrible cries. The sight and sounds of that night will never leave me, but the most abiding memory will be of the police, in front of the Grand Hotel, struggling with photographers who were trying to get inside to take photographs.

At first we thought that the damage had been done by a missile from the sea and, indeed, it looked as if this could well have been the case. Jock Bruce Gardyne joined me as I looked at this extraordinary spectacle. He told me that he had got up, shaved, washed and dressed in a leisurely fashion and then made his way out of the hotel. By this time, there was quite a large crowd milling about, a crowd that included many Cabinet Ministers. I particularly remember Keith Joseph resplendent in his silk paisley dressing gown.

I hurried to the Metropole, a new hotel not far from the Grand. There we set up a Party headquarters. Many people were of the opinion that the conference should close. Margaret Thatcher had been taken from the Grand to secure premises not far away. There had, however, been a hitch as she was leaving. First the police sent out of the hotel a double, in case there were marksmen hiding nearby. A head was seen to rise over a parapet, Margaret Thatcher's departure was delayed. John Selwyn Gummer had raced to her side.

Gummer was much praised for the attention that he paid to those who were injured. He then returned to Brighton where he assisted the police in dealing with the devastation that prevailed. However, neither Michael Spicer, his deputy, nor I had had any knowledge as to his whereabouts at the time. Tony Garner, the party's chief agent, having escaped from the Grand Hotel wearing his dinner jacket but no tie and odd shoes, bravely returned into the wreckage with the police to find a list of those who were staying there. Then together the police and Garner went to their operations room where they found

Gummer. Gummer then rang the Prime Minister who predictably told him that the conference must go on. After some discussions about security for that morning, Garner returned to the hall where his Central Office agents had gathered. Garner described the police operations room as a grim place. The names of the dead and seriously wounded were written up on a board as news came through.

Those who worked for Gummer did not know whether there would be another attack or not. What they did know was that members of the Party's organisation were the likely targets. No sooner had an office been set up in the Metropole, than we all had to vacate that hotel because there was a bomb warning. It was a frightening night for a number of people who held comparatively junior posts in the Party. They were the people who held that conference together. Michael Spicer showed a talent for leadership that I had never seen before.

Amongst the many problems of opening the conference on time the following morning was that most of the hierarchy of the Party had nothing to wear. We had to get them clothes, and quickly, and we decided the answer was to open Marks & Spencer as early as possible.

I had, with a number of other people, found my way to Edward Du Cann's rather grand suite in the Metropole. I used his telephone to ring Romilly – she usually watches the early morning news and I did not want her imagining that I was dead. Then I rang the security of Marks & Spencer's head office, explained what had happened and asked that the Managing Director telephone me at the Metropole. In time, he rang back. The lines were blocked; he had had trouble getting through. The Manager of their local branch would be on duty at seven; his staff would join him as early as they could. I spread the word amongst Brighton's taxi drivers that anyone without clothes was to be brought to M&S. I would, I told them, settle the fares. Luckily I had a considerable amount of cash on me. Standing outside the Marks & Spencer store, I waited for the first taxis and soon they came thick and fast. I paid them off and sent them back for more of our people. Inside clothes were found for all those who needed them. I am proud to say that they never looked smarter. In all the hurry, I had forgotten my tie. A friend of mine, Geoffrey Parkhouse from the *Glasgow Herald*, lent me his. It was a Garrick Club tie and, in those days, I wore no other. The £10,000 bill for the clothes was paid by Central Office. It was quite illuminating afterwards to note which members of the Party and the Government asked to pay for their new clothes and which members let the matter pass...

The conference opened on time, and that afternoon we set off for home. Gummer's secretaries spent the weekend at my home, instead of going back to their flats in London. They were in a considerable state of shock. Nineteen days after the attack on Margaret Thatcher's life, Mrs Gandhi was assassinated.

There had been bomb threats to the conference before and when I think of one particular instance now I turn cold with fear. It was during a conference session when I had taken over from Peter Thorneycroft on the conference platform. The Chief Agent passed me a note. 'There is a bomb warning. Shall I clear the hall?' I told him to search the hall discreetly but let the conference continue. I sat and watched as the Party's agents went up and down the rows of delegates, searching handbags and looking under seats. I took the decision to carry on, for if I had not then our conference would have been continually interrupted. I do not think I would make the same decision today.

In time, Gummer was moved from Central Office. I came to the conclusion that Gummer was not the choice of Margaret Thatcher, but rather the choice of John Wakeham and the Whips, many of whom were Gummer's close political friends. His appointment and Parkinson's fall were just two more steps along the pretty road that her enemies constructed, a road that led to her downfall.

Once again, I was in Australia when Margaret Thatcher telephoned me with welcome news. John Selwyn Gummer was to be replaced by Norman Tebbit. I was delighted. And then came the bad news. For some inexplicable reason, Jeffrey Archer was appointed Norman Tebbit's deputy. I have never really discovered how Archer got this job. I can only accept the explanation given in Margaret Thatcher's memoirs.

12

Politics 1984–91

Norman Tebbit was as good a Chairman as John Selwyn Gummer was a bad one. When I arrived back in London a week or so before the Party Conference, I wandered into Norman's office to greet him. 'There is only one problem,' Tebbit told me, 'Margaret has made Jeffrey Archer my Deputy. We will just have to control him.' I did not realise at the time quite how prophetic these words were.

Not even Norman Tebbit could control Jeffrey Archer. The man seemed to have an unending capacity for saying what he thought, without taking the precaution of thinking. He bounced about the place, full of energy and ostentatious formality. 'Good morning, Chairman,' he would say to Norman, almost standing to attention and saluting. It was not long before he was encouraging the few Conservatives that remain in Northern Ireland to start a Conservative Association. This was definitely not Party policy at the time. Tebbit knew nothing of Archer's initiative, and the Northern Ireland Office were equally in the dark. Archer was reprimanded and put firmly in his box, but like the Jack, it was not long before the lid was thrown open and his cheeky face was up and grinning again. The man could not be controlled. He had no hesitation in telling all and sundry how close he was to Margaret Thatcher as, indeed, he now tells everyone of his close relationship with John Major. I do not know how Archer gets on with Major, but if he really is that close to the man, then that might account in some way for the erratic and unfortunate nature of so many of the Prime Minister's statements. As far as Margaret Thatcher is concerned, there is no mention of Jeffrey Archer at all in the first volume of her memoirs and in the second volume only one, and that on page 422. I quote: 'Norman needed a Deputy Chairman who would be able to make those visits to the party around the country which Norman's health precluded him from doing. Only someone with a high profile already could do this successfully, and I decided that Jeffrey Archer was the right choice. He was the extrovert's extrovert. He had prodigious energy; he was and remains the most popular speaker that the Party has ever had. Unfortunately, as it turned out, Jeffrey's political judgement did not always match his enormous energy and fund-raising ability; ill considered remarks got him and the party into some awkward scrapes, but he always got himself out of them.' The thinking was right, the choice of man totally wrong. All courts – and prime ministers have courts, just as do Kings and Queens – need their share of jesters, musicians and jugglers. The myth about Archer is that he was a member of Thatcher's court. The fact is that he was not.

As for Archer's fundraising achievements, they were negligible. He occupied himself mainly with high-profile auctioning of signed whiskey bottles at Party functions. He played little part in raising the £10 million or so that it cost each year to run Central Office. Archer is a clever man – he must be to construct such a blatantly transparent myth about himself. Every time evidence is produced that his myth is transparent, it is dismissed on the basis that no man would pretend to a life so easily debunked. Oddly likeable, Archer adds to the pleasures of life and many people have been the recipients of his open hospitality. I only hope, for the sake of Britain, that no politician, hearing only good of the man, mistakenly gives him again a job of any political consequence. To do that would once more put both Party and nation in considerable jeopardy.

Norman Tebbit bore the cross of Archer with considerable fortitude. I am not such a kindly spirit, and hoped that Archer would soon turn his attention elsewhere than Central Office, although sadly there was no hope of his promotion to a junior minister. In 1985 help came one morning at breakfast time and, as help often does, it came in the most unlikely form. Gordon Reece and I were taking our breakfast in the Palace Hotel in Bournemouth, where the Party Conference was being held that year. At another table in the same room was David Montgomery, then Editor of the *News of the World*, breakfasting with an elegant young woman. Across the room Jeffrey Archer ate his breakfast with two men, neither known to me. The elegant lady rose from her table and came across to join Gordon Reece and myself. She introduced herself as Grania Forbes, the new Political Editor of the *News of the World*. She had, she said, an

embarrassing story about Jeffrey Archer. It was alleged, and subsequently proven to be groundless, that Archer had been consorting
with prostitutes. We were fairly surprised at this tale. She went on
to allege that a young member of Archer's office had taken a large
sum of money to pay off a lady whom she believed was blackmailing
Archer. This pay-off, it was claimed, had taken place on Victoria
station. 'Have you told Archer this?' Gordon Reece asked. 'He denies
it,' she replied. Grania Forbes had only a week or so before joined
the *News of the World*, having previously been the Palace Cor-
respondent for the Press Association. She was completely thrown by
the story with which she was now dealing. I was sorry for Archer
caught up in this scandal, although it did not turn out so badly for
him. As Margaret Thatcher pointed out, Archer, while he often got
his Party and himself into awkward scrapes, always got himself out
of them. He got out of this particular scrape with the highest libel
damages ever awarded at that time. Of his Party being financially
compensated for the embarrassment, I have no recall.

Archer's resignation was more than enough of a reason for Norman
Tebbit and myself to open a bottle of champagne. We were then able
to get on with the business of winning the next election, without
reading the early edition of the *Evening Standard* each day in terror
of finding yet another Archer gaffe uttered the evening before at a
meeting in some remote part of the British Isles.

Lord Young was spending more and more time at Central Office as
the 1987 election approached. He had been a special adviser of the
Department of Trade and Industry, and a protégé of Keith Joseph. In
1985, he entered the Lords and became Secretary of State for
Employment. Unlike Jeffrey Archer, Margaret Thatcher set considerable store by David Young's opinions.

As the campaign opened, rival factions began to line up. On one
side were Norman Tebbit and Michael Dobbs, his right-hand man
and by then Chief of Staff in Central Office, on a holiday from
Saatchi & Saatchi where he worked. On the other side were David
Young and Tim Bell, who had recently left Saatchi & Saatchi. There
was at the time considerable animosity between Tim Bell and the
Saatchis, although this has now passed and they are all friends again.
It is hard enough for a Chairman to run a political campaign even
when the whole of his office is on his side. In this campaign there
was no pretence: the two camps were openly hostile. My position
was quite clear: I worked for Margaret Thatcher. When she favoured

Tebbit, I favoured Tebbit; when she favoured Young, then I favoured Young.

My relationship with Tebbit was not helped at the time by the fact that during the Westland crisis I had commissioned a series of polls that showed the personal importance of Margaret Thatcher to victory at the next election. Geoffrey Tucker and John Banks had sold me the idea of a new approach to polling that their firm had developed. I spotted, at once, how I could use this system to help Margaret Thatcher, who was under attack. Tebbit had returned to hospital to have yet another in a series of operations necessary subsequent to the injuries he received from the Brighton bomb. Rumour was rife in the Party that Heseltine would force Margaret Thatcher to resign over Westland. Denis was said to have begun to pack his bags. Margaret Thatcher remarked to me that Christmas, as we sat alone on Christmas night, that she could not see what all the fuss was about. Why on earth were hours of the Cabinet's time being spent on debating the future of such a small company as Westland, a company that the state did not even own? Heseltine, she said, was capable of anything. She saw his overwhelming ambition as an evil force. Norman Tebbit's right-hand men were Michael Dobbs and Robin Harris, the Director of the Conservative Research Department. It was believed that they were at his bedside planning his campaign for a leadership contest, if Margaret Thatcher should fall. This cannot have helped his relationship with her at the time and, taken alone, must have tempted Margaret Thatcher to favour David Young.

John Banks, a man whom I had expected to be discreet, told the authors of the official account of the 1987 election and they published what he told them about his wonderful polls and how he was working for the Conservative Party. I had not told Tebbit anything about them. In the event, Neil Kinnock made a complete mess winding up for the Opposition in their censure debate. Margaret Thatcher survived and the Westland crisis went away leaving only two casualties: Michael Heseltine, who left the Cabinet, and his opponent, Leon Brittan, who resigned two weeks later. Margaret Thatcher had supported Brittan against Heseltine, but this seemed to cut no ice with Brittan. He grumbled like mad at the way he was shabbily treated. Since then he has done everything he can to sabotage Margaret Thatcher.

A few days after the censure debate, I was having a drink in the

bar of Bucks Club. On the other side of the room was Harold
Macmillan, whom I barely knew. He was drinking with his biogra-
pher, Alistair Horne. Horne came over and asked me to join them.
Macmillan began to tell me what a disaster Neil Kinnock was. 'His
speech at the debate on Westland was completely hopeless,' Macmillan
said. He then made the speech that he would have made if he had
stood in Kinnock's shoes. 'How lucky Margaret Thatcher is,' I said,
'that you are on our side.'

Macmillan, of course, was highly critical of Margaret Thatcher's
greatest reform, privatisation. Privatisation, he said, during his maiden
speech in the Lords, is akin to selling the family silver. Margaret
Thatcher said privately that, unlike the Macmillans, her family did
not have any silver to sell. Macmillan, having finished taking apart
Neil Kinnock and putting down Margaret Thatcher in the process,
sent Alistair Horne to get another round of drinks. Turning to me he
said, 'I always knew that Blunt was a spy. We used him as a double
agent. We were feeding him a lot of rubbish. The Russians became
suspicious so I went to see the Queen and arranged with her to make
him a Knight of the Royal Victorian Order to show the Russians
how highly we regarded him.' Alistair Horne returned and Harold
Macmillan changed the subject. I was surprised at Macmillan's
remarks about Blunt because they were contrary to all that had been
published on the subject.

Later I was tangentially involved with spies in a most curious
way. Shortly after I came out of hospital and was recuperating in
my South Audley Street flat, I had an unexpected visit from Victor
Rothschild. I let him in and slowly the old man climbed the stairs
to my first-floor flat. He sat in an armchair and came straight to
the point. He had information about Peter Wright, whose memoirs
the Government were desperately trying to suppress, and he asked
me to give this to Margaret Thatcher. Would I pass these papers
to her? He handed me a bundle of papers and a bottle of Mouton
Rothschild's excellent claret. 'In future, when I communicate with
you I will sign myself "Claret".' Having delivered his message he
left straight away. I took the papers without reading them to
Downing Street and left them there. Whether they ever reached
Margaret Thatcher or not I have no means of knowing. A few
weeks later, I received a letter saying, 'Do you want more of the
same, Claret.' I had enjoyed Lord Rothschild's claret greatly. So I
sent a message saying, 'Yes.' Sure enough, another bundle of

papers was delivered, but this time without the accompanying bottle of claret.

The crunch in the 1987 election came on Wobbly Thursday. Young described how, on meeting Tebbit in Downing Street, he took him by the lapels and shook him. If this was true, Young was lucky that Tebbit was ill. Young insisted that the campaign must immediately change direction. Look at the opinion polls; they were wobbling all over the place. Young had completely turned my theory on its head. He used the fact that the polls wobbled that Thursday as a reason to make trouble and put himself in charge of the campaign. However, as I had told him that they would, the polls returned to the Conservative lead the next day and all went ahead as Norman Tebbit had planned it.

The night of the election I dined with David Young at San Lorenzo's in Beauchamp Place. Young was appearing on the BBC's coverage of election night. Not long after he had left, I received a panicky telephone call from him. The BBC exit polls showed that the Tories had lost. Later Young believed that this was a sinister BBC plot. Personally, I believe that someone was just trying to make him look foolish.

After the victory there were again rumblings in the Party. No one had expected Margaret Thatcher to win a third victory. The putative successors got out their calculators and worked out that they might have to wait another five years, making them five years older, and that much less likely to become the Party's new Leader. Young men calculated that this victory put them in the race. The old enemies, the Wets, were largely exterminated. The new battle appeared to be about shades of right-wing opinion.

I had, as usual, spent the summer in Australia. I had not felt well as we drove from Broome to Darwin through the Kimberleys. Along the Gibb River Road, which was barely a track, are a number of small lakes and waterfalls in rocky country inaccessible by motor vehicle. We – my two eldest daughters, two girlfriends of theirs, Romilly, Snowy, Charlie Diesel and myself – decided to walk to one of these lakes called the Bell Gorge.

That morning we had breakfasted at just after six a.m. at Derby in an outback hotel with outback staff and outback food. 'Are you off the street?' the waitress asked. 'Yes,' we replied. It was, in this type of hotel, quite normal to be asked to share a table to save dirtying another table cloth. There were enough of us on this occasion, however, to warrant a table to ourselves. I ate a plate of kidneys and bacon covered in a brown sauce, fried bread, potatoes, beans and tomatoes, toast and marmalade, all washed down with a mug of coffee. The sun was hot as we walked to the Bell Gorge. Down a steep slope, climbing over rocks we reached the water. The girls stripped off their clothes and stood under the waterfalls; Snowy and Charlie swam in the clear water of the small lake; I sat on a rock feeling short of breath and sick.

For some days my left arm had ached. I believed that the pain came from my posture at meals, that my chair was too low or my table too high. As we set out to climb back to our vehicles, I lagged behind. I felt pain in my chest and was violently sick. Snowy came back and helped me. My illness we all put down to a heavy breakfast and the hot sun. I drove on and two days later, after two nights sleeping in the bush, we reached Darwin.

From Darwin we went back to Broome and a political battle over my idea of building an airport. A public meeting was called and I had an overwhelming majority 1,200 to 6, or something of that order. A petition in favour of the airport was circulated, and over 2,000 signed. I put the petition on the fax machine and sent it continuously to all the government ministers in Perth. All weekend we sent this petition, time and time again. On Monday, when their staff returned to work, the ministers' fax machines were all out of paper and their floors were covered with copies of my petition. It was all to little avail. The government was paralysed by fears of the past. They did not dare to do anything that in any way could be construed as helping men such as myself, regardless of whether what we were trying to do was sensible or not. In my case I did not need their financial help, just for them to resist the temptation to hinder my plans. I flew to Sydney and then to Canberra. The Federal politicians were keen to see my airport built. Then it was back to London and to a difficult Party Conference.

By this time I had Lord Beaverbrook as my Deputy and he was, I may say, a considerable help to me. At the Party Conference I felt tired and ill. On the Monday after the conference I visited my doctor, who sent me to a heart specialist. By Thursday I was in the Wellington Hospital having an angiogram. The best artery that I had leading to my heart was working at forty per cent of its capacity, the worst ten per cent. 'Do not even get out of bed,' the heart specialist told me. 'I want to get a really good surgeon, and I want him to operate tomorrow and he will need to be fresh. This is going to be a long job.' I was, on the whole, rather relieved by this news. At least I knew what was wrong with me.

The next day Gareth Reece operated on my heart for eight and a half hours. When I woke in the intensive care unit of the Wellington Hospital, I asked how it had gone. 'Six by-passes,' he replied. 'Bloody heck,' I mumbled and dozed off. The nurses kept waking me and I was desperately thirsty, so they gave me cubes of ice made from lime juice to suck, which I thought a wonderful invention. As I lay I could hear the voices of Romilly and Olga Polizzi, who both sat with me all night. A few days later, out of curiosity, I asked Gareth Reece what my heart was like. 'It's a hard little heart,' he answered and seeing my distress at this news, for who wants the world to know that their heart is both small and hard, he went on, 'I hate those large floppy hearts that fall between your fingers when you lift them out.' As if to reassure me further, he continued, 'You have a really big chest. I was right up to my elbows in there looking for your heart.'

Romilly slept in my room when I was out of intensive care, and it was wonderfully reassuring to have her there. My family visited me, as did Margaret Thatcher, who had rung Romilly several times while I was being operated on, seeking news and offering help. Cecil Parkinson came, as did David Young, who arrived the day after Black Monday, when the stock market had crashed. Within ten days I was out of hospital. I was lucky. I spent six months recovering from the operation, during which time Max Beaverbrook did my work at Central Office. The protégé of David Young, Beaverbrook was in fact an emissary announcing Young's imminent arrival. Norman Tebbit retired, and I got on with the work of raising money.

The Treasurers had rules that any donation from an individual was a matter kept confidential between the donor and Treasurers. This was the rule long before I arrived at Central Office and I sincerely hope that rule will always be kept. A citizen in Britain is entitled to privacy as to which political party they support at the ballot box, so why should they declare which political party they support financially? As for the people who give away other people's money, such as directors of companies who make donations to political parties from shareholders' funds, the law says quite clearly that such a donation must be declared in the accounts of the company concerned. The onus for deciding whether a donation is political or not lies with the directors of the company who give the donation. It is not the responsibility of the Treasurers of the Conservative Party, or any other political party, to decide whether a donation should be declared. Such a donation comes from the after-tax income of the company, as do dividends to shareholders. There are, on all sides of politics, fringe groups who receive money from various sources. The Labour Research Department and the Centre for Policy Studies are two of them, Aims of Industry and the Conservative Industrial Fund are two more. The European Movement is a political body but cross-party in its aim, as is Bill Cash's European Foundation. It is with these bodies that the clear arrangements on disclosure of donations become muddled. For the record, I have no recall of any funds passing from Aims of Industry to the Conservative Party while I was Treasurer. Those who demanded certain assurances from the Party for their cash were unacceptable. There is only one valid reason for giving money to a political party and that is to help the party of your preference be elected so that you, along with the rest of the nation, can enjoy the supposedly beneficial results of that party's government.

In recent years, there has been much talk of rich foreigners supporting the Conservative Party. It is true that foreigners, some richer than others, do. In my day they mostly owned companies in Britain. These people have succumbed to the blandishments of successive governments of all shades of opinion to invest in Britain. These investments help the British economy and employ large numbers of the British people. Why should these companies not support the British political system and British political parties? As for wealthy Sheiks and Serb businessmen, I never came across either of these bringing suitcases of money into Central Office. A suitcase is a useless way to deliver a large sum of cash; a cheque is far more convenient. In my time, these mysterious foreigners were but the fantasy of fixated Labour politicians. The scale of the whole operation at Central Office at that time did not need this sort of money. In any case, I had been instructed by Margaret Thatcher to be most circumspect in whom I took money from.

I had only one rule: the Party needed money to encourage people to vote Conservative at elections. If the money I took was in any way likely to lose the Party votes and so put the winning of elections in jeopardy, then far better send that money away.

During the 1987 election campaign, I received a message from Dr Armand Hammer. Would I call and see him at Claridges? I arrived, knocked on the door of his suite, the door opened and a skinny old man stood there in only his underpants. 'Come in, I am Dr,' he commanded. I was given a large glass of whisky and told how much the Queen loved him. 'You want money,' he said. This remark was not a question. 'Yes,' I said, 'money would be helpful.' 'If you go to Geneva, I have two thousand pounds in cash that you can have.' I left Dr Hammer, thanking him profusely, and did nothing about his gift. For all I know, the money is still waiting in Geneva. I did, however, leave several hours later clutching his biography. I have never read it, I cannot believe that there is much more in it than he told me that day.

It would be ridiculous to claim that mistakes were not made during my time as Treasurer. Asil Nadir was a mistake – not the taking of his money, for at the time he was highly respected as a successful businessman who had just won the Queen's Award for Industry. The mistake I made was meeting him only once. I should have got to know Asil Nadir and I might just have felt uneasy about his money.

Octave Botnar I knew well. He seemed to me an admirable man, who had no desire to meet politicians or attend grand dinners. Botnar is a man who worked in Britain for many years and was pro-British in every respect. He supported numerous British charities and, as far as I am aware, asked for nothing in return. His dispute was with the Inland Revenue. Eventually he settled that dispute, unlike Asil Nadir, who is accused of fraud. I have great respect for Octave Botnar while I have only contempt for Nadir. These were both mistakes that made headlines in the press long after I left Central Office.

For the fifteen years I was Treasurer, longer by far than any other Treasurer in the Party's history, life was comparatively peaceful. That is not to say that I did not have other problems. Sitting in my bath early one morning in 1979, I was reading the *Daily Mirror*. I always read the tabloids in my bath, for I have short arms and the bottom half of the *Guardian* used to get sopping wet. The broadsheets I read at breakfast. Since I first started in Central Office, I have read all the newspapers each day and I still do. This particular morning, I had a terrible hangover. I looked at the front page of the *Daily Mirror* and there was a photograph of a man I thought that I recognised. As my eyes focused, I realised that the man was me. One of my representatives in the northeast of England had written to a number of companies asking for money. There was nothing wrong with this; it was his job to write to people asking for money. But the text of his letter went something like this: 'The new Conservative Government has given all of you grants for your businesses. How about giving some money to the Conservative Party?' That this letter was sent is clearly wrong. There cannot have been a more clean-cut case of asking for money for the wrong reasons. I hurried to Smith Square and waited somewhat nervously for Peter Thorneycroft who, after he had settled himself at his desk, in the most casual way dismissed the problem. This had nothing to do with him or the Prime Minister. This was a problem with my department and I, as Treasurer, must deal with the press. At one o'clock I sat in a studio at the BBC with Robin Day. I was ready for an inquisition. I told the truth. My representative was wrong. It was pure ignorance that had led him to write this letter. He was a good man who had been on this occasion particularly stupid. I had explained to him that what he had done was wrong. Would I sack my representative? No, I would not sack him, because his intention was not evil. He understood that what he had done was wrong and he would not repeat the mistake. Ignorance was the cause of the whole affair. In any case, he was old and would find it hard to get any new employment. The matter passed over and did not make the next day's papers. I recall this event to illustrate how matters like this should be dealt with.

Nowadays the Chairman speaks for the Treasurers, they are directly responsible to him. This is a great mistake, as what the Chairman needs are Treasurers capable of speaking for themselves. Furthermore, had the incident of 1979 got out of control, Margaret Thatcher would have sacked me – an easy enough course to take. Under John Major's new rules, she would have had to sack Peter Thorneycroft, a totally different and far more dangerous operation.

Because the Conservatives have been in power for over sixteen years and most of that time raised all the money that they needed to win elections, the Labour Party are convinced that there are spurious motives attached to the actions of those who support the Conservatives financially. The Labour Party are only just beginning to realise that nearly the whole of British industry and a large part of the population will pay almost anything to keep them out of power. The reward for financial support to the Conservative Party is simply not to have to put up with a Labour government.

In 1983, I bought 3,000 copies of the Labour Manifesto. The

Labour Party were delighted and released the information to the press. I merely tagged the relevant pages and sent the documents to potential donors and money rolled into the Conservative coffers.

During elections it was my habit to arrive early and open the Treasurer's mail. I knew which letters had cheques enclosed because I could feel the paper clips. In 1987 I opened two letters consecutively, one from a vast industrial company, whose Chairman made his excuses and sent no cheque, the other from a man who had bought his council home and feared that the Labour Party might take it off him. He enclosed £200. I copied both letters and the cheque, later that day giving these copies to Margaret Thatcher. I pointed out that our support was where support really counted, for it is people not industries who vote on polling day. The most cost-effective way for a political party to win votes is by fundraising, for if a person only gives as little as ten pence it means that he or she will vote for your party.

The Labour Party always imagined and has often said that the Conservative Party sold honours. Lloyd George sold honours, or rather Maundy Gregory did on his behalf. Lloyd George was of the opinion that when you sold a man a baronetcy that was the end of the matter, the Government had no further commitment, that in the end this system was cleaner and of greater honesty than that of selling favours. The Conservative Party did not sell honours or favours while I was Treasurer. The evidence clearly shows that top industrialists receive honours, and that the companies where these top industrialists work often give money to the Conservatives. Separately both conclusions are accurate; to link them is a dangerous error. I quote only two examples. Sir James Goldsmith and Sir James Hanson, now Lord Hanson. Both of these men's companies contributed to the Conservatives, both of these men received their knighthoods under Labour governments. I am sure that if party political donations were abolished it would not change the complexion of the Honours List one jot nor tittle.

Only once was I propositioned to secure an honour. My office received an invitation for me to take tea at a house in Hampstead. I had known the people concerned for some years and had approached the husband on many occasions and he had always refused to give a donation. I was intrigued. I arrived at the house at about five-thirty p.m. and was greeted with great enthusiasm. The husband was seriously ill, tucked up in a chair, his legs stretched out on a stool. The house, a large one, was well-furnished with antiques and memorabilia. The wife opened a bottle of Dom Perignon champagne – this was in the days before I only drank the Macallan whisky. She handed me a glass of champagne and a plate of smoked salmon. The husband asked after my family and the wife passed round more champagne, more smoked salmon and then came the question: if they gave the Party a large sum of money, could I be sure that the husband would receive a knighthood? It was all terribly sad: the sick husband, the nervous wife, the wealth and the kindness that they were showing me. I tried, in a way that avoided pomposity, to explain that what they were asking me to do would constitute a criminal act. Returning to 32 Smith Square, I wrote an account of this incident and my negative reaction. I signed it, sealed it in an envelope and posted it through the letterbox of the Treasurer's safe which was in the wall of Henry Lee's office. Central Office has been turned upside down since I left, so probably some other department now has Henry Lee's old office and has inherited his wall safe. My letter should still be inside that safe. Some weeks later the man concerned died.

Raising money had its ups and downs. Once, at the beginning of 1987, Jock Bruce Gardyne came into my office holding a cheque in his hand. 'Look at this disgusting cheque.' I looked at the cheque. It was made out for five pounds. 'Do you see who it is from?' I knew the man, as did Jock. He ran a large and well-known shop in Covent Garden. I telephoned the man and Jock and I, climbing into a taxi, went straight to his premises. Shown in to the chairman's office we sat and explained the dangers of Labour government and the benefits that would follow when the Tories took over again. 'I can see that I have been a trifle mean,' the man said, as he pulled another five pounds from a purse and handed it to me. I was flabbergasted. We left and I used the money to pay the taxi fare back to Smith Square. It was only as I grew in confidence that I dared use that wonderful quotation from Weizmann, then President of Israel, who had just been given a donation that he regarded as derisory. Handing back the cheque he remarked, 'Too small for a bribe, too much for a tip.'

The highlight of my career raising funds for the Conservatives came a year after I had given up the job. In 1991 Chris Patten asked me to come and see the Prime Minister with him. The meeting took place in John Major's office at the House of Commons. He was late; I waited patiently. 'Would I help them out?' There was a rich man who had been very generous to the Party during my years as

Treasurer. I knew this man. The Party's funds were in a desperate state. A large donation would be most helpful. Would I see if I could persuade this man to make such a donation? As far as I was aware, only the three of us knew about this matter. I saw the gentleman concerned the next evening and he generously gave me a large cheque. I carefully put the cheque in my pocket and hurried out to dinner. The next morning I walked to Smith Square. It was a fine sunny day and as I crossed Hyde Park, on a whim I pulled the cheque out of my pocket. For the first time, I became aware that I was carrying no ordinary cheque but a bearer's bond for half a million pounds. Any mugger or casual thief who waited to attack me would have made a rather larger haul than he might have expected. I reached Knightsbridge and caught a taxi to Smith Square, then sought out Max Beaverbrook, gave him the cheque and Henry Lee gave me a receipt, which I gave to the man concerned.

By this time only six people knew of the cheque. Yet some months later I found the details of the transaction in a Sunday newspaper. Max Beaverbrook I know to be discreet, Henry Lee's discretion is without question. The donor had no intention of informing the press and neither had I. The fact of the matter was the existence of the cheque had leaked. From this episode, there is no doubt that John Major as Prime Minister has played a greater part in the acquiring of donations than is good for either him or the Party itself.

David Young put his hat in the ring as the future Chairman, but Willie Whitelaw would have none of it. John Wakeham, now married to my former secretary, Alison, would have none of it. I backed Young and we were beaten. Young took the job of Deputy to Kenneth Baker, the new Chairman, as a consolation prize. He then bought the building that stood next door to 32 Smith Square. Remodelling Central Office, he gave Kenneth Baker the vast office that Baker felt he deserved. Never a day went by that some ambitious person did not apply to Baker or the Prime Minister for my job as Treasurer. The job that no one had wanted in 1975 seemed, by 1989, to be on everyone's shopping list.

Anthony Meyer opposed Margaret Thatcher. He did not win but he changed the rules. There was now no moral barrier that stopped members of the Parliamentary Party from competing for the leadership while the Leader was still Prime Minister. It was now considered good form to shoot at Commanders-in-Chief. Margaret Thatcher's campaign was run from my house in Great College Street. There were defects in that campaign. Ian Gow, for one, was worried, and came to me to talk about those defects. George Younger made a report for Margaret Thatcher. Ian Gow had resigned over the Anglo-Irish Agreement and unfortunately did not have the influence that he had had before. I visited Margaret Thatcher and told her that it was widely felt that Charles Powell and Bernard Ingham did her little good these days. Would she not get rid of one of them as a sacrifice to the Party?

Margaret Thatcher refused. Charles, she said, was indispensable at helping her with her workload; she made no mention of Ingham. Fine men they both were and are, expert in their own fields, but neither of them knew anything about the Conservative Party. Neither of them understood how the Party worked or how to spot the signs of discontent amongst members of the Party, nor for that matter how to set about diffusing the anger that was being stored up.

Christmas 1989, I spent at Chequers. We watched the fall of Communism in Romania on the television. Margaret Thatcher's words were that it was all happening too quickly. She was at odds with the mood of the country. Always far sighted, she was way ahead of most other politicians on the collapse of Communism. Despite having played a crucial part in bringing that collapse about, she was sceptical about the immediate aftermath. The world wanted to celebrate and talk of peace dividends; Margaret Thatcher spoke of the dangers that came from the collapse of Communism. She believed that we should be well armed and that our defences, such as NATO, should be kept in good repair.

Her Cabinet were wildly enthusiastic about Europe. She saw the dangers and seemed to be dragging her feet. She was beginning to realise that, just as there was more to the collapse of Communism than a peace dividend, so there was more to our position in Europe. Some of the European nations had hidden agendas. By 3 October the following year, Germany was reunified. This came about without the other states of Europe being consulted. Margaret Thatcher was way ahead of her Cabinet, her Government and her electorate.

By May 1990, I had left my home at West Green. I had for some years been a target of the IRA and my house was vulnerable to attack. Some instinct encouraged me to move. I also moved my

London residence. A week or so later in my new London apartment, I woke as usual just before six a.m. I switched on the television and as I began to increase the volume, a house ruined by a bomb blast came on the screen. Romilly, sitting in bed beside me said, 'That's West Green.' So it was. Our last home had been blown apart by an IRA bomb. It was an incredibly strange feeling, sitting there looking at a ruined house where, had we not left, we would have died. The telephone rang. It was the Prime Minister. She had also just seen the six a.m. news. She was very kind about the whole business. I am compelled to write, however, that I did not feel too badly about the house for I and my family were still alive. The bomb, twenty pounds of Semtex, which is a large bomb, had exploded under the window where Margaret Thatcher had stayed only four months before. That room was next to Skye's bedroom. Next the police called. 'Do not move. Do not touch anything in the apartment,' they said and, rest assured, we did not touch anything. In minutes, they arrived with dogs and equipment. Our apartment was thoroughly searched. Soon the press began to ring me. 'What can you say under these circumstances?' I simply said, 'It is a shame that the IRA, these days, are going around blowing up beautiful old houses.'

Margaret Thatcher had visited West Green several times before, on the first occasion when our daughter Skye was very small. Skye took Margaret Thatcher by the hand and led her into the garden to play hide and seek. When I noticed that the Prime Minister was not around, I set out to look for her. Nobody seemed to know where she was. I found Margaret Thatcher in the garden, hiding behind hedges as Skye searched for her. Margaret Thatcher's Special Branch men and women were trying to keep track of her as she entered into the spirit of Skye's game. Margaret Thatcher is naturally good with small children, treating them like miniature adults, which is what small children really enjoy.

I have many memories of West Green. Many were the parties that we held there, a magic house filled with ghosts and parties held years before. General Hawley, who commanded the English cavalry at Culloden, built that house and over the garden door inscribed the words in Latin, 'Do as you feel inclined.'

The best party I ever gave was on my wedding night. I had that day married Romilly Hobbs, and had discovered the nature of love, a sense of being together even when you are apart, so intimate that it defies description. That day, with friends, I decorated a table that followed three of the walls of my drawing room. We collected from the garden all the old implements – buckets, baskets, hoes, rakes, spades, forks and watering cans – which we painted white. All of this was arranged the length of the table and amongst them we placed heaps of vegetables, cabbages, artichokes, melons, potatoes, cucumbers and pineapples, also painted white. The house was filled with roses and lilies in crude country pots. Willie Cochrane, the piper, played. Albert Roux cooked a dinner that was as near a miracle as it is possible for a chef to make with food. The party wandered on; the night was boiling; it was a warm October; the rooms were lit with candles; music echoed through the house as we ate with our friends. Romilly and I were tired and happy.

When my daughter, Skye, was christened I gave a party there. Long tables were laid out on one of the three lawns that stepped upwards away towards seventeenth-century stone sculptures and a clipped hornbeam hedge to the park land beyond. Formal chairs from the dining room were set at the tables, covered in the finest linen. Silver was laid out and glass from Venice. Waiters served as twenty-five or so members of my family sat with the child's godparents to take lunch before the christening. The mix of the formal table setting and the rustic atmosphere of the garden worked wonderfully.

Often we had parties in the garden and if the weather was uncertain we dined in the house filled with flowers. Before and after dinner, we walked between the box hedges and the night-smelling flowers of the garden, along yew alleys, through walled gardens, past ponds and fountains. Lunch on the Sundays when Romilly and I were at home was usually a considerable event. Twelve guests would be invited for twelve-thirty, and champagne would be served in the drawing room while I cooked the first two courses of lunch. Romilly used to cook the puddings: steamed treacle pudding or spotted dick with custard, baked jam roll or various tarts. Romilly, a considerable expert on food, taught me to cook. When I lived at West Green, with its kitchen that had a great fireplace, sofas, a television and a large pine refectory table, where we lived and often ate, quite apart from a range of cookers and a team to wash up – my enjoyment of cooking was enormous. Lunches tended to stretch towards the early evening, filling Sunday afternoon neatly, a time that I found a black part of a week. The table would be decorated with seasonal fruit, cheeses and nuts. There were fresh herbs from the garden, flowerpots filled with cut flowers and clear glass vases from Venice with herbs. The cutlery was eighteenth-century steel with stained ivory handles. The lace tablecloths were piled one overlapping another. West Green was a perfect house for parties, a wonderfully romantic house with just a touch of fear about the place.

I also gave parties at Conservative Party conferences at Brighton, Bournemouth and Blackpool. These started as small intimate affairs. Invitation was by word of mouth. The conversation was indiscreet, but no one ever reported that conversation. When Margaret Thatcher was Prime Minister she never attended my parties at conferences nor, for that matter did she ever come to my parties when she was Leader of the Opposition. I did not invite her, nor would I invite John Major if I gave these parties now. The purpose of these parties was not to prove how well I knew a Prime Minister, or how many important people I could pack into one room. My parties were there to set a tone of friendship with certain key members of the press, to give a feeling of goodwill in a small way to a vast conference. I kept no lists of those who came – they were a mixture of press, politicians and industrialists who seemed to enjoy the parties, which were held in the sitting room of my suite. There was plenty to eat – lobster, oysters, chicken legs, that kind of thing – and plenty to drink. People came back each year. I invited people to my parties because so many of them were, and happily still are, my friends. Their importance, or lack of it, was of little interest to me then or now.

Some years before I had suggested to Margaret Thatcher that Garel-Jones be sacked as a Whip, for I and others felt he was systematically recommending for promotion the Prime Minister's enemies. Margaret Thatcher told me that there was little point. Garel-Jones had told her that for family reasons he had soon to resign his seat. Garel-Jones is still in the Commons, while Margaret Thatcher is wasted in the Lords. It is interesting to note that Tristan Garel-Jones who, on the face of it, played such a part in the politics of the 1980s, is only mentioned three times in the second volume of Margaret Thatcher's auto-biography and those occasions between pages 830 and 854 do not do him much credit. Garel-Jones must have moved about his politics quietly and in secret.

I was not the first to suggest to the Prime Minister that either Charles Powell or Bernard Ingham should go. Gordon Reece had given her the same advice. Foolishly, Gordon gave his advice by telephone and telephones in Downing Street have many ears. Two of

those who listened to Gordon Reece's advice were Charles Powell and
Bernard Ingham. The lines in and out of Parliament in the battle for
the leadership of the Tory Party were not clearly drawn. The issue
of whether Margaret Thatcher should stay as Prime Minister had its
supporters, the likes of Tebbit, Parkinson, Ian Gow, Nicholas Ridley
and myself. Ranked against her were Michael Heseltine and his
followers. The spring of 1990 was an uneasy time, the summer one
of sadness for Thatcher's followers. On 6 June our house was blown
up, on 14 July Nick Ridley resigned, on 30 July Ian Gow was
assassinated. Ian Gow's funeral was, unlike Airey Neave's, a sad
affair. Romilly and I travelled to the funeral with Cecil and Anne
Parkinson. The church was crowded. As the Last Post was played,
the tannoy system crackled. It sounded like gunfire. Gunfire crackled
in the ranks of the Conservative Party. By 2 August Iraq had invaded
Kuwait. On 1 October Geoffrey Howe resigned.

During the third week of September, I visited Margaret Thatcher
to tell her that Britain was beginning a serious recession. This had
been brought to my attention rather sharply by the fact that my
antiques and curiosity business, which usually turned over a figure
approaching £100,000 a week, was suddenly only doing £2,000
worth of business. I had also noticed how quiet London was. The
Burlington Arcade, for example, had nobody in it when I walked
down it one Wednesday afternoon. I made some enquiries and found
that there were several shops to lease in that arcade, the first that
had been on the market for years. Margaret Thatcher was impressed
by the anecdotal evidence. I also told her that the interest rate was
too high, and that it was crucifying the small traders. She agreed
with me and said that was why she had joined the ERM. She had
been persuaded by John Major that to do so would allow interest
rates to be brought down. I was told later by Charles Powell that
the Prime Minister had mentioned my views on the approaching
recession to her Cabinet. They dismissed them as the opinions of an
eccentric.

Later, when John Major became Prime Minister, I was invited to
No. 11 Downing Street to dine with the Lamonts. Norman was now
the Chancellor of the Exchequer. He did not agree that a recession
was approaching and pointed out that what appeared to be a recession
was the effect of the Gulf War. I disagreed with him and argued that
the effects of the Gulf War were masking what was really happening
to the economy. 'When the Gulf War ends the Government expects

the economy to recover. In fact, what will happen is that the economy will continue to sink deeper into a recession.'

Lamont said all this was rubbish. I told Lamont that the recession would only be made worse by the drop in the value of property caused by high interest rates. Property in the 1980s was the collateral that banks sought as security for loans to businesses. Each time the value of property dropped, more and more businesses had a deficiency in their security. The banks, as a result, foreclosed and, having to right off bad debts, were forced to ask their good debtors to repay loans as they needed the cash to top up their balance with the Bank of England. The situation could only get worse. I suggested that he might consider trying something similar to the action that George Brown took in the 1960s, which was to ban all new office developments. This had little effect on the people who were building office buildings, because there was already an over-supply, other than to put the value of their empty properties up. The market was safe and the virus of falling property values did not spread to the rest of the economy. Lamont dismissed this as complete rubbish, which turned out to be his general attitude to any words that might be construed as criticism. Of course, Lamont did not understand what I was on about, for he knew little about running a business and nothing about property development and the vagaries of the market.

I was talking to a Government that did not want to admit that a recession existed and so, to their minds, one did not exist. They were a Government of Chums and as is the way with chums, they did not want to spoil each other's fun. When Norman Lamont told me that my views were rubbish, he added, 'By the way, there is no recession technically.' Technically, he may well have been right, but people in the country were losing their homes through repossession, their jobs and their savings through negative equity. If that is not a recession, I do not know what is. John Major began by saying that if his management of the economy was not hurting, it was not working. These must surely be amongst the most callous words ever uttered by a British Prime Minister. When he finally admitted the fact that there was a recession, he said, 'This recession will be shallow and short.' The only part about the recession that was shallow and short was its cause – Norman Lamont. Then John Major set about turning, for the first time but not the last, events that were forcing policy on him.

At the Lamonts' dinner table, Romilly sat next to her host. 'How do you feel now that you are Chancellor of the Exchequer?' Lamont replied, 'I am excited and I intend to prove that I am right and that my critics are all wrong.' I do not recall Mr Lamont being able to do that, nor anything like it. More to the point, however, was Romilly's reply: 'Norman, I hope you remember that you are gambling with our money.'

Both Norman Lamont and John Major lost, in time, the biggest gamble of all, the ERM. It cost the nation billions and the people got not so much as a hint of an apology let alone a ministerial resignation. How strange politics are. Having made two blunders on an unprecedented scale, Lamont goes about the country as an important figure whilst explaining that John Major made him back the wrong horse. If I seem a little testy when I write of John Major who, after all, appointed and supported Lamont, this sorry tale may go some of the way to explain why. As for the British economy, it is now recovering, I am inclined to believe, rather than headed for an unprecedented boom. The Conservative Government will no doubt try to claim credit for these good times. They – John Major and his Cabinet – brought about a terrible recession by the policy of aligning our currency with Germany's. The boom that is coming is the consequence of changing that policy – this is how economic cycles are made.

When Heseltine was finally goaded into challenging Margaret Thatcher by Bernard Ingham, Tristan Garel-Jones visited my house in Great College Street where Margaret Thatcher had set up her campaign headquarters, to offer his help to the late Peter Morrison. Peter turned him away. So Douglas Hurd became the beneficiary of Garel-Jones's help. He did not win either, nor did Michael Heseltine. Even Margaret Thatcher was forced to resign and Garel-Jones's close friend, John Major, became Prime Minister.

I had retired as Treasurer on 15 July 1990, exactly fifteen years after I had joined Margaret Thatcher as the Treasurer of her Party. The last year had for me been extremely tiresome. I had been ill and had worked too long at Central Office. Too many Members of Parliament were finding people who would give the Party money, too many businessmen believed that to be Treasurer of the Conservative Party was just the job for them. Senior officials in Central Office were in the pay of businessmen and promoting their interests, and I felt that the place was out of control. Kenneth Baker sat resplendent in his magnificent office. A warning was given to me about a particular businessman, and I passed the message on to two members of the Cabinet who were closely associated with him. Within hours, my words were repeated to this man. Fifteen years was too long. I was beginning to fight the old battles, all over again.

I saw Margaret Thatcher and told her that I was supposed to change my life after my operation in 1987 and here we were in 1989 and, if anything, my lifestyle was now more stressful than it ever had been.

There had been considerable debate about who should have the job when I left. I was in favour of Henry Keswick, whom I believe would have made an admirable Treasurer, but his appointment was opposed by David Young, who soon left politics to become a director and then Chairman of Cable and Wireless. Young's motive for stopping Henry, I believed, was to enable his protégé Max Beaverbrook, my Deputy, to be made Treasurer instead. Max did the best that he could, but he is not nor will he ever be Henry Keswick. Henry Keswick is a man apart. Cunning, clever, tough and a determinedly right-wing Conservative, he had the contacts for that job and the knowledge of how to ask for money. He is a man who has great style. Max Beaverbrook is kind, considerate, helpful, eager for the chase, but hesitant at the kill. I was to stay for six months to see Max Beaverbrook settled into the job as Treasurer.

I did not attend the Conference that year. I was tired after all those years of politics, the last thing that I wanted was to be plunged right into the heart of the Conservative Party again. The leadership contest was fought out amongst parliamentarians; I heard what was going on second hand through my secretary, Shana Hole, who worked on Margaret Thatcher's campaign team. Shana is an excellent woman who served me well, going on to become the political adviser to Richard Ryder, John Major's first Chief Whip.

The news from the Thatcher campaign was depressing. Peter Morrison, once Deputy Chairman of the Conservative Party and then the Prime Minister's PPS, was no Ian Gow, who had once held the same job. The campaign appeared to be going well, but I was uneasy. I put this down to a natural pessimism that I have about the results of elections of all kinds. The Prime Minister played no part in the campaign for her re-election as leader of her Party, as she rightly believed that she had served that Party for fifteen years and this was no time to plead for support. She trusted her parliamentary party to support her.

I left England to join Romilly in Italy. We were, that day, to lunch with friends just outside Bologna. No sooner had I passed through customs at Bologna than Romilly told me that No. 10 Downing Street had called. I telephoned them at once and was informed that the Prime Minister would like me to dine with her at Chequers, on the Saturday night. I accepted. Romilly and I had our lunch, then drove to Venice to spend the night, and the next morning I set out for England. That afternoon I picked up Gordon Reece, who was another guest invited to Chequers, and that evening we drove there together. Unusually, dinner at Chequers was a stilted affair. The Prime Minister was distracted, for she had to go to Paris the next day for a conference on security and cooperation in Europe. The other guests were members of her campaign team. The Prime Minister hurried everyone through dinner and we all drank coffee in the drawing room. Kenneth Baker stood and made a speech pledging undying loyalty which, to be fair to him, he showed when push came to shove. Peter Morrison stood and took a piece of paper from his pocket. He had in his hand the numbers and he was happy to announce that the Prime Minister had won. The Prime Minister thanked them fulsomely and they were all shown into the night. Gordon Reece and myself were asked to stay behind. We, the three of us, moved into the Great Hall, where a warm fire was burning. The Prime Minister ordered champagne for Gordon and whisky for both of us.

'I have heard all this before,' she said. 'This is exactly what they told Ted.' Neither Gordon nor I made any effort to reassure her that Morrison's figures were correct. We just did not know. We had played no part in the whole unfortunate proceeding. As we drove back to London, Gordon and I barely spoke to each other. On 20 November, the First Ballot was held. I waited with Kenneth Baker and one or two others for the result in the Prime Minister's office at the Commons. Margaret Thatcher had missed the necessary majority by two votes. If Ian Gow had been alive, she would have had that majority. If Ian Gow had been alive, the margin would never have been that narrow. If Ian Gow had lived, I wonder if Geoffrey Howe would ever have made that speech, for they were close friends.

Margaret Thatcher returned to London the next day. She intended to fight the next round, much to the surprise of many of her supposed supporters. They took the view that she must be persuaded not to commit this folly, to go quietly. It was a nasty moment for John Major when Margaret Thatcher put his hand to the fire by asking him to second her on the Second Ballot. His hesitation of a few moments on the telephone when asked that question speaks more than a thousand words.

That morning Gordon Reece, Tim Bell and myself visited John Wakeham, who was the Prime Minister's new campaign manager. He appeared helpful and even optimistic, but by the evening I had begun to wonder if he had seen his role as campaign manager or undertaker. Wakeham had in the past expressed the view that he would himself make an admirable Prime Minister. His performance on television during the 1983 election led Willie Whitelaw and myself who watched it together to take a different view. 'Terrible, terrible, terrible, quite terrible,' muttered Willie Whitelaw, which from a man who usually said, 'Wonderful, wonderful, wonderful, quite wonderful,' at the least opportunity, was condemnation indeed.

At lunchtime that day Tim Bell, Gordon Reece and myself lunched in the private room at Mark's Club. David English and Conrad Black joined us. We discussed what could be done, and Tim Bell tried to telephone John Major. Norma Major answered the phone and told him that her husband's mouth was too sore to speak to anyone which, in retrospect, seems surprising because he managed to speak to Margaret Thatcher later in the day and Jeffrey Archer appears to have had conversations with him as well. His reluctance to speak to Bell, who explained to Norma Major that we were gathered together trying to help Margaret Thatcher, has always seemed strange. I cannot help wondering sometimes about his miraculous recovery the next day to fight his own campaign for the leadership of the Conservative Party. Try as I may, I cannot understand why John Major's teeth gave him no trouble from the beginning of July, when Parliament broke up, to November when the leadership elections occurred. John Major's action of going off to have his wisdom teeth fixed at the same time as he was proposing Margaret Thatcher in a leadership contest was an action that, given the most charitable interpretation, seems extremely casual. Perhaps the blame really lies with his dentist, who failed to warn John Major that his wisdom teeth were likely to give him trouble. I do hope that the Prime Minister no longer uses this man, for the nation could be put in dire straits should his advice be so terribly wrong again.

I was due to see Margaret Thatcher at seven o'clock that evening and then to take Denis out to dinner. During the afternoon Margaret Thatcher was busy seeing members of the Cabinet; their various reactions are chronicled in her autobiography. These reactions make fascinating reading and do little credit to most of her Cabinet. Margaret Thatcher, who had never let the fact that somebody disagreed with her politically stand in the way of their promotion if they had talent, was now paying the political price for her generosity of spirit.

The Prime Minister was late coming back to Downing Street. I sat with Charles Powell. At about seven-thirty his telephone rang. It was a call from her office at the House of Commons. Would he please start drafting a resignation statement? Twenty minutes later the doorman at Downing Street warned us that the Prime Minister was returning. I stood in the hall with Charles Powell and waited. The Prime Minister came through the front door and asked me to follow her to the lift. We went straight up to the flat where Denis was waiting in the sitting room. Denis offered me a drink and Margaret told him of the day's events. 'One by one they came in and with a couple of exceptions, they all told me the same thing. Of course, they will support me but they will not campaign on my behalf and that I cannot win. Except for Ken Clarke. He was straightforward and came to the point; he said I should go.' 'To hell with them, they don't deserve you,' Denis remarked. The Prime Minister turned to me. What did I think? 'You can win, and what is more, you can win the next election, but you must consider is the battle worthwhile. You will have to govern with a hostile Cabinet.' In victory, Margaret Thatcher would have had to sit with a Cabinet whose support was at best tenuous. This treachery that was afoot was no new treachery, it had been long in the planning. In truth, the vote of the backbenchers was meaningless. Margaret Thatcher's fate was sealed when her Cabinet deserted her en masse.

Denis and I left for Mark's Club, where Olga Polizzi and William Shawcross were already sitting at the table. Carol joined us later with her great friend, Albina de Boisrouvray. When I saw Carol enter the restaurant, I got up quickly from the table, took her upstairs and explained what had happened. I have always had the greatest respect for the courage of the Thatcher family and how they conduct themselves in public. That evening confirmed that I was right in my judgement. Denis and Carol ate their dinner and were amusing guests while under considerable strain: we were the only three people at the table to know what was going on. The sheer dignity with which both Carol and Denis conducted themselves that evening was breathtaking.

Next morning, I was to have breakfast with Stephen Fay and Henry Porter, both eminent journalists. We met at the Fox and Anchor in Smithfield. After we finished breakfast I told them that the Prime Minister had resigned; we then listened to the official announcement on my car's wireless. I do not think that the Conservative Parliamentary Party really knew what it had done. They were, I believe, caught up in a world of their own, a world from which they have not yet broken free. Only a considerable defeat will clear their heads and start them thinking again. It was so in the past and it is so now. Only the defeats of 1945, 1964 and 1974 made the Parliamentary Party stop to think; only those defeats revitalised the voluntary party, which was at its greatest strength in the postwar years of the 1950s following the defeat of 1945. The same is true of the years after 1964, and there was a great surge in Conservative Party membership after the defeats of 1974 and during the years of Thatcher's opposition that followed those defeats. Lost in its own little world, the Conservative Parliamentary Party forced the resignation of its greatest peacetime leader, a woman who had won three general elections and two leadership contests, being undefeated in a third. Not only did the Conservative Parliamentary Party dispense with the service of one of its greatest and most charismatic leaders, but they did this while she was still Prime Minister and the nation was at war.

13

Not, I hope, the
Last Chapter

The end of Margaret Thatcher's premiership came suddenly. Deals were done and John Major was in place in Downing Street. It is strange to write that an event you almost expected was a shock when it came. For me, however, that was the truth of the matter. Margaret Thatcher set up camp in my Great College Street house. At first she seemed dazed, unable to find enough work to fill a day that only a week before was not long enough for all the work in hand. 'It is like the death of a close relative for her,' a doctor friend told me. As for myself, I was distressed, for this was not the way that her term as Prime Minister should have ended.

Life, however, went on. The first of a number of problems was the sacks of letters that came in for Margaret Thatcher. Central Office sent over two girls who worked at these letters. Alex Mennell, a stalwart of Central Office from Parkinson's days of glory, was seconded by her employer Peter Palumbo to help, and she was invaluable.

A few nights after Margaret's resignation, I found myself back in the same room at Mark's Club, this time the guest of Conrad Black. My fellow guests were Margaret Thatcher and Henry Kissinger. The topic of conversation was who was the best agent to handle the publication of her autobiography and then the scale of fees that could be charged to various organisations for making speeches at functions. It was strange to hear these two great politicians talk of the mundane facts of how to earn a living when I would have expected them to speak of Presidents and Heads of State.

On her resignation, Mitterrand sent Margaret Thatcher a painting as a present and, much to the irritation of Downing Street, immediately invited her to lunch. It was ironic really, for the supposed antagonism between her and the other European leaders was amongst the reasons given by many of her colleagues for getting rid of her. Those months after the resignation were a difficult time. There were many actions Margaret Thatcher took that irritated Downing Street and many they took that infuriated her.

The next election came and John Major won. In theory, he was now his own man, out from under the shadow of his predecessor. In truth, he had never been under that shadow. Far better for him if he had been. John Major, for all his time in power, has always been the prisoner of the Cabinet of Chums. They, like mischievous children playing with a rag doll, pull him this way and that, pulling off an arm here, a leg there. And so it was with both his policy and the members of his government. The policy went one bit at a time until only an incomprehensible muddle was left. His government went one member at a time, each loss the result of a scandal. As for his majority, the Liberals and the Labour Party took care of that. The change of leader that was to cleanse and unite the Conservative Party left only bitterness; each member of the Cabinet, with one exception, never daring to challenge John Major, each of them awaiting his downfall for the opportunity to take his place.

During the years after her resignation I saw even more of Margaret Thatcher than during her years as Prime Minister. Once, dining with her and Denis, Romilly and Carol were with us, Carol asked her mother why she had promoted John Major. 'He was very good at doing what I asked him to do. I assumed that he believed in what he was doing.'

There were two questions that I had long wanted to ask Margaret Thatcher. There was no need to back track over the stale ground of Tristan Garel-Jones or his chums, why warnings were ignored, friends neglected and enemies promoted. All of that was inevitable. Knowing both the natures of Thatcher and Garel-Jones, she would always promote on a basis of ability, and he often recommended her enemies as the ablest people available to do a job. Garel-Jones spoke with the Whip's voice. As a consequence, he was believed.

In the end, it was her friends who failed Margaret Thatcher, not her enemies who brought her down. In their hearts they doubted, doubted that she would win that election in 1992, doubted that she was truly capable of carrying on, doubted the wisdom of her policies and, in particular, the Poll Tax. All this suited the well-laid plans of her enemies, who waited for just such an opportunity.

I had very little interest in chewing over this old cud with Margaret

Thatcher. What really interested me was, firstly, why she signed the Anglo-Irish Agreement that led to the resignation of Ian Gow. 'It was the pressure from the Americans that made me sign that Agreement.' I was not totally surprised. The second question to which I wanted an answer, was why she signed the Single European Act. That Act has not been interpreted as she intended, was the answer. I suppose, looking at the facts, she should not have trusted her successor to ensure that it was interpreted as she intended. To say that Margaret Thatcher was tricked is too easy an answer and certainly not the one she gave me. It so happened that when the Cabinet of Chums took over they were all gung-ho on Europe. By the time John Major discovered that the public did not share their enthusiasm, it was too hard to put the genie of the Single European Act back in the bottle, too easy for his acolytes to blame Margaret Thatcher for signing it, too easy, as well, to paint Margaret Thatcher as a bitter woman angry at loss of office and to shout this facile refrain every time that she has a word of criticism for the government.

Margaret Thatcher has long ago recovered from her anger and hurt at the treachery of her colleagues. Nowadays, she delights in earning a healthy living from her books and lectures. As for position, today Margaret Thatcher's words are listened to the world over, people flock to see her when she travels, her prestige seems to grow everywhere except amongst the chattering classes of Britain, but then this was ever so. As for myself, I long ago got over my anger at the Conservative Parliamentary Party's great treachery. However, having seen how people can act given the opportunity, it would be folly not to take notice of that experience.

There are people in politics that I like and admire, as there are people in politics that I dislike and despise. Those people whom I dislike, I am afraid will have to receive the force of my distaste, for that is how I am. Margaret Thatcher came to power with a victory over Ted Heath. John Major came to power by a victory over Margaret Thatcher. Her victory was won with battle openly declared, fought with passion, the risks of that battle terminal to her career had she lost. John Major's victory was won by stealth.

As for the Conservative Party, when I joined them as their Treasurer in 1975, I was a Conservative by instinct and habit. I was never an activist, climbing my way up some Party ladder. It was to join Margaret Thatcher's 'Long March' that I went to work in 32 Smith Square. I am still, by instinct, a Conservative; the habit, however, has now been broken. I am more searching in my enquiries these days as to how the Conservative Party conducts itself. I feel that I have remained much the same in my views, but that the Party has crept away, like some husband slipping from his lover's bed, in the early hours of morning, to return to his wife. Margaret Thatcher's Long March culminated in 1979 with the Conservative Party being seduced back to Conservatism from the near-Socialist philosophy to which it had been married during the previous twenty-five years. While I am sad that the political ideals of Thatcherism are one by one first reviled and then discarded by those to whom they handed office, I have few personal regrets.

Margaret Thatcher changed my life, as she did the lives of so many other people. Today I write and travel, I still collect, currently only ties, marble beads and political badges. I try to keep my collecting under control. Slowly but remorselessly, however, the collection of odd-shaped stones in our house grows and grows. I have, however, changed many of my views over the years.

Many years ago I gave up going to the Church of England and after a long period in which religion played no part in my life, I started attending Catholic churches. I am now a regular churchgoer; I feel better when I have been to church. To me, birth, life and death all seem the greatest of miracles.

I am still interested in politics and occasionally active, though most of the time I just write about politics. I am still blessed with an endless curiosity about people, places and things. I live in continental Europe; I revel in the beauty of that place and the vast quantity of man-made masterpieces that are there. I have, however, after years of looking at man-made beauty come to believe that it is only human beings who are really important. Finally, I have come to the conclusion that there is no masterpiece in this world that is of greater importance than the meanest member of mankind who would destroy it.